the **Hockey Drill Book**

DAVE CHAMBERS

Human Kinetics

Library of Congress Cataloging-in-Publication Data

Chambers, Dave, 1940-
  The hockey drill book / Dave Chambers.
    p. cm.
  ISBN-13: 978-0-7360-6534-4 (soft cover)
  ISBN-10: 0-7360-6534-2 (soft cover)
  1. Hockey--Training. 2. Hockey--Coaching. I. Title.
  GV848.3.C43 2007
  796.355--dc22   2007016091

ISBN-10: 0-7360-6534-2
ISBN-13: 978-0-7360-6534-4

Developmental Editor: Kevin Matz; **Assistant Editor:** Laura Koritz; **Copyeditor:** Pat Connolly; **Proofreader:** Anne Meyer Byler; **Graphic Designer:** Robert Reuther; **Graphic Artist:** Kim McFarland; **Cover Designer:** Stuart Cartwright; **Photo Asset Manager:** Laura Fitch; **Photo Office Assistant:** Jason Allen; **Art Manager:** Kelly Hendren; **Associate Art Manager:** Alan L. Wilborn; **Illustrator:** Denise Lowry; **Printer:** Versa Press

Human Kinetics books are available at special discounts for bulk purchase. Special editions or book excerpts can also be created to specification. For details, contact the Special Sales Manager at Human Kinetics.

Printed in the United States of America   10   9   8   7   6   5   4   3   2   1

Human Kinetics
Web site: www.HumanKinetics.com

United States: Human Kinetics
P.O. Box 5076
Champaign, IL 61825-5076
800-747-4457
e-mail: humank@hkusa.com

Canada: Human Kinetics
475 Devonshire Road Unit 100
Windsor, ON N8Y 2L5
800-465-7301 (in Canada only)
e-mail: orders@hkcanada.com

Europe: Human Kinetics
107 Bradford Road
Stanningley
Leeds LS28 6AT, United Kingdom
+44 (0) 113 255 5665
e-mail: hk@hkeurope.com

Australia: Human Kinetics
57A Price Avenue
Lower Mitcham, South Australia 5062
08 8372 0999
e-mail: liaw@hkaustralia.com

New Zealand: Human Kinetics
Division of Sports Distributors NZ Ltd.
P.O. Box 300 226 Albany
North Shore City
Auckland
0064 9 448 1207
e-mail: info@humankinetics.co.nz

the
Hockey Drill Book

DAVE CHAMBERS

Contents

Drill Finder

(continued)

*Skills: BS for backward skating, C for checking, FS for forward skating, P for passing, SA for skating agility, Sh for shooting, and St for stickhandling.

Drill Finder *(continued)*

(continued)

*Skills: BS for backward skating, C for checking, FS for forward skating, P for passing, SA for skating agility, Sh for shooting, and St for stickhandling.

Drill Finder (continued)

(continued)

*Skills: BS for backward skating, C for checking, FS for forward skating, P for passing, SA for skating agility, Sh for shooting, and St for stickhandling.

Drill Finder (continued)

Foreword

I am not surprised by the depth and quality of Dave Chambers' *The Hockey Drill Book* or at the potential for this book to be a coach's or player's best reference and guide.

I first met Dave in a football locker room at St. Michael's High School in Toronto. A senior student and football and hockey scholarship athlete, Dave took me, a 15-year-old boy, under his wing. I learned much about athleticism, leadership, and competition from this veteran player. I followed Dave's career as he developed into a world-class hockey player on Canada's national team in the 1960s.

But Dave's greatest contributions to the game of hockey would come after he moved from playing to coaching. Dave developed into a top teacher, coach, and mentor in the game. Dave's coaching experiences are wide and varied—he's coached at all levels, including the NHL and in many nations.

The game of hockey is a wonderful team sport that requires a strong blend of physical and mental skills for competition. Players must develop a solid base of fundamentals—skating, shooting, passing—even before beginning to learn how to play the game. It is clear that unless athletes have developed the basic individual and technical skills, they will not be able to master the more complex and tactical team skills necessary for competing and winning at a high level.

Most coaches agree that their prime duty is to help players become the best they can be. A coach constantly searches for ways to provide the information, preparation, guidance, and leadership to assist individual athletes in their skill development and to help a group of athletes come together and play as a team. This is where Dave's book becomes *the* coach's bible. Drills are the primary coach's tool by which both individual and team skills are taught and learned. A coach at any level, in any country, can use Dave's drills to structure a practice to meet the needs of the individual or group learning the game. This marvelous collection of drills, gathered over many years and from many philosophies of teaching and playing the game, can also inspire coaches to create their own drills to meet their specific needs as they arise. Beyond that, this book is a useful companion to players of any skill level wishing to develop. The drills are varied and intuitive so that anyone could pick up this book and flip to an area he or she wishes to improve to find several easy-to-follow drills designed for a range of skill levels.

The organization of the book proceeds as if Dave Chambers is creating a practice. The first chapter addresses communicating with the players and teaching them the necessary skills. Then it moves on to planning and developing a practice, building it by beginning with basic individual skills, and progressing to more complex, competitive team skills. The next chapters contain drills that address all phases of the game, while always building on fundamentals, in an order that reflects his recommended practice structure.

As I said, I am not surprised by the success of Dave Chambers as a hockey man. Nor am I surprised at the quality of his book. *The Hockey Drill Book* will always have a place on my coaching desk.

Pat Quinn

Preface

Today's hockey merges the style of play from many hockey cultures, including Russia, Canada, the United States, Sweden, Finland, the Czech Republic, Slovakia, and Switzerland. At the professional level, the game is changing in ways that require players to have more skill and speed, and these changes will filter down to all levels of hockey. *The Hockey Drill Book* is a compilation of drills I have used and observed in North America and Europe over the last 35 years that can be used to provide the training that players need to compete effectively in this new brand of hockey. The book includes proven drills used by coaches of top professional and national teams as well as amateur coaches from many countries. These leading-edge drills incorporate all the principles of today's modern hockey—speed, agility, passing, transition, and shooting—that will hone and polish the skills and techniques players need so that they can succeed.

The drills in *The Hockey Drill Book* can be used by coaches at all levels. The book is designed to help coaches plan and structure practices by providing a multitude of drills that they can incorporate into their practices. The chapters of the book are organized so that drills from chapters 2 and 3 can be used to teach players the basic skills, like skating, passing, stickhandling, and shooting, and the later chapters move on to drills teaching team play, from the basic one-on-one to complex systems, transitions, and defensive play. Within each chapter, the drills also progress from simple to complex. The progression of chapters and of drills within chapters allows players to master the simpler drills and then move up to the more complex and challenging drills used at the higher levels. Always keep in mind that players at all levels need to master the fundamentals.

Dave Chambers

Key to Diagrams

○   Forward or player

●   Defensive forward

▲   Defenseman

△   Offensive defenseman

⊘ ◮
⊗ ◭   Different color sweaters

G   Goaltender

⟶   Player skating without the puck

〰➤   Player skating with the puck

- - - ➤   Pass

⟹   Shot

∿➤   Lateral movement

| | | | | | Lateral movement cross steps

⟶|| Stop

∿•➤   Drop pass

∿∿∿   Backward skating

∿∿∿∿   Backward skating with the puck

△ ⊙   Offensive or defensive player starting with the puck

✕   Cone

⋰⋱   Pucks

⟲   Curl

�   Pivot

⊣   Screen, pick, or block

ⓒ   Coach

↺   Tight turn – 180°

>   Against (as in 2 > 1)

chapter 1

Running Effective Practices and Drills

"How you practice is how you play." The quality of a team's practices will determine the quality of the athletes' skills, conditioning, and mental preparation as well as team tactics and strategy. Running effective practices and drills is one of the most important aspects of coaching. Good performance in games is the result of good practices, which require careful planning and hard work from you, the coach, and dedication and motivation from the athletes. You need to develop weekly, monthly, and season plans that outline the team's practice sessions and identify the drill progressions that will be used throughout the season.

Planning the Practice

You need flexibility in designing your team's practices. Each practice is one part of the total season plan. Every practice should include working on individual skills (technical), team play and systems (tactical), and conditioning. In addition, the strategy aspect of the game should be addressed in practices, especially with older athletes. Also allow time in each practice to work on weaknesses and problems that have arisen in past games or practices. The following list provides some guidelines to consider in designing your practices.

Guidelines for Designing and Running Effective Practices

- Have a weekly, monthly, and season plan for the general progression of skills and team play.
- Set goals and objectives for each practice. Make sure your players, assistant coaches, and support staff are aware of these goals and are involved in the planning process.
- Plan your practices to suit the age and skill level of your players.
- Progress from basic skill practices to more complex and challenging practices.
- Have a good progression from practicing skills to working on team play in each practice.
- Teach new skills and new drills early in practice.
- Make practice and drills applicable to game situations.
- Keep all players active and include the goaltenders in all drills.
- Give clear and concise instructions throughout the practice.
- Make sure you have the players' attention when you are speaking, and maintain eye contact with the players. Position the players in the best formation to hear you speak (usually a U formation).
- Explain and demonstrate skills and drills clearly. Have the players begin the drills quickly after the demonstration.
- Don't talk too long. One to two minutes at a time is enough for explanations of skills and drills.
- Use all of the ice surface if possible.
- Use smaller groups when working on individual skills so that the players can have more repetitions.
- Involve your assistant coaches in all aspects of the practice.
- Observe, evaluate, and give feedback throughout the practice. Assistant coaches should also be involved in this process.
- Be positive and upbeat. Greet your athletes using their first names before or at the start of practice. Early in the practice, use verbal communication more frequently to show enthusiasm and to establish a good rapport.
- Include a warm-up and cool-down in each practice. The warm-up should include general skating and dynamic stretching (slow movements to fast movements), and the cool-down should include static stretching (slow movements that are held for 30 seconds at the end point).
- Before the practice, have the players do individual stretching off ice to save on ice time.
- Use conditioning drills at or near the end of each practice.
- Stop a drill if you observe a general error or a lack of effort.

© PETR JOSEK/Reuters/Corbis

- Explain new drills before practice if you want to save on ice time.
- Include a fun drill in each practice.
- Place a rink board on the side-board glass for on-ice instruction.
- Have between 40 and 50 pucks available for each practice.
- If time permits, have certain players work on specific skills with the assistant coaches after the formal practice ends.
- Evaluate each practice with the assistant coaches and team leaders when finished.
- Demand excellence.

Types of Practice and Practice Structure

Before determining which type of practice to conduct on specific days, know the amount of ice time available for each practice, the number of practices per week, and the ratio of practices to games. Ideally, each practice should last 1 to 1.5 hours. Professional, junior, and college teams usually have 2 hours of ice time available to them, but at lower levels, a team may have only 1 hour. In some situations, two teams may even have to share an hour of ice time. Schedule your practices accordingly. If you can't fit all the skills into one practice, spread them over the practices for the week, or even the month.

A Typical Practice

A typical practice should include work on skill development, team play, and conditioning. For younger age groups (under 10 years old), the team should focus more on the basic skills of skating, passing, shooting, and puck control, with less emphasis on team systems. Teams with older players still work on fundamentals but should spend more time on game situations and team play than the younger age groups. Practices can include the following:

- Individual skills and techniques
- Offensive play
- Defensive play
- Special teams (power play, penalty killing, face-offs)
- Conditioning
- Having fun

Here is an example of the sequence of activities in a typical practice. A variety of drills for each skill can be performed. And, as mentioned before, depending on the amount of time you have and the age group you're coaching, you may not be able to cover everything in a single practice. But remember, each practice should include stretching and one individual and team warm-up drill at the start, and a fun drill or game toward the end. And always make time for your players to cool down.

1. Dressing room dynamic stretching and instruction
2. Individual warm-up—skating, passing, puck control, and dynamic stretching
3. Team warm-up—full ice with shooting
4. 1v1
5. 2v1
6. 2v2
7. 3v1
8. Breakouts
9. Positional skills—forwards, defense, goalies
10. Scrimmage
11. Fun—conditioning relay
12. Cool-down—including a group discussion with the coach and static stretching

Theme Practices

With high-level teams that have many practices, you can design "theme" practices. For example, a theme practice may focus only on offensive play, defensive play, or special teams.

- **Offensive Practice.** In an offensive practice, the team would focus on quick puck movements, passing, receiving, shooting, scoring goals, going to the net, breakouts, and various offensive situations. The practice would be high tempo and would include little defensive resistance, such as in 2v1 and 3v1 drills with regroups and neutral zone counters. This gives players the space to execute offensive skills without resistance (resistance is added in other practices that focus on defensive tactics).

- **Defensive Practice.** In a defensive practice, the team would focus on forechecking, backchecking, defensive zone play, and defensive team play. For teams that practice daily, this type of practice is usually used once a week. A defensive practice may also be conducted when a team has displayed poor defensive play and must focus on this specific aspect of the game.

- **Special Teams Practice.** Special teams practice is extremely important in today's game because referees call more obstruction penalties. The day before a game is often a good time to focus on power plays and penalty killing because this type of practice is usually not exhausting. If practice time is limited, this aspect of the game should be included in a regular practice.

Other types of practices are fun-only practices (with special games) and simple (no-brainer) practices. The simple type of practice is a good choice after tough games—the practice is short and includes basic, fast-moving, noncomplicated drills. These kinds of practices aren't used often, but they can give players a chance to take it easy when necessary.

You need to decide what aspects are to be emphasized in each practice. The weekly, monthly, and season plans should be the guide to well-designed practice sessions.

Designing and Using Effective Drills

The development and implementation of appropriate drills are the keys to effective practices. And since drills are the primary tool a coach has to help players practice and perfect important skills techniques, good drills are paramount. To help athletes improve their individual skills and team play, select the most effective drills and place them in the proper order within the practice plan. Your ability to do this will determine the team's level of success. Below is a common and effective teaching progression to help you choose and then implement drills into your practices. There are drills in this book that address each of the skills and strategies listed. Pick drills that focus on each area below in the order provided. Drills focusing on basic skills and fundamentals should be at the beginning of practice as they are most important. Then progress towards more advanced drills, as illustrated. As previously mentioned, younger players, just starting out, should focus almost entirely on the basics, like skating, puck control, passing, and shooting. For older, more advanced players, you can incorporate drills that develop offensive and defensive zone play and power play and penalty killing strategies.

- Skating
- Puck control
- Passing and receiving
- Shooting
- Checking
- Goaltending
- Breakouts
- Regroups
- Offensive zone play
- Defensive zone play
- Power play
- Penalty killing
- Face-offs

Clearly explain or demonstrate the drill you are using to work on a skill. You can demonstrate or give instruction on how to perform drills during the practice before each drill and during skill practice. Some coaches prefer to explain drills before practice begins, especially with older athletes. Keep instructions brief in order to maximize ice time and activity during practice. To communicate effectively, remember the KISS principle: "Keep it simple and specific." After you demonstrate the skill, the athletes should practice the skill immediately. Athletes can practice the skill alone, in pairs, or in groups, depending on the drill.

Also remember that athletes need to know how they are doing in their efforts to learn skills. Provide specific feedback during and after the practice of a skill. As the athletes practice the skill, you and coaching assistants should circulate among the athletes, giving feedback and correction. Group corrections can be given on common errors. In most cases, feedback should be positive, emphasizing correct movements and helping athletes correct or refine incorrect movements. Athletes learn more quickly in a positive environment.

The drills used for practicing the skills should be challenging and as game-like as possible. If there is a large difference in skill levels within a team, you may want to match players of similar skill levels in practice. If the difference in skill level on a team is small, this type of matching is not necessary.

Following are some guidelines for the development of drills:

© Glenn Campbell/Icon SMI/Corbis

Guidelines for Developing and Using Effective Drills

- Drills should be suitable to the age, skill level, and physical maturity of the players.
- Drills should have a specific purpose and should meet the objectives of the practice.
- Drills should relate to the skills used in the game.
- Drills should follow a progression moving from simple to complex.
- Drills should challenge the skill level of each player.
- As much as possible, drills should be interesting, competitive, and fun.
- Drills should be designed to get maximum participation from all the players.
- Drills should have an optimal number of repetitions for each player. For drills used to work on basic skills, you may need to divide the players into smaller groups so that each player gets more repetitions.

- Explain each drill clearly and demonstrate how the players should practice the skill. The explanation and demonstration should take no longer than two minutes.
- When you are explaining the drill, the players should be positioned so that each player has a clear view of you.
- Drills should be varied and innovative. Have a series of drills and a variety of drills to accomplish the same purpose (for example, two-on-one, three-on-two).
- With older athletes, you may be able to combine several skills in the same drill (for example, one-on-one combines with a two-on-two backcheck drill).
- You and your assistant coaches should give individual feedback and encouragement to the players during each drill.
- Give each drill a name. After using a drill a number of times, you can save time by quickly putting the players into the drill simply by calling out the name of the drill (without explaining and demonstrating each time).
- You can introduce and explain new drills in the dressing room to save time on the ice, especially for teams with limited practice time.
- Do most drills at a high, gamelike tempo.
- Do the drills correctly. When you observe major errors or a lack of effort, stop the drill and correct the errors for the group. The drill can then be restarted.
- Each drill should have a clearly stated purpose.
- Drills should have a conditioning effect facilitated by intense work followed by rest for each repetition.
- Drills should follow a progression that flows from one skill to the next (for example, two-on-one followed by three-on-one, and so on).
- Drills should be run for an optimal amount of time (usually five to eight minutes). The drills should be long enough for an appropriate number of repetitions, but they should not be too long because the players' attention and intensity will diminish.
- Use all of the ice surface for each drill to maximize participation.
- Evaluate the success of the drills after each practice.
- Be flexible. A drill may not be working because it is too complex or wasn't explained correctly. When this occurs, you might have to change or improvise a drill during the practice.
- If the practice turns out to be too long or too short, you might need to add or remove a drill from the practice plan.

Remember, effective drills should lead to improvement in the players' individual skills and team play. The key to good, well-planned practices is your ability to design and implement effective, progressive, and interesting drills.

chapter 2

Warm-Up Drills for Skating, Passing, and Stickhandling

The drills described in this chapter are designed for the beginning of practice and include stretching exercises, skating agility, puckhandling, passing, and small-area games. The goalies can take part in these nonshooting drills, or they can warm up with stationary shooting with a coach or another player (with a goalie in the goal area at each end of the rink). (See chapter 14 for goalie specific drills.)

Normally, one warm-up drill without shooting is sufficient at the beginning of each practice. These drills usually include some stretching, skating, passing, and stickhandling, and should last for five minutes. These warm-up drills assume that the players have been taught the previously mentioned basic skills and that the players are able to repeatedly perform these basic skills correctly. The drills in this chapter progress from skating and stickhandling to passing and receiving. In addition to providing practice of the basic skills, the warm-up drills without shooting are designed to stretch and warm up the muscles—and possibly prevent injuries from overstretching during quick movements. The stretching should start with slow movements and progress to quicker active stretching.

1   SKATING BETWEEN THE BLUE LINES

Players should skate around the rink at three-quarter speed, executing the following four skating maneuvers:

1. Sprint between the blue lines.
2. Skate backward between the blue lines.
3. Skate forward in and out between the blue lines—*in* from the first blue line to the center circle and *out* to the next blue line.
4. Skate backward in and out between the blue lines—*in* from the first blue line to the center circle and *out* to the next blue line.

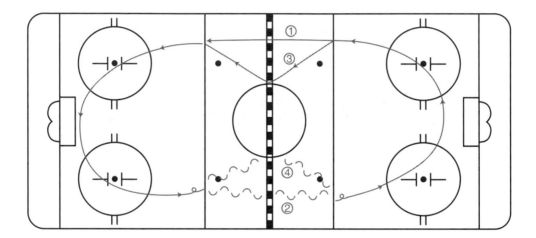

2 SKATE AROUND THE RINK: VARIATIONS ON THE WHISTLE

The following four skating variations should be executed in the order shown:

1. Skate fast and then slow on each whistle.
2. Skate forward and then backward on each whistle.
3. Pivot toward the boards and go in the opposite direction on each whistle. (Note: All players turn toward the boards in the same direction.)
4. Stop on the whistle and go in the opposite direction.

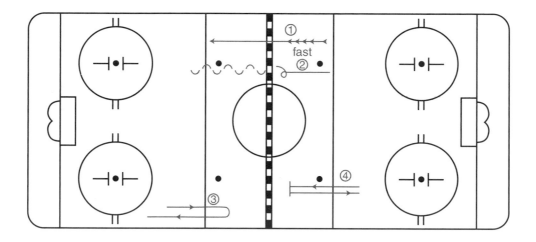

3   DIAGONAL SKATE: FORWARD AND BACKWARD

Players should start at the goal line and skate the following sequence:

1. Skate forward diagonally to the near blue line.
2. Skate backward diagonally to the center line.
3. Skate forward diagonally to the far blue line.
4. Skate backward diagonally to the goal line.
5. Skate forward the length of the ice to the starting position at the goal line.

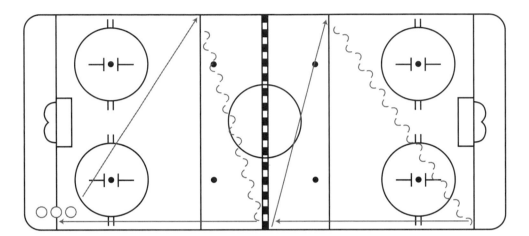

4 DIAGONAL SKATE: CROSSOVER STEPS

Players should start at the goal line and skate the following sequence:
1. Skate forward diagonally to the near blue line.
2. Skate using crossover steps along the blue line.
3. Skate forward diagonally to the center line.
4. Skate using crossover steps along the center line.
5. Skate forward diagonally to the far blue line.
6. Skate using crossover steps along the blue line.
7. Skate forward diagonally to the goal line.

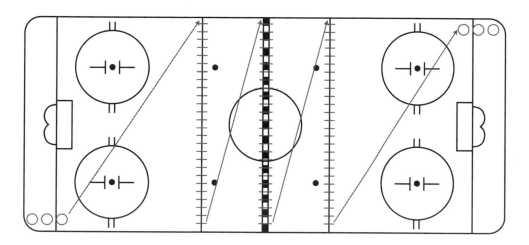

5 WARM-UP SKATE: FORWARD, BACKWARD, PIVOT

Have players start at the goal line and skate the following sequence:

1. Skate backward to the hash marks at the circle.
2. Pivot and skate forward to the side boards at the blue line.
3. Pivot and skate backward to the center circle.
4. Pivot and skate forward to the side boards at the far blue line.
5. Pivot and skate backward to the hash marks at the face-off circle.
6. Pivot and skate forward to the corner boards at the goal line.

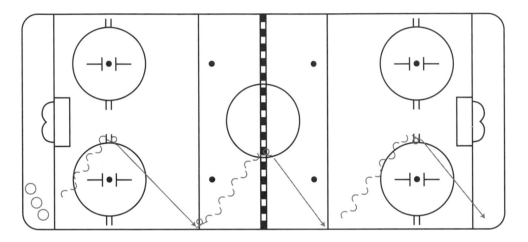

6 WARM-UP SKATE: ZIGZAG

1. Skate in a zigzag pattern down the ice by skating forward, stopping, skating backward, stopping, skating forward, stopping—alternating down the ice.
2. Players can go in partners, with the partner skating behind all the way down the ice and alternating on the next sequence.

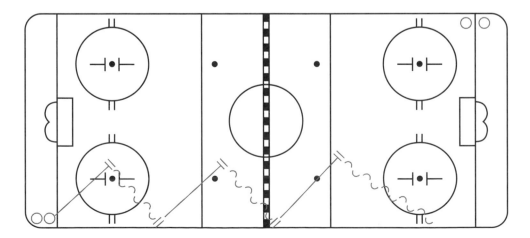

AGILITY WARM-UP

Have players start at the goal line and skate the following sequence:

1. Sprint to the near blue line.
2. Perform lateral crossover steps along the blue line.
3. Sprint to the far blue line.
4. Perform lateral crossover steps along the blue line.
5. Skate backward to the near blue line.
6. Pivot and sprint forward to the goal line.

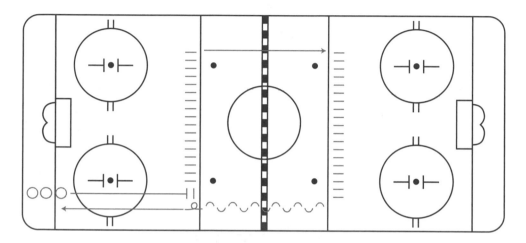

8 WARM-UP SKATE: BACKWARD, FORWARD, BACKWARD

Player 1 and player 2 begin at opposite corners of the same goal line and skate the following sequence:

1. Skate backward to the blue line.
2. Pivot and skate forward diagonally to the far blue line.
3. Pivot and skate backward to the goal line.

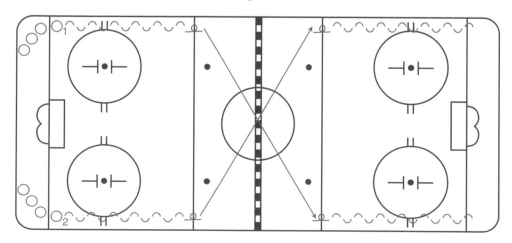

9 SKATE THE CIRCLE: SHORT SPRINT

Players should start at the blue line and skate the following sequence:

1. Skate backward around half of the center circle.
2. Pivot and skate forward around the second half of the circle.
3. Sprint to the far goal line.

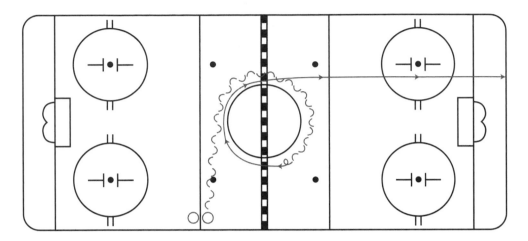

10 SKATE THE CIRCLES

Start from the goal line and skate once around each circle in the order shown.

Variation

Skate forward clockwise around circles 1, 3, and 5, and skate forward counterclockwise around circles 2, 4, and 6.

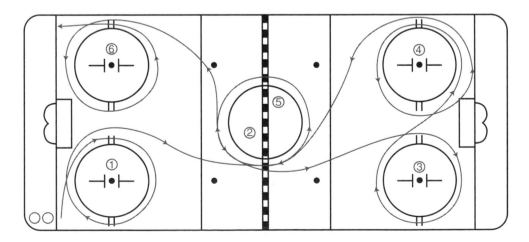

Stations are set up on the ice as shown. Players should start one at a time and skate through all eight stations in progression. When the first player has moved to station 2, the next player starts.

> Station 1: Backward crossovers
> Station 2: Lateral crossovers
> Station 3: Tight turns
> Station 4: Backward skating
> Station 5: Forward crossovers
> Station 6: Lateral crossovers
> Station 7: 360-degree turns
> Station 8: Backward crossovers

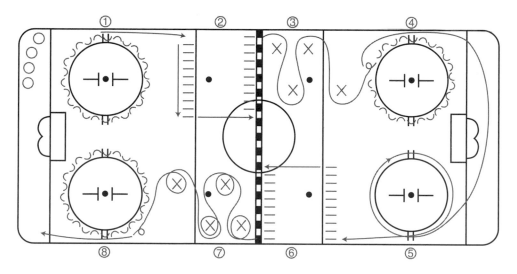

Stations are set up on the ice as shown. Players should rotate through the stations (rotate every two minutes).

Station 1: Tight turns

Station 2: Lateral crossovers, backward skating, pivots

Station 3: Backward and forward crossovers

Station 4: Agility circle—lateral crossovers, forward and backward skating, forward and backward crossovers, pivots

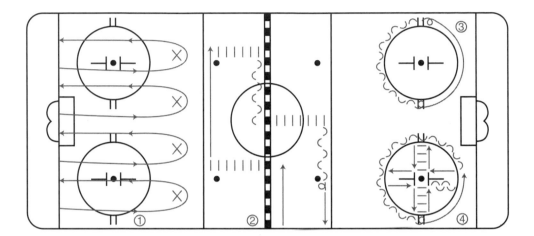

13   WARM-UP AGILITY CIRCUIT

Stations are set up on the ice as shown. Players should rotate through the stations, spending about 40 seconds skating at each station.

Station 1: One-foot zigzag

Players skate a zigzag pattern on one foot—first left foot, then right foot.

Station 2: Ride the stick

Players put the stick between their legs and glide between the blue line and the goal line.

Station 3: Shoot the duck

1. Players squat down with one leg extended out in front and the other in a bent-knee position.
2. The players glide from the goal line to the blue line with the left leg extended forward.
3. They return with the right leg extended forward.

Station 4: Jump the stick

Players jump over the stick—which is lying on the ice—with one foot, alternating from left to right.

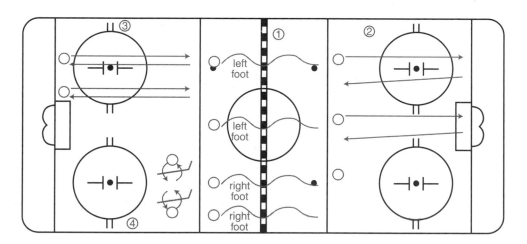

WARM-UP AGILITY SKATE

Each player has a puck. On the whistle, each player skates the following sequence:

1. Skate three strides forward.
2. Skate three strides backward.
3. Skate chop steps sideways each way.
4. Pivot and skate forward three strides.
5. Skate easy until the next whistle, when the drill is repeated.

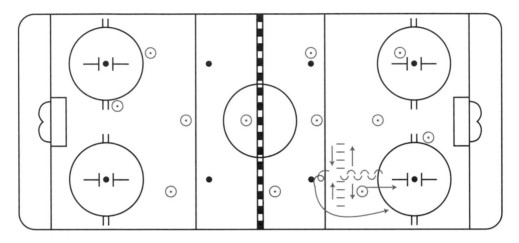

WARM-UP STICKHANDLING

1. Players skate at half speed.
2. On the whistle, the players skate at full speed in a confined space while stickhandling.
3. On the next whistle, players again skate at half speed.
4. The drill continues in this pattern. The high-speed stickhandling should last for 20-second intervals with 20 seconds of rest.

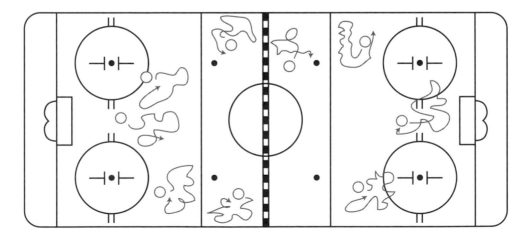

16   SKATE AROUND THE RINK WITH PUCKS

Players can practice puckhandling by skating around the rink and executing the following skills in this order:

1. Stickhandle.
2. Put the puck in the skates. Kick the puck to the stick. Pass the puck back to the skates. Repeat.
3. Pass the puck to a partner using quick passes, with one touch each time.
4. Three players pass the puck. One player skates backward, and the other two players skate forward.
5. On the whistle, play 1v1 against a partner, anywhere on the ice.

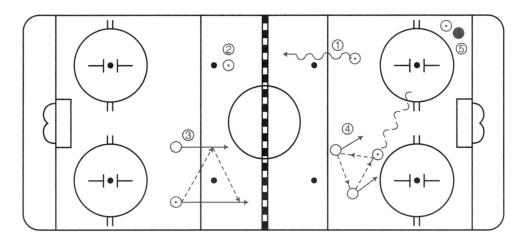

WARM-UP SKATE: TIGHT TURNS, CROSSOVERS, PUCK PROTECTION

1. On the whistle, players skate around two cones. The players use crossover steps and tight turns while protecting the puck.
2. Players work in pairs. While one player skates, the other rests. (Use 20-second intervals.)

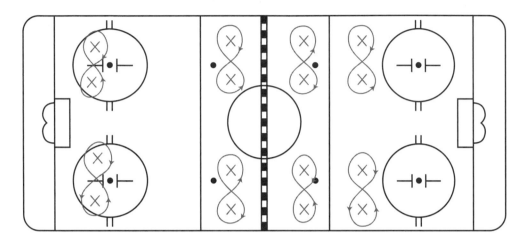

NEUTRAL ZONE SCRAMBLE

1. Five players with pucks begin behind each goal line. The groups skate from opposite ends with their pucks and stickhandle in the neutral zone in all directions.
2. On the whistle, the two groups of five players skate to the opposite ends while stickhandling with the pucks.

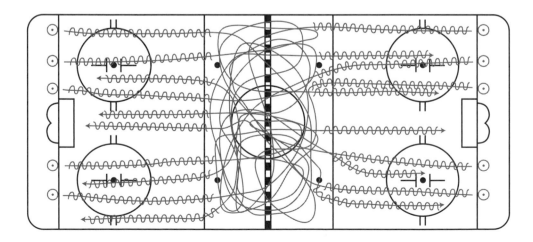

19   WARM-UP AGILITY WEAVE

1. Cones are placed in the neutral zone.
2. Player 1 and player 2 start from opposite ends with a puck and stickhandle around the cones.
3. On the whistle, player 1 and player 2 go over the far blue lines and shoot at the opposite end from where they started.

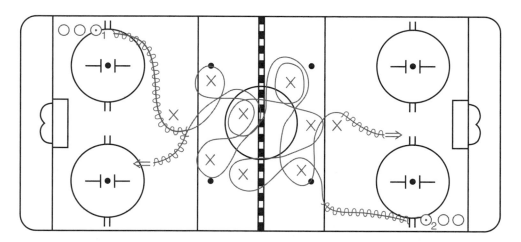

20   STICKHANDLE DRILL

1. All players stickhandle with their own puck between the blue lines.
2. Players try to knock the puck free of another player's stick while controlling their own puck.
3. If a player's puck is knocked off, the player is out and must go outside the blue lines.
4. Two coaches limit and make the space smaller and smaller between the blue lines until one player is left in control of his or her puck and the others are out.

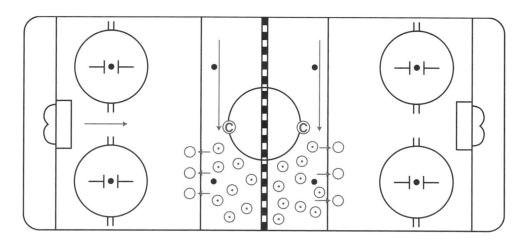

Form three groups and set up in three zones of the ice. Each group does the following:

1. The first player with the puck passes across the ice to the opposite player, follows the pass, and takes the position of the player receiving the pass.
2. The player receiving the pass then passes across the ice to the next player and follows the pass to the next position.
3. The drill continues with the same pattern.

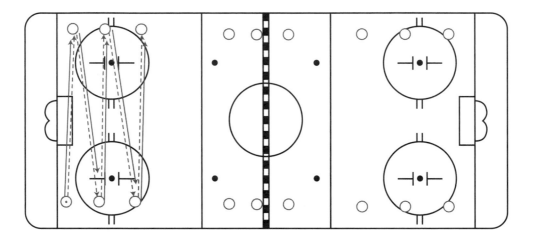

1. Two players skate down the middle of the rink passing the puck.
2. When they approach the goal line, both players turn toward the boards and change direction, heading back toward the end of the rink where they started.
3. The players skate the length of the rink while making rink-wide passes to their partner.

Variation

The two players skate backward down the middle of the rink passing the puck. They turn outward toward the boards and skate forward the length of the ice passing the puck.

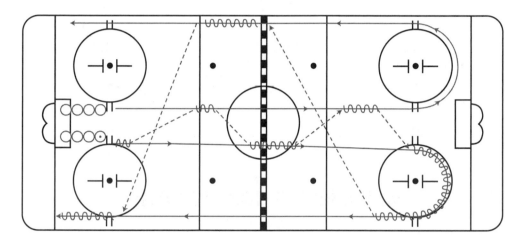

GIVE-AND-GO

1. Players take stationary positions along the boards on each side of the rink.
2. On each side of the rink, a player with the puck starts behind the goal line and skates the length of the ice, exchanging passes with the stationary players.
3. After receiving and giving a pass, the stationary players move to the next stationary position.

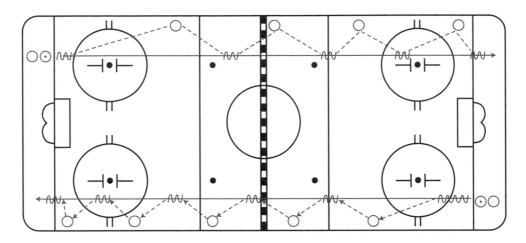

WARM-UP ONE-TOUCH PASSING

1. Groups of five or six players are in three zones.
2. One player in each zone one-touch passes with each of the other players, including the goalie.
3. After the player has one-touch passed with each player, the last player passed to goes next.

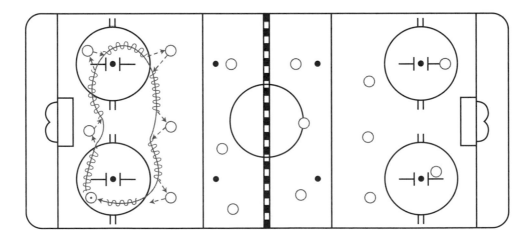

Station groups of four players at each of the 5 circles. At each station have the groups perform one of the following:

> Station 1: Stand around the circle and one-touch pass around and across the circle.
>
> Station 2: One-touch pass but follow the pass and change positions with the receiver of the pass.
>
> Station 3: Players are on their knees passing the puck around and across the circle.
>
> Station 4: Players can only backhand pass around and across the circle.
>
> Station 5: Play "monkey in the middle," with one player in the middle trying to intercept the pass. If the player in the middle is successful, the player whose pass was intercepted must trade places with the middle player.

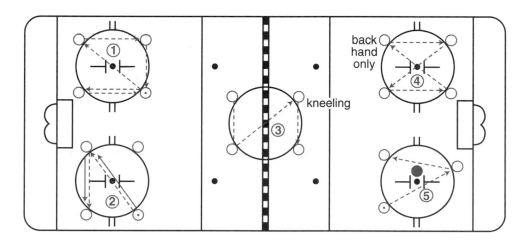

1. Player 1 skates backward out of the center circle and receives a pass from player 2.
2. Player 1 pivots with the puck and then skates a figure eight while exchanging passes with player 2.
3. Player 1 finishes skating the figure eight by returning to the center circle.
4. Player 2 then skates backward from the center circle and skates a figure eight while exchanging passes with player 3.
5. This drill is done from both sides of the center circle.

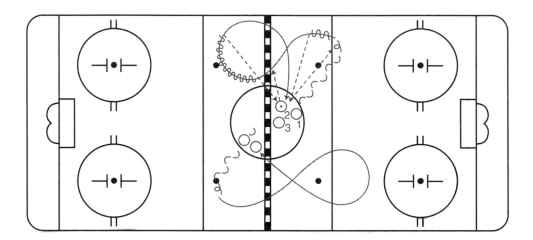

OUT OF THE MIDDLE:
EXCHANGE PASSES WITH TWO DEFENSEMEN

1. Forward 1 skates backward out of the center circle with the puck and exchanges one-touch passes with forward 2.
2. Forward 1 pivots and exchanges passes with defenseman 1 and defenseman 2, who are at the top of the face-off circles at opposite ends of the rink.
3. Forward 1 returns to the center circle, and forward 2 starts skating the same pattern.
4. This drill is done from both sides of the center circle.

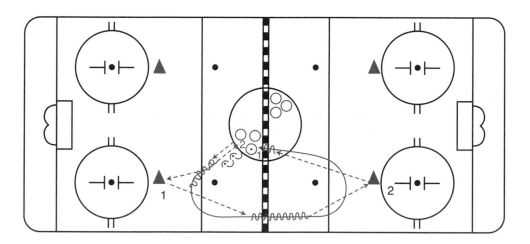

Players setup in lines at the top of the face-off circles on both sides of the rink. The drill can be run using any of the following sequences, or players can cycle through all of them in an order specified by the coach:

Sequence 1

Two players skate toward each other, exchange one puck, and skate to the opposite line.

Sequence 2

Two players, each with a puck, skate toward each other, exchange pucks, and skate to the opposite line.

Sequence 3

Two players from the opposite lines exchange passes and return to the same line. The players turn toward the middle to receive the passes.

Sequence 4

Two players from the opposite lines skate to the far blue line, turn toward the boards, and receive a puck from the opposite line. They return to the line they started at and pass to the next player, who repeats the drill.

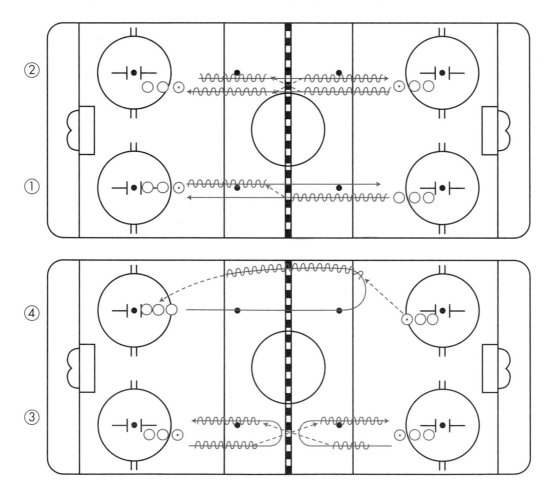

29   NEUTRAL ZONE EXCHANGE: 2V0

Two players from two lines at the same end exchange passes as they skate to the far blue line, where they exchange a pass with a player in the opposite line. The two players then exchange passes as they return 2v0 to the end they started at.

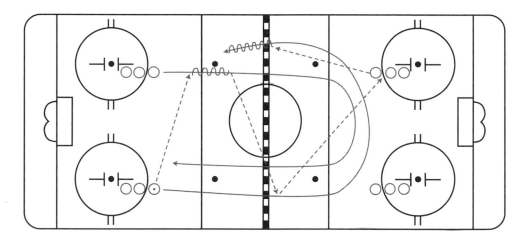

30   NEUTRAL ZONE EXCHANGE: 3V0

1. Three players start at one end at the top of the face-off circles.
2. The players exchange passes while skating to the far blue line.
3. The players exchange a pass with the player in the middle of the far blue line, and then the three players take the return pass and skate back to the starting position while exchanging passes.
4. As soon as the player at the far blue line exchanges the pass, that player and two others start out 3v0 and repeat the drill from the opposite end.

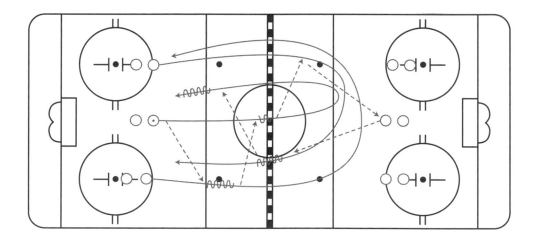

31   WARM-UP PASSING AND RECEIVING CIRCUIT

Stations are set up on the ice as shown. Players rotate through the stations every 40 seconds.

Station 1: Follow the pass

1. Player 1 passes to player 2.
2. Player 1 follows the pass.
3. Player 2 passes to player 3.
4. Player 2 follows the pass, and so on.

Station 2: Monkey in the middle

1. Player 1 tries to intercept a pass.
2. If a pass is intercepted, the passer goes to the middle.

Station 3: Shuttle

1. Player 1 skates forward with the puck.
2. Player 2 skates backward.
3. Player 1 passes to player 2.
4. Player 2 then skates forward, and player 1 skates backward.

Station 4: Figure eight passing

Player 1 skates around the cones in a figure eight pattern, exchanging passes with player 2.

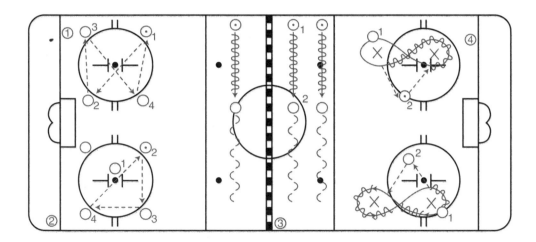

CIRCLES: 1V1, 2V1, 3V1, 2V2, 3V2

Station groups at each of the 5 circles. At each station have the groups perform one of the following:

Station 1: Pairs of players play 1v1 within the circles. The offensive player starts with the puck. The defensive player tries to get control of the puck and get it out of the circle. All players must stay inside the circle.

Station 2: Same drill but with three players playing 2v1.

Station 3: Same drill but with four players playing 3v1.

Station 4: Same drill but with four players playing 2v2.

Station 5: Same drill but with five players playing 3v2.

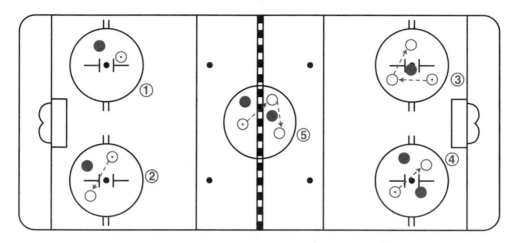

CROSS ICE: 3V3

1. Players play 3v3 cross ice in three zones using the open end of a cone as the goal. (The cones are placed horizontally on the ice with the open end facing inward.)

2. A goal is scored by passing the puck into the open end of the cone.

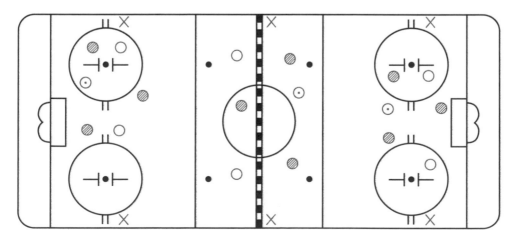

1. Three players try to keep the puck away from three opposing players for 30 seconds in the neutral zone. (On the coach's whistle, the players change with three of their teammates who are lined up on the blue line.)
2. The three players pass to each other, or they can pass to players on their team who are standing on the blue line.
3. The players on the blue line must pass back to one of the three players and not to another player on the blue line.

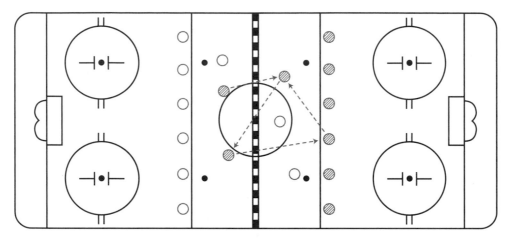

35   FULL-ICE BOGGLE WITH TWO PUCKS

1. All the players are on the ice and play with two pucks. (Goalies are used for this drill.)
2. No icings or offsides are called, and the first team to score 10 goals is the winner.
3. When the second puck is scored, the coach puts two more pucks on the ice.
4. Shooting is only allowed near the goal, and no slap shots are allowed.

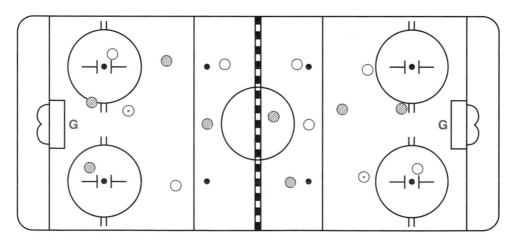

1. Two 5v5 games are played, one at each end of the rink, inside the blue lines. In each game, the opposing teams shoot at the same goalie and must stay inside the blue line.
2. When a team gains possession of the puck, they must pass the puck two times before shooting.
3. If the puck goes outside the blue line, the other team gets possession, and the coaches give a new puck to the other team.

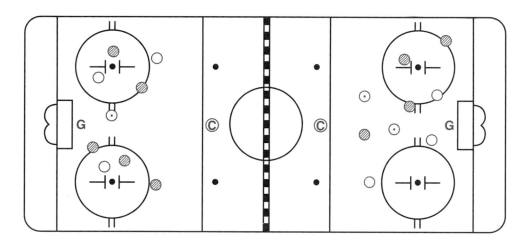

chapter 3

Warm-Up Drills With Shooting

The drills presented in this chapter are usually done at the beginning of practice to help the players—including the goalies—warm up and prepare for the rest of practice. Only one drill from this chapter should be needed per practice and it should usually follow a drill from chapter 2. The drills in this chapter include passing, skating, puckhandling, and shooting. They are also designed to give the goalies an opportunity to face a good number of shots to ensure that they are warmed up and prepared for the remainder of the practice.

For these drills, slap shots should be taken from no closer than the blue line. Slap shots from closer in can travel at speeds the goalie cannot react to, which can lead to injuries for the goalies. For shots closer to the goal, players should use wrist shots. Also, two-on-zero and three-on-zero drills should include only one or two passes inside the blue line to make the situations as gamelike as possible—in a game, only one or two passes are usually made inside the blue line before a shot is taken on goal. More passes than that only increases the likelihood of a turnover. Spend about five minutes of practice time on warm-up drills with shooting, and watch the players to make sure they are using correct techniques.

37 SHOOT, ONE-TOUCH PASS, NEXT SHOOTER

1. Player 1 skates with the puck and shoots, then turns and skates back to the same line, exchanging a one-touch pass with player 2.
2. Player 2 repeats the drill.
3. The drill is done at both ends.

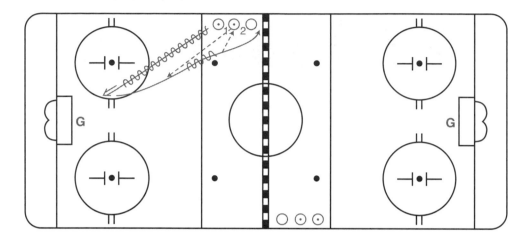

38 PUCK EXCHANGE (WITH STATIONARY PLAYER) AND SHOOT

1. The player with the puck inside the blue line one-touch passes with the stationary player at the center circle.
2. The player then loops toward the boards, takes a return pass from the stationary player, and shoots.

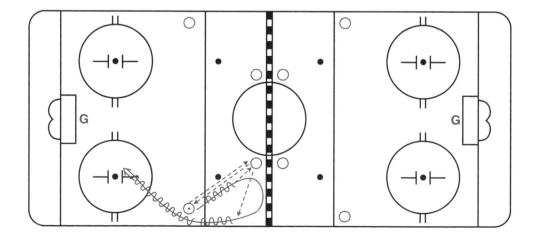

AGILITY, PASS, SHOOT

1. Player 1 skates to the corner, gets a puck, and passes to player 2.
2. Player 1 skates to the blue line, pivots, skates backward to the center line, pivots again, and skates forward over the blue line.
3. Player 1 then cuts in toward the net, receives a pass from player 2, and shoots.

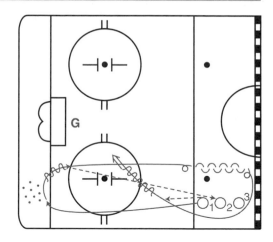

40 BACKWARD, ONE-TOUCH PASS, PIVOT, SHOOT

1. Player 1 skates backward with the puck and one-touch passes with player 2.
2. Player 1 then pivots, skates forward around the cone, and shoots.
3. Player 3 starts the next sequence of the drill with player 4.
4. The drill is done at both ends of the rink.

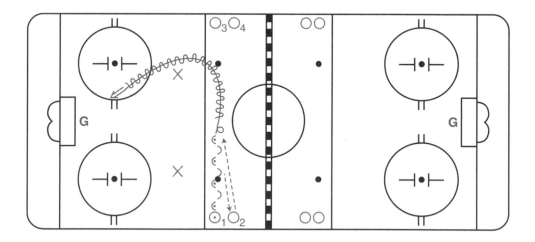

41   ONE-TOUCH PASS AND SHOOT

1. Player 1 starts with the puck, skates across the rink along the blue line, one-touch passes with player 2, skates around the cone, and shoots.
2. Player 2 then starts the same drill from the side boards at the opposite side.

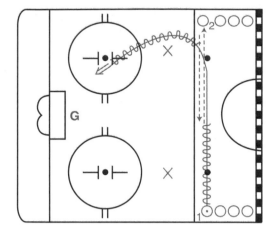

42   TWO ONE-TOUCH PASSES AND SHOOT

1. Player 1 starts with the puck, skates backward from the boards, and one-touch passes with player 2.
2. Player 1 then pivots, skates forward, and one-touch passes with player 3.
3. Player 1 takes the return pass, skates around the cone, and shoots.
4. Player 3 then starts the same drill from the opposite side boards with player 4.

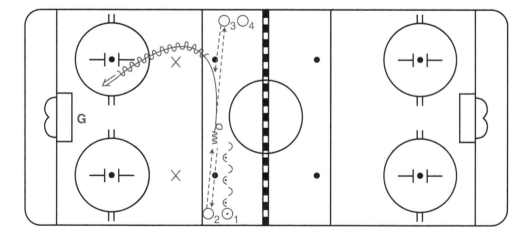

43   SWEDEN, THREE ONE-TOUCH PASSES

1. Player 1 skates backward with the puck and one-touch passes with player 2.
2. Player 1 pivots, skates forward, and one-touch passes with player 3.
3. Player 1 skates around the cone, one-touch passes with player 4, and shoots. (Player 1 then takes the place of player 4.)
4. Player 3 starts the next sequence of the drill.
5. The drill is done at both ends of the rink.

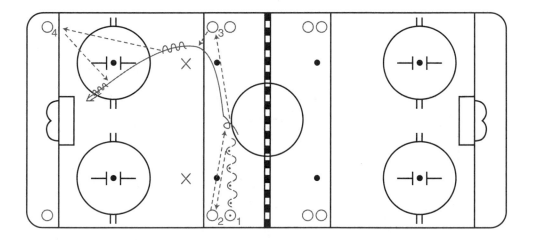

1. Player 1 skates with the puck from the blue line and passes diagonally to player 2 at the goal line. Player 2 returns the pass.
2. Player 1 skates toward the neutral zone and passes to player 3 at the center line. Player 3 returns the pass.
3. Player 1 pivots 360 degrees, skates over the blue line, and shoots.
4. Player 1 takes the position of player 2. Player 2 takes the position of player 3. Player 3 goes to the side boards.
5. Player 4 goes next and passes with player 5 and player 6.
6. The drill is done at both ends of the rink.

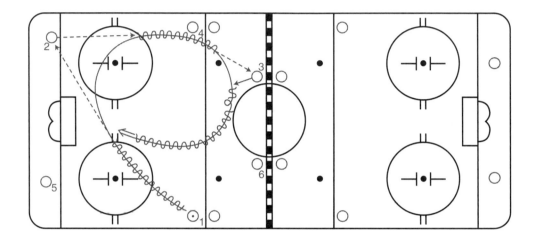

NEUTRAL ZONE CURL

1. Player 1 skates across the ice without a puck and receives a pass from player 2.
2. Player 1 pivots, skates backward with the puck, pivots, exchanges passes with player 3, and shoots.
3. Player 2 starts the same drill from the opposite side.
4. The drill is done at both ends of the rink.

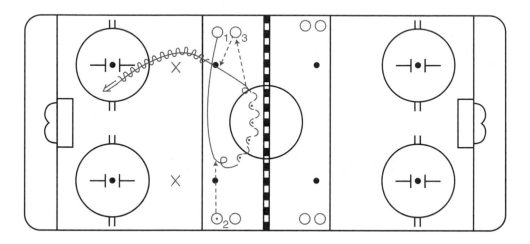

46

FOLLOW THE PASS

1. Player 1 passes to player 2.
2. Player 1 follows the pass to player 2's line.
3. Player 2 passes to player 3.
4. Player 2 follows the pass to player 3's line.
5. Player 3 passes to player 4.
6. Player 3 follows the pass to player 4's line.
7. Player 4 shoots and then goes to player 1's line.

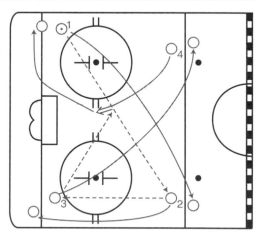

1. Player 1 passes to player 2.
2. Player 2 passes to player 3.
3. Player 3 passes to player 4.
4. Player 1 skates around player 2, cuts down the middle, receives a pass from player 4, and shoots.
5. Player 1 replaces player 4, and the other players rotate one position backward toward player 1's starting position.

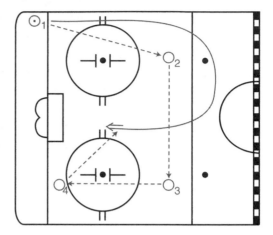

48   MIDDLE PEEL-OFF: 1V0, 2V0

Players should line up at center line and, on the coach's command, perform one of the following two sequences:

Sequence 1

1. Player 1 curls toward the boards from the center circle and receives a pass from player 2.
2. Player 1 skates around the cone and shoots.
3. Player 2 then curls to the opposite boards, takes a pass from player 3, and shoots.

Sequence 2

1. Player 4 and player 5 curl toward opposite boards, and one of these players receives a pass from player 6.
2. Player 4 and player 5 skate around the cones, go 2v0, and shoot. (Only one pass is allowed after player 4 and player 5 pass the cones.)

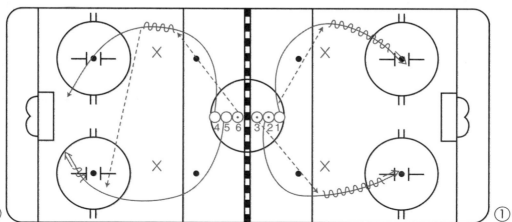

1. Player 1, player 2, and player 3 loop out of the corner inside the blue line. Each player has a puck.
2. Player 1 skates wide toward the far boards and shoots.
3. Player 2 skates to the middle and shoots.
4. Player 3 turns toward the near boards and shoots on the near side.
5. All three players go to the opposite corner.
6. Three new players start from this opposite corner.
7. The drill is done at both ends of the rink.

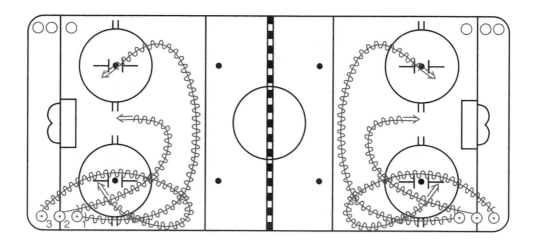

RUSSIAN STICKHANDLE, TWO SHOTS

1. Two players with pucks come from each side and stickhandle in the neutral zone on each side of the rink.
2. On the whistle, both players on each side go over the blue line and shoot in succession.

Variation

The two players on each side of the rink pass and receive one puck in the neutral zone. On the whistle, they go 2v0 and shoot.

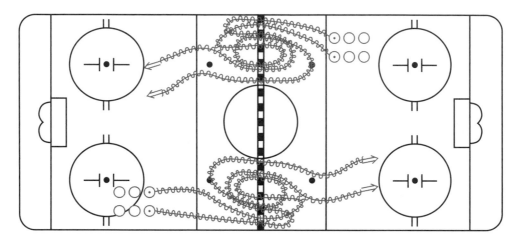

MINNESOTA SCRAMBLE AND SHOOT

1. Five players with pucks begin behind each goal line.
2. The groups skate from opposite ends with their pucks and stickhandle in the neutral zone in all directions.
3. On the whistle, all 10 players skate with their puck and shoot at the opposite end from where they started.

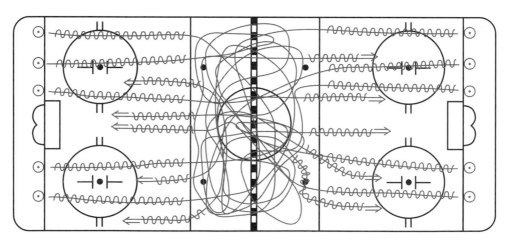

52   SWEDEN NEUTRAL ZONE DIAGONAL

1. Player 1 skates backward with the puck, pivots, skates forward around the center circle, and exchanges passes with player 2.
2. Player 1 finishes skating around the circle and shoots at the end opposite from where the drill started.
3. Player 2 then starts the next sequence of the drill, and player 1 goes to the line diagonally opposite to the line he or she started in.

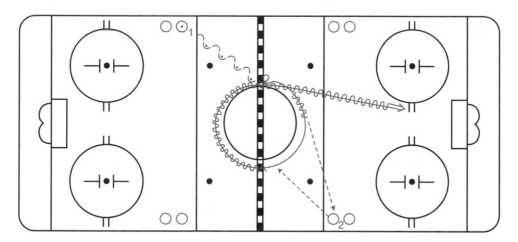

53   FINLAND CIRCLE

1. Player 1 skates around the center circle, receives a pass from player 2, and shoots at the far end.
2. Player 3 starts the next sequence of the drill.
3. Player 1 goes to the line opposite from the line the drill started at.

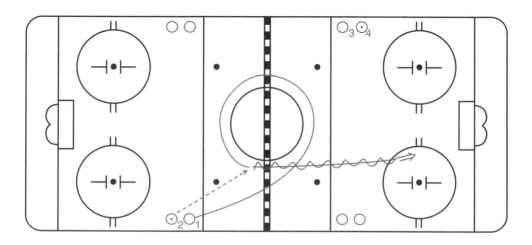

1. Player 1 skates through the neutral zone and one-touch passes with player 2.
2. Player 2 passes to player 3.
3. Player 1 skates back through the neutral zone and receives a pass from player 3.
4. Player 1 skates over the blue line and shoots.

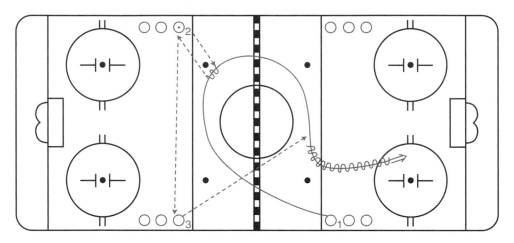

1. Players start in four groups at the blue lines.
2. Player 1 passes the puck to player 2, then skates over the far blue line and takes a return pass from player 2.
3. Player 1 pivots, skates backward with the puck, pivots, skates forward, exchanges passes with player 3 and player 4, and shoots.
4. Player 4 starts the next part of the drill by passing to player 3 and repeats the same pattern. The players return to the same line they started at.

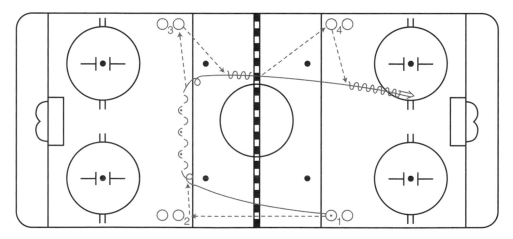

1. Player 1 skates backward and one-touch passes with player 2, then pivots and one-touch passes with player 3.
2. Player 1 circles to the center line, receives a pass from player 2, and shoots at the goalie.

Variation

The same sequence is followed but with a give-and-go pass from player 4 or player 5 before shooting.

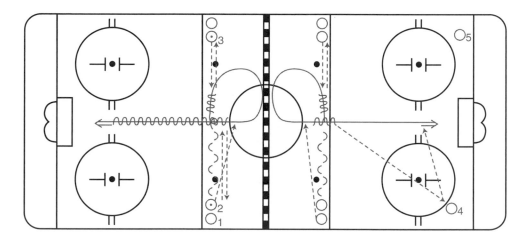

1. Player 1 and player 3 skate along the two blue lines with pucks and pass to player 2 and player 4 at the same time.
2. Player 1 and player 3 then skate toward the far blue line at opposite ends of the rink.
3. Player 2 and player 4 skate out from the boards with the puck and pass to player 1 and player 3, who go in and shoot.
4. Player 2 and player 4 skate along the blue line with new pucks and repeat the same sequence that player 1 and player 3 just completed.

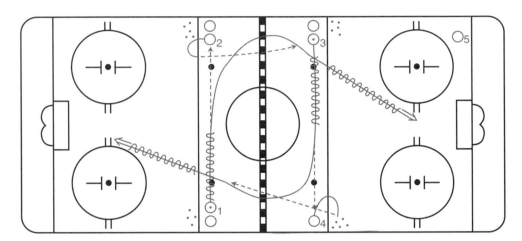

1. Player 1 skates backward from the blue line, pivots, skates to the corner, and gets a puck.
2. Player 1 skates down the boards; executes give-and-go passes with player 2, player 3, and player 4; and then shoots.
3. After shooting, player 1 goes to player 4's position. Player 4 rotates to player 3's line, player 3 rotates to player 2's line, and player 2 goes to player 1's line at the starting position.
4. The drill is continuous on both sides of the rink.

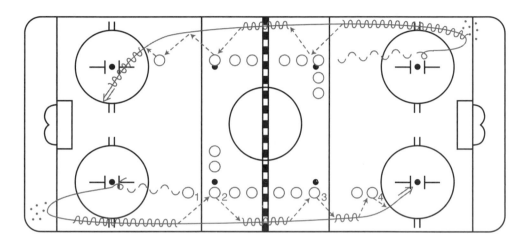

59   GOALIE PASS UP

1. Player 1 skates over the blue line and shoots.
2. The goalie stops the shot, controls the rebound, and passes to player 2 at the side boards next to the face-off circle.
3. Player 1 loops across inside the blue line and takes a pass from player 2.
4. Player 1 passes to player 3.
5. Player 3 continues the drill by shooting at the goalie and repeating the same sequence as player 1.

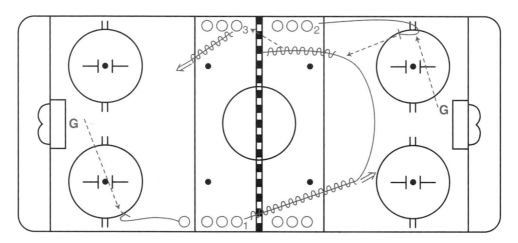

60   STRETCH, 2V0

1. Player 1 skates through the neutral zone and receives a pass from player 3.
2. Player 2 skates through the neutral zone, cuts to the middle of the ice, and takes a pass from player 1.
3. Player 1 crosses behind player 2, and they go 2v0 with only one pass inside the blue line before shooting.

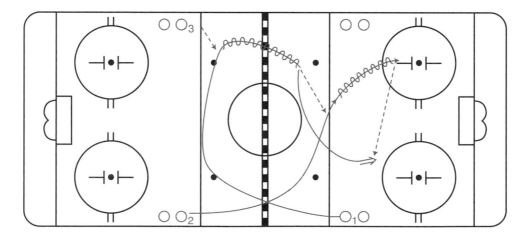

61   SHORT PASS, WIDE PASS

1. The goalie passes to player 1.
2. Player 1 passes to player 2—either a short pass, with player 2 skating across the ice (inside the near blue line), or a wide pass, with player 2 skating down the ice on the wide side.

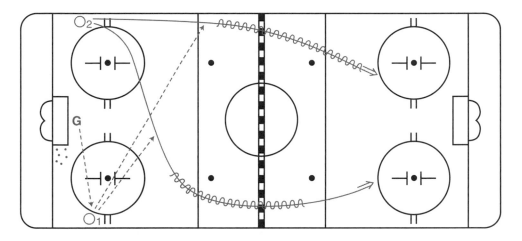

62   RUSSIAN STRETCH, 2V0

1. Player 1 starts the drill by skating in from the blue line and shooting.
2. Player 1 then goes to the corner, gets a puck, and passes to player 2, who has delayed and then skated across just outside the blue line (starting from the same line as player 1 started from).
3. Player 1 skates up the ice and joins player 2 for a 2v0 at the far end. (Only one pass is allowed before shooting after the players cross the blue line on the 2v0.)
4. Player 3 and player 4 start the next sequence of the drill using the same pattern. The drill is continuous.

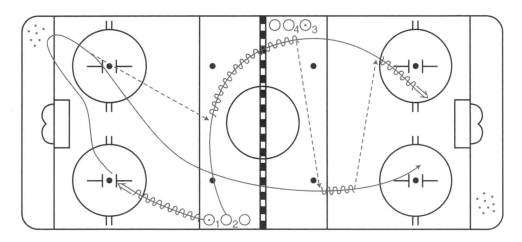

1. Player 1 and player 2 skate around the face-off circle, and they both shoot on the goalie.
2. Player 1 and player 2 loop toward the corner, take a pass from a coach, and go 2v0 at the far end of the rink. (On the 2v0, only one pass is allowed inside the far blue line before shooting.)
3. Player 3 and player 4 do the drill simultaneously from the opposite corner.

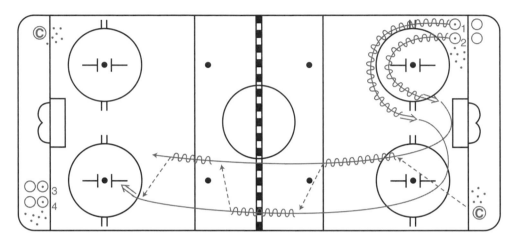

64 THREE OUT OF THE CORNER, CURL AT THE LINES

1. Three players come out of a corner of the rink, and each player loops around a cone at the blue lines and center line and shoots at the end the players started from.
2. The drill is done at both ends of the rink.

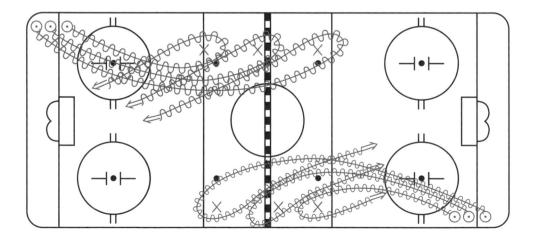

CALGARY, 3V0

1. Player 1, player 2, and player 3 each have a puck. They skate out of the corner and shoot in succession at the near end.
2. All three players skate to the near blue line and get a second puck, then skate the length of the ice and shoot in succession at the far end of the rink.
3. Player 4, player 5, and player 6 then come out of the diagonal corner and repeat the drill going in the opposite direction.

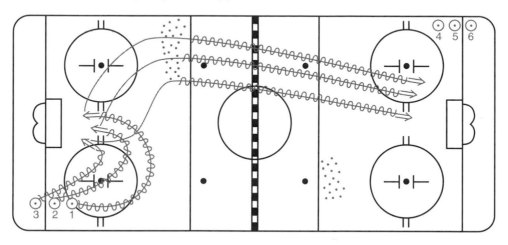

TIMING, 3V0

1. Player 1 skates the length of the ice and shoots, then goes to the corner to get another puck.
2. Player 2 skates inside the far blue line.
3. Player 1 passes to player 2.
4. Player 3 skates to the near blue line and takes a pass from player 2.
5. Player 3 shoots, and player 1 and player 2 skate to the net for a rebound.

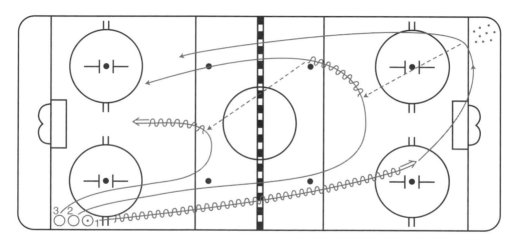

CAROUSEL, DROP PASS

1. Player 1 skates without the puck, loops inside the far blue line, and receives a pass from player 2.
2. Player 1 skates with the puck and drop passes to player 2.
3. Player 2 passes back to player 1, who skates the length of the ice and shoots.
4. Player 2 skates over the far blue line, loops, takes a pass from player 3, and repeats the sequence.
5. The drill starts from alternating diagonal corners at both ends.

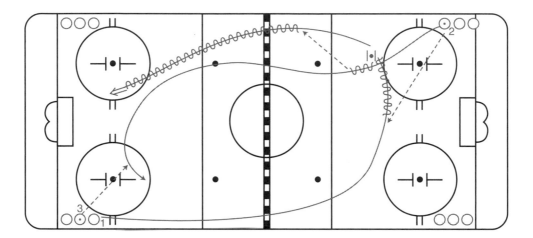

68 DOUBLE CAROUSEL, SECOND SHOT

1. Player 1 skates over the far blue line, loops at the top of the circles, receives a pass from player 2, skates the length of the ice, and shoots.
2. Player 1 then circles back to the far blue line, takes a second pass from player 2, skates down the rink, and shoots a second shot.
3. After passing the second time to player 1, player 2 starts the same sequence and receives two passes from player 3.

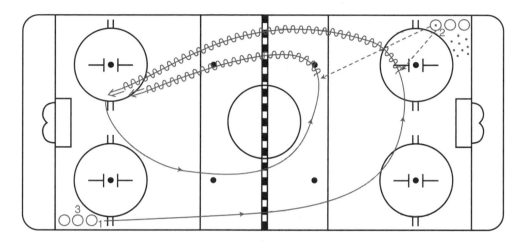

69 1V0 WITH BACKCHECKER CHASER

1. Player 1 skates over the far blue line and receives a pass from player 2, who has moved toward the middle of the ice.
2. Player 1 skates the length of the ice with player 2 chasing and shoots.
3. Player 2 swings around and receives a pass from player 4.
4. Player 2 then skates the length of the ice with player 4 chasing as a backchecker.
5. The drill is continuous.

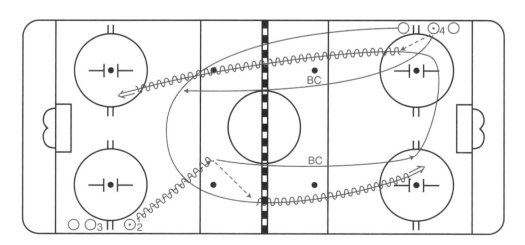

1. Player 1 shoots to start the drill and skates across to the opposite circle to receive a pass from a coach.
2. Player 2 loops from the center of the blue line and receives a pass from player 1.
3. Player 2 skates over the far blue line and shoots.
4. Player 1 chases player 2.
5. Player 2 skates across and receives a pass from a coach.
6. Player 3 loops from the center and receives a pass from player 2.
7. Player 3 skates over the far blue line and shoots, and player 2 chases.
8. The drill begins at both ends simultaneously.

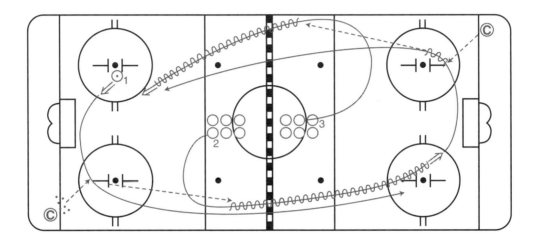

71   D AND F THROUGH THE MIDDLE, 1V0

1. Defenseman 1 skates through the center circle and takes a pass from forward 1, who has also skated through the center circle.
2. Defenseman 1 skates backward with the puck and then passes to forward 1, who has looped toward the blue line at the end he or she started from.
3. Forward 1 goes over the blue line and shoots.
4. Forward 2 then passes to defenseman 2 in the same pattern, and the drill is continuous.

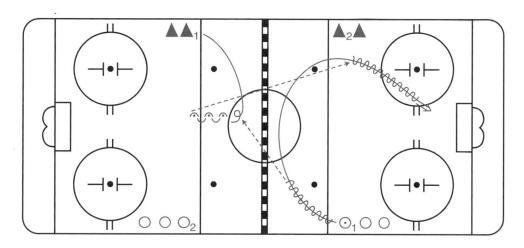

72   SWISS, FROM THE MIDDLE, FIGURE EIGHT

1. Player 1 skates backward from the center circle with the puck and exchanges one-touch passes with player 2.
2. Player 1 then pivots, skates forward in a figure eight while exchanging passes with player 2, and shoots.
3. The drill is done on both sides of the rink.

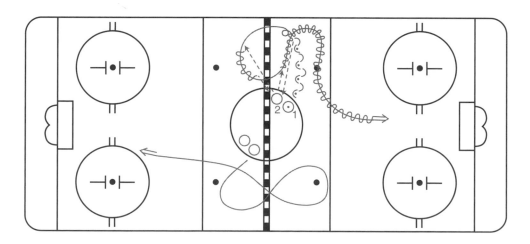

SWISS, MIDDLE, D TO D, SHOOT

1. Forward 1 and forward 2 start in the center circle with pucks.
2. Forward 1 passes to defenseman 2.
3. Defenseman 2 passes to defenseman 1.
4. Forward 1 curls toward the boards and receives a pass from defenseman 1.
5. Forward 1 goes to the far end and shoots.
6. At the same time, forward 2 runs the same drill with defensemen 3 and 4 on the other side of the rink.
7. The drill is continuous.

Variation

Forward 1 and forward 2 go at the same time and pass to defenseman 1, who then passes to defenseman 2.

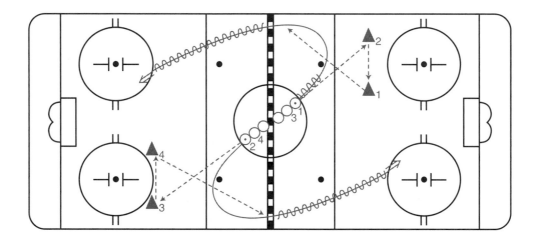

1. Forward 1 passes to defenseman 1.
2. Defenseman 1 passes to defenseman 2.
3. Defenseman 2 passes to forward 1.
4. Forward 1 and forward 2 skate to the far end of the rink; forward 1 skates behind defenseman 2, and forward 2 skates in front.
5. Forward 3 skates diagonally across to the center line and curls back.
6. Forward 1, forward 2, and forward 3 go 3v0 at the end they started from.
7. Forward 4, forward 5, and forward 6 start the next sequence from the opposite end by first passing to defenseman 2. The drill is continuous.

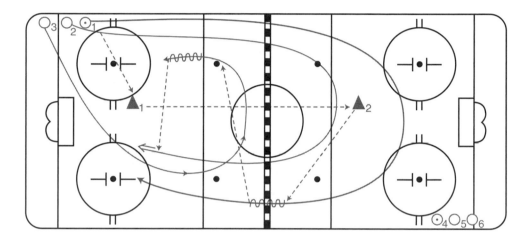

1. Defenseman 1 skates backward out of the center circle and passes to forward 1, who has skated and looped at the opposite blue line.
2. Forward 1 skates with the puck and shoots at the end where he or she started.
3. Forward 1 then goes to the front of the net.
4. Defenseman 1 follows forward 1 and receives a pass at the blue line from a coach.
5. Defenseman 1 shoots, and forward 1 screens or deflects the shot.
6. Forward 2 and defenseman 2 perform the same sequence at the same time.
7. The drill is continuous.

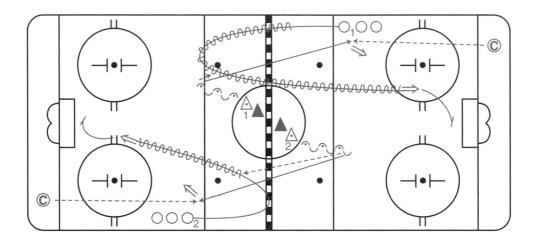

D TO D PASS, ROTATE 1V0

1. Forward 1 skates with the puck toward the far blue line and passes to defenseman 2.
2. Defenseman 2 passes to defenseman 1.
3. Forward 1 loops counterclockwise toward the far boards and receives a pass from defenseman 1.
4. Forward 1 shoots at the end where he or she started.
5. Forward 2 skates the same pattern at the opposite end and passes to defenseman 4.
6. Defenseman 4 passes to defenseman 3.
7. Defenseman 3 passes to forward 2, who shoots at the far end of the rink.
8. The drill is continuous. The defensemen rotate in and out, with defenseman 5 and defenseman 6 rotating clockwise in the next sequence.

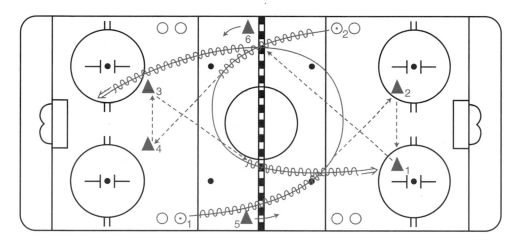

1. Forward 1 starts with the puck.
2. Forward 1 and forward 2 start at the same time and skate toward defenseman 1 and defenseman 2.
3. Forward 1 passes to defenseman 2.
4. Defenseman 2 passes to defenseman 1.
5. Forward 1 and forward 2 either cross or curl toward the side boards, take a return pass from defenseman 1, and go 2v0 at the end of the rink where they started. (Only one pass is allowed inside the blue line.)
6. Forward 3 and forward 4 start the next sequence by passing to defenseman 3 and defenseman 4.
7. Defenseman 5 and defenseman 6 rotate in for the defensemen.

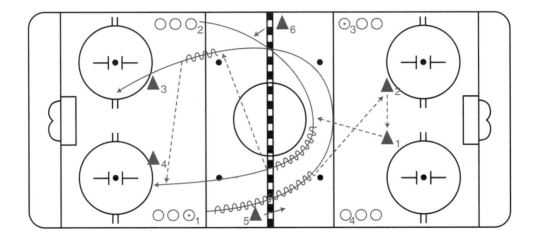

1. Defenseman 1 starts at the blue line, skates forward to the center line, stops, and skates backward.
2. Forward 1 starts with a puck at the opposite blue line, skates toward defenseman 1, and passes the puck to defenseman 1 as defenseman 1 skates backward.
3. Defenseman 1 passes the puck back to forward 1, who has curled toward the middle of the ice.
4. Forward 1 skates in and shoots, and then curls back toward the center line.
5. After passing to forward 1, defenseman 1 goes to the corner, gets a puck, and makes a long pass to forward 1 at the center line.
6. Forward 1 goes in and shoots a second shot.
7. Forward 2 and defenseman 2 perform the same sequence at the same time on the other side of the rink. The drill is continuous.

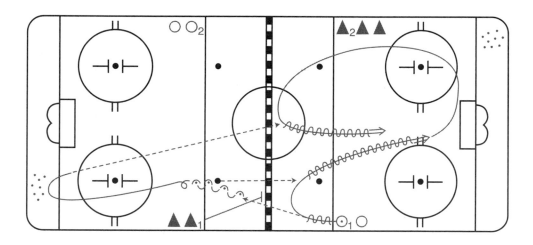

1. Forward 1 passes to defenseman 1, who has skated to the center line.
2. Defenseman 1 skates backward with the puck and passes to forward 1, who loops across inside the center line.
3. Forward 1 goes over the blue line and shoots.
4. After shooting, forward 1 turns back, loops inside the center line, and takes a second pass from defenseman 1, who has pivoted, skated to the corner, and received a puck from a coach.
5. Forward 1 shoots again and then stops in front of the net.
6. Defenseman 1 skates to the far blue line, receives a pass from another coach, and shoots.
7. Forward 1 screens or deflects.
8. Forward 2 and defenseman 2 perform the same drill simultaneously from the other side.

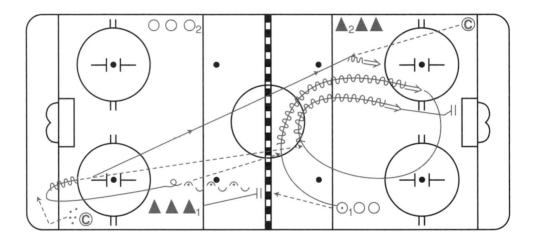

1. Defenseman 1 skates to the center line, pivots, skates backward, and receives a pass from defenseman 2.
2. Forward 1 skates to the center line, curls back, and takes a pass from defenseman 1.
3. Forward 1 goes over the blue line and shoots, then goes to the corner to get another puck.
4. Defenseman 1 skates to the far blue line after passing the puck to forward 1.
5. Forward 1 passes the puck to defenseman 1 inside the blue line, and defenseman 1 shoots.
6. Forward 1 goes to the front of the net for a screen or deflection or rebound.
7. Defenseman 3 and defenseman 4 repeat the same drill with forward 2 shooting at the opposite end of the rink.

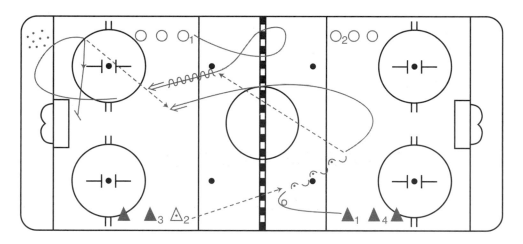

DRIVE FOR THE NET, 1V0

1. Player 1 skates across the ice, receives a pass from player 2, skates around the cone at the far blue line (while keeping the feet moving), and shoots.
2. At the same time, player 3 skates across the ice, receives a pass from player 4, skates around the cone at the far blue line, and shoots.
3. Player 2 and player 4 go next, repeating the same pattern from the opposite side.

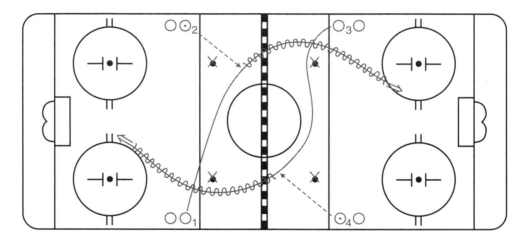

DRIVE FOR THE NET, 2V0

1. Player 1 and player 5 skate across the ice at the same time.
2. Player 1 receives a pass from player 2 and skates around the cone at the far blue line.
3. Player 5 skates through the middle to the net.
4. Player 1 either shoots or passes to player 5 for a shot.
5. Player 3 and player 6 go next, repeating the same pattern.

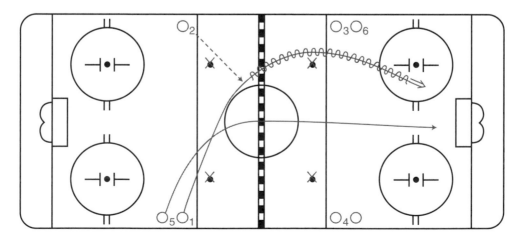

83   DRIVE FOR THE NET, 3V0

1. Player 1 skates across the ice, receives a pass from player 2, and skates around the cone at the far blue line.
2. Player 5 skates through the middle to the net.
3. Player 7 delays, then skates down the side boards over the far blue line and cuts to the middle of the ice.
4. Player 7 receives a pass from player 1 and shoots.
5. Player 3, player 6, and player 8 go next, repeating the same pattern.

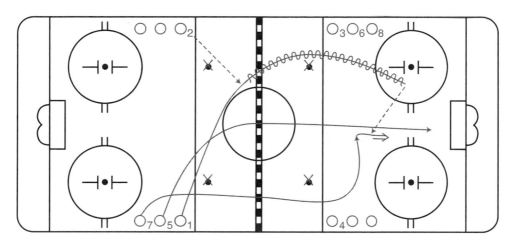

84   TEAM CANADA, STRAIGHT GIVE-AND-GO

1. Players are in four lines at the blue lines.
2. Player 1 skates with the puck and passes to player 2.
3. Player 1 receives a return pass from player 2 and shoots at the end opposite from where he or she started.
4. The same drill is run on the other side of the rink.

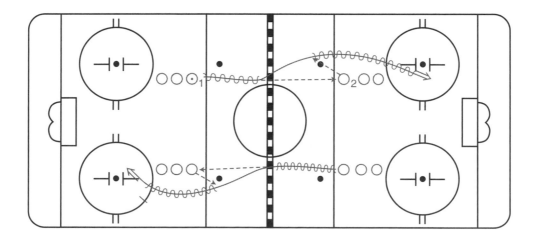

85   TEAM CANADA, REVERSE GIVE-AND-GO

1. Players are in four lines at the blue lines.
2. Player 1 skates with the puck toward player 2 and passes the puck to player 2.
3. Player 1 skates to the far blue line, loops toward the side boards to reverse direction, receives a return pass from player 2, and then skates back to the other end and shoots.
4. The same drill is run on the other side of the rink.

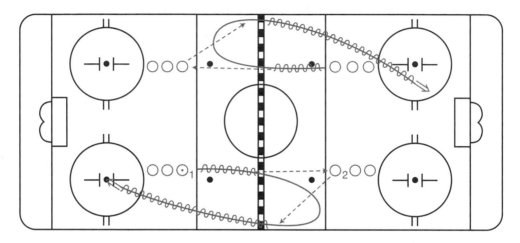

86   TEAM CANADA, CUT TO THE MIDDLE

1. Players are in four lines at the blue lines.
2. Player 1 skates toward player 2 and passes the puck to player 2.
3. Player 1 skates to the far blue line, loops toward the boards to reverse direction, and receives a return pass from player 2.
4. Player 1 cuts to the middle of the ice at the blue line and shoots.
5. The same drill is run on the other side of the rink.

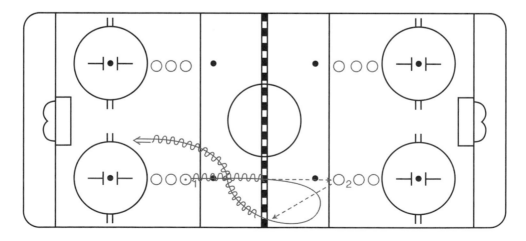

87 TEAM CANADA, SKATE AROUND THE CENTER CIRCLE

1. Players are in four lines at the blue lines.
2. Player 1 passes diagonally across to player 3.
3. Player 2 skates around the center circle and receives a pass from player 3.
4. Player 2 skates to the far end and shoots.
5. At the same time, player 4 passes diagonally to player 5, and player 6 skates around the center circle and receives a pass from player 5.

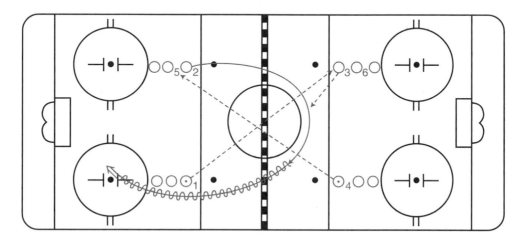

88   TEAM CANADA, 2V0

1. Players are in four lines at the blue lines.
2. Player 1 passes to player 2.
3. Player 2 passes to player 3.
4. Player 1 and player 4 skate to the far blue line, loop, take a return pass, and go 2v0 in the opposite direction.

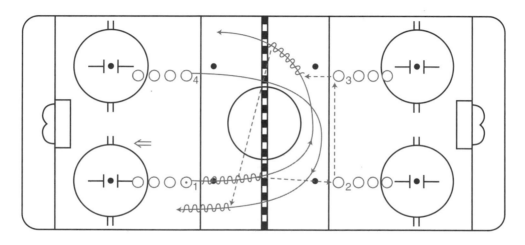

1. Forward 1 passes to defenseman 1.
2. Forward 1 skates to the far blue line, turns toward the side boards, loops back, takes a return pass from defenseman 1, and skates in for the shot.
3. At the same time, forward 2 passes to defenseman 2, loops toward the boards at the far blue line to reverse direction, and receives the return pass for the shot.
4. The drill continues with forward 3 passing to defenseman 1 and forward 4 passing to defenseman 2.

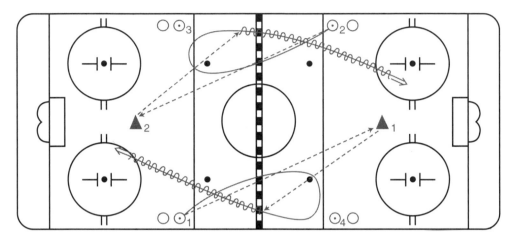

1. Forward 1 passes to defenseman 1.
2. Forward 1 skates around the center circle and receives a return pass from defenseman 1.
3. Forward 2 loops at the far blue line and comes back for a 2v0 with forward 1. (Only one pass is allowed inside the blue line during the 2v0.)

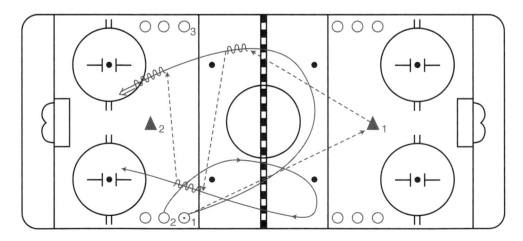

1. Forward 1 passes to defenseman 1.
2. Forward 1 skates around the center circle and receives a return pass from defenseman 1.
3. Forward 2 skates toward the far blue line and loops back toward the boards.
4. Forward 3 skates across from the far boards under the center circle.
5. Forward 1, forward 2, and forward 3 go 3v0.
6. Forward 4, forward 5, and forward 6 go next, repeating the drill from the other end.

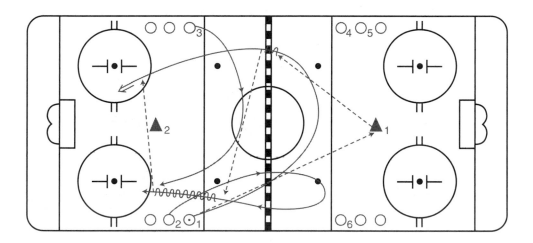

This drill is the same as the previous three Winnipeg drills, with the exception of having two defensemen. For example, in the 1v0 Winnipeg, Two Defensemen drill, the following sequence would be followed:

1. Forward 1 passes to defenseman 1 and skates to the far blue line before looping back.
2. Defenseman 1 passes to defenseman 2.
3. Defenseman 2 passes to forward 1, who skates back to the other end and shoots.

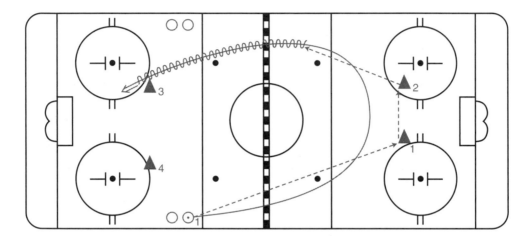

STRETCH, 2V0

1. Player 1 skates in and shoots, then goes to the corner and gets another puck. Player 1 passes to player 2, who is skating across inside the blue line.
2. Player 3 curls and skates to the far blue line to receive a pass from player 2.
3. Player 3 skates across the blue line and shoots.
4. Player 2 follows player 3 and looks for a rebound.
5. Player 2 goes to the corner and gets a puck.
6. Player 4 and player 5 come off the boards and player 2 passes to player 4.
7. Players 4 and 5 go 2v0 at the opposite end.
8. The drill is continuous.

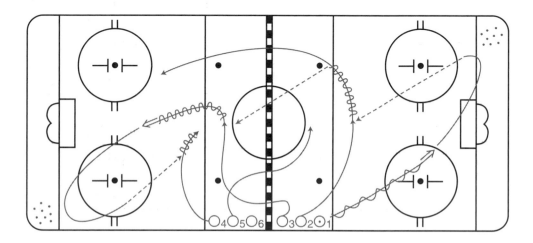

KAMLOOPS, 1V0 SHOOTING

1. Forward 1 and forward 2 start from diagonal corners of the rink. They both skate to the center circle and get a puck.
2. Forward 1 passes to defenseman 2.
3. Forward 2 passes to defenseman 1.
4. Forward 1 and forward 2 turn and curl toward the boards, take return passes from defenseman 2 and defenseman 1, go back to the end of the rink they started from, and shoot.
5. Forward 3 and forward 4 go next from opposite corners.

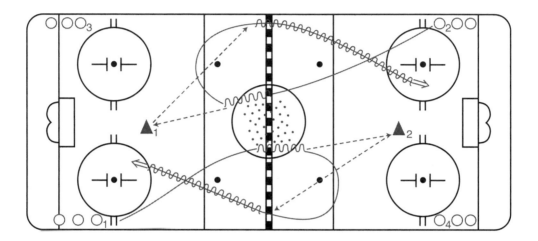

KAMLOOPS, 2V0 PASS AND SHOOT

1. Forward 1 and forward 2 skate at the same time toward the center circle. One of the two players gets a puck and passes to defenseman 2.
2. Forward 1 and forward 2 turn, curl toward the boards, and take a return pass from defenseman 2.
3. Forward 1 and forward 2 go 2v0 at the end of the rink they started from. (Only one pass is allowed before shooting after they pass the blue line in the offensive zone.)
4. Forward 3 and forward 4 go next and pass to defenseman 1.
5. The drill is continuous.

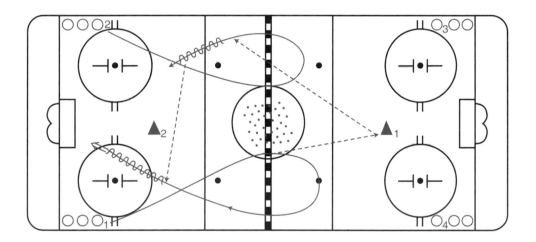

1. Player 1 and player 2 shoot to start the drill and then go to the corners to get another puck.
2. Player 3 and player 4 come from the side boards and curl to the middle, where they receive passes from player 1 and player 2.
3. Player 5 and player 6 curl toward the boards and receive passes from player 3 and player 4.
4. After passing, the players who made the passes go to the line of the players passed to.
5. The drill is continuous.

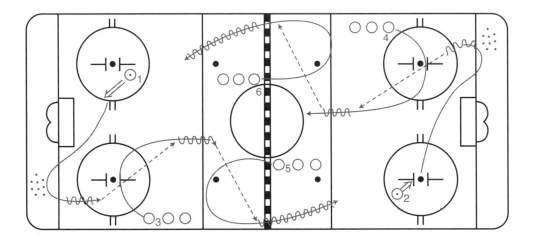

1. Player 1 and player 2 shoot to start the drill and then go to the corners to get another puck.
2. Player 1 and player 2 make long passes to player 3 and player 4, who have curled toward the center line from the side boards at opposite blue lines.
3. Player 3 and player 4 shoot and then go to the corners to get another puck, which they pass to the next two players coming off the boards.
4. The drill is continuous.

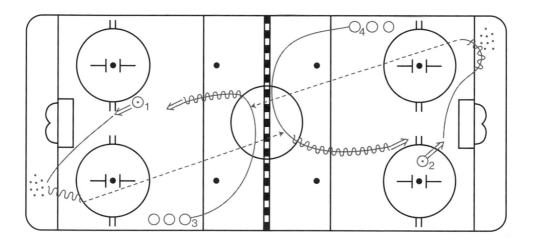

CZECH 1V0

1. Players line up at the side boards, and pucks are placed in the four corners. Put three cones in the middle of the ice so players going 1v0 in opposite directions don't collide.

2. Player 1 and player 2 come off the side boards, go toward opposite ends—skating into the top of the circles—and receive a pass from a coach or a goalie to start the drill (see figure 1).

3. Player 1 and player 2 loop back, skate the length of the ice, and shoot.

4. After shooting, player 1 and player 2 go to the corners, get a puck, and pass to the next player coming off the side boards (see figure 2).

5. The next players going offensive should wait until the shooting player gets the puck in the corner, and should skate to the top of the circle to receive the pass.

6. The drill is continuous.

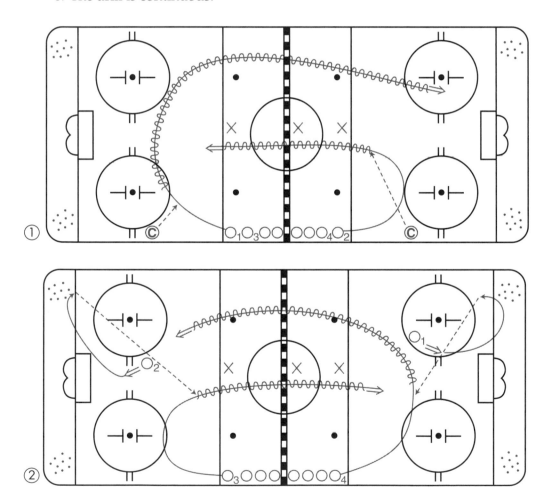

1. Player 1 and player 2 come off the side boards and receive a pass from a coach to start the drill.
2. Player 1 and player 2 loop back, skate the length of the rink on a 2v0, and shoot. (Only one pass is allowed inside the blue line during the 2v0.)
3. The player who doesn't shoot goes to the corner and starts the next sequence by passing to player 3 and player 4, who have waited until the player going to the corner has the puck and then swung inside the top of the circles to receive the passes.
4. Player 3 and player 4 go 2v0 to the far end of the rink.

Variation

Three players come off the side boards performing the steps above, making it a 3v0.

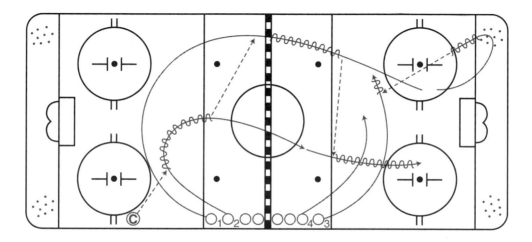

chapter 4

One-on-One Drills

One-on-one situations occur frequently in the game of ice hockey. They may occur along the boards, in the corners, in front of the net, or away from the boards. The drills in this chapter can be used to practice these situations, including one-on-ones that go full ice and those that take place in a small space.

For these one-on-one drills, make sure that the attacking players skate at full speed or use a change of speed to beat the defender. Different offensive moves that players should work on when performing these drills include moving to either side of the defender (on the backhand or forehand side), using curl moves, faking a shot and going wide, and using a head fake one way and going the other way. Offensive players may also practice moving the puck diagonally between the defender's stick and skates or using the defender as a screen when shooting. Passing the puck to a teammate is always a better option than trying to beat an opponent one on one.

The defender should always try to close the gap between the defender and the attacker in open ice. Defenders need to work on their backward skating speed—a defender should attempt to skate backward at the same speed as the attacker and be in a balanced position to react quickly to any change in movement by the attacker. In the corners or along the boards, the defender should try to pin the attacker, or if the player has full control and is moving from the boards or corner, the defender should try to contain the attacker's movement. The defender should keep the head up and watch the opponent's chest instead of the puck. If the defender is looking only at the puck, the defender's head is down, which gives the defender little chance to stop the attacker's body if the puck gets by the defender. With the new rules in ice hockey regarding the use of the stick, defenders must be sure that the stick is on the ice and held with one hand; the elbow should be bent so the defender is ready to poke check the attacking player if possible. If the poke check is not effective, the shoulder check is used both in open ice and when pinning an opponent. If the poke check is effective, it knocks the puck away, making the body check unnecessary. The hip check is another option, but it is a high-risk check and must be executed properly because a missed hip check leaves the defender out of the play. Therefore, pivoting and turning with an opponent when the player goes wide is usually more effective than the hip check.

100   AROUND THE RINK, 1V1

1. On the whistle from the coach, two players go 1v1 for 30 seconds.
2. On the next whistle, the players skate around the rink passing the puck.
3. On the next whistle, they go 1v1 again.

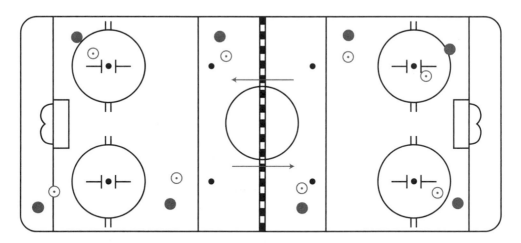

101   1V1 STRAIGHT

1. Defenseman 1 and defenseman 2 skate forward with the puck from the blue line on opposite ends of the rink.
2. Defenseman 1 and defenseman 2 pass the puck to forward 1 and forward 2 at the goal line.
3. Forward 1 goes 1v1 against defenseman 1, and forward 2 goes 1v1 against defenseman 2.
4. The drill is started each time with a whistle from the coach.

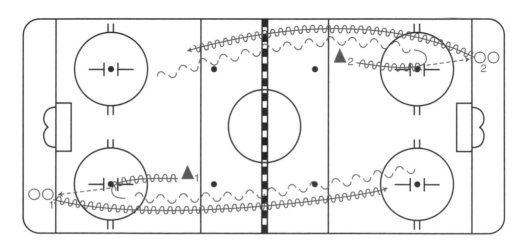

1. Forward 1 starts at the boards near the face-off circle, skates over the far blue line, and receives a pass from defenseman 2.
2. Defenseman 1 skates forward around the center circle, pivots, and skates backward.
3. Forward 1 goes 1v1 against defenseman 1.
4. After passing the puck to forward 1, defenseman 2 skates around the center circle; forward 2 skates to the far blue line, receives a pass from defenseman 3 and comes back to go 1v1 against defenseman 2.
5. The drill is repeated from the opposite end of the rink, with other players lined up to pass to them.
6. The drill can alternate from each end for the 1v1, or players at both ends can go at the same time. If players from both ends go, the next defenseman at each end passes the puck to the forward coming inside the blue line.

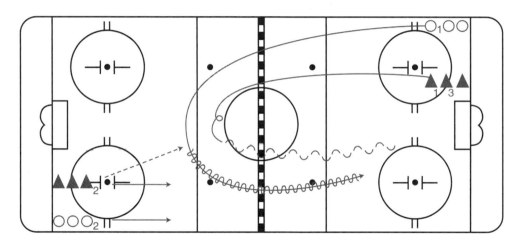

1. Forward 1 starts at the goal line and passes the puck to defenseman 1, who is at the blue line.
2. Forward 1 skates to the front of the net to screen or deflect.
3. Defenseman 1 skates along the blue line to the middle and shoots.
4. Forward 2 then passes a puck to forward 1.
5. Forward 1 goes 1v1 against defenseman 1, who skates backward to the opposite end of the rink.
6. Forward 3, forward 4, and defenseman 2 do the same drill simultaneously at the other end of the rink.

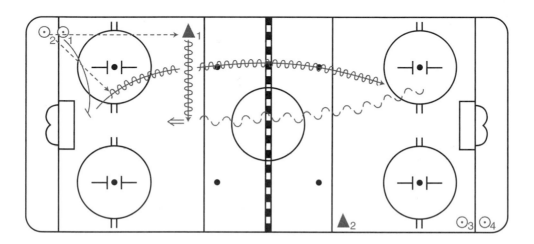

1. Forward 1 one-touch passes with defenseman 1, who skates backward out of the center circle.
2. Forward 1 skates a figure eight and exchanges passes with defenseman 1, who mirrors the skating pattern of forward 1.
3. When forward 1 completes the figure eight in the neutral zone, forward 1 goes 1v1 against defenseman 1.
4. Forward 2 and defenseman 2 do the same drill simultaneously from the other side of the center circle.

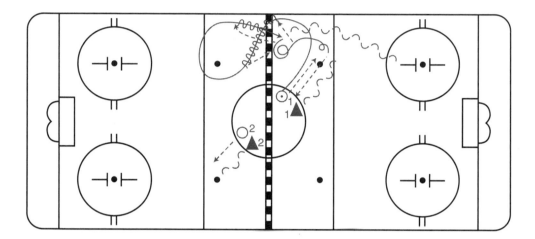

PASS TO DEFENSEMAN, PASS TO COACH, 1V1

1. Defenseman 1 skates backward out of the center circle and takes a pass from forward 1.
2. Defenseman 1 pivots, skates forward, and passes to forward 1, who skates out of the center circle.
3. Forward 1 skates a figure eight and exchanges passes with the coach.
4. After passing to forward 1, defenseman 1 pivots at the center line, skates backward, and defends against forward 1 in a 1v1.
5. Forward 2 and defenseman 2 perform the same drill simultaneously from the other side of the center circle.

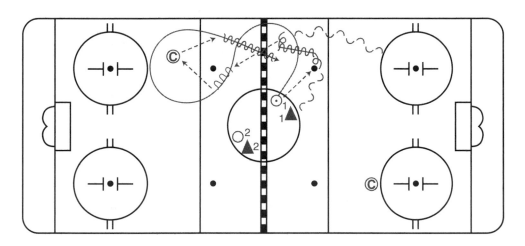

1. Defenseman 1 and defenseman 2 skate diagonally backward out of the middle at opposite sides, pivot, and get a pass from the coach.
2. Forward 1 and forward 2 skate to the far blue line, loop wide, and take passes from defenseman 1 (who passes to forward 2) and defenseman 2 (who passes to forward 1).
3. After passing, defenseman 1 and defenseman 2 skate diagonally across the ice, and the players go 1v1—forward 1 goes 1v1 against defenseman 1, and forward 2 goes 1v1 against defenseman 2.
4. Each repetition of the drill begins on a whistle from the coach.

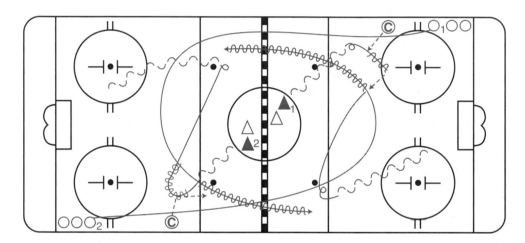

1. Forward 1 and forward 2 skate with pucks toward the far blue lines.
2. Forward 1 passes to defenseman 1, and forward 2 passes to defenseman 2.
3. Defenseman 1 returns the pass to forward 1, and defenseman 2 returns the pass to forward 2.
4. Forward 1 and forward 2 loop and skate back with the puck.
5. After passing, defenseman 1 and defenseman 2 skate forward to the blue line, pivot, and skate backward.
6. Forward 1 then goes 1v1 against defenseman 2, and forward 2 goes 1v1 against defenseman 1.
7. The drill begins simultaneously from both sides.

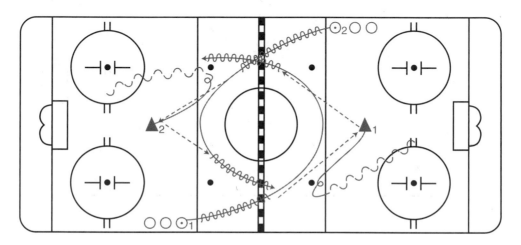

1. The coach shoots the puck in the corner.
2. The forward skates in from the blue line, gets the puck, and skates in a zigzag motion from the corner.
3. The defenseman skates forward, pivots, skates backward, and mirrors the forward's movement until the top of the face-off circle.
4. The forward then goes 1v1 against the defenseman to the far end of the rink.
5. The drill goes in both directions at the same time.

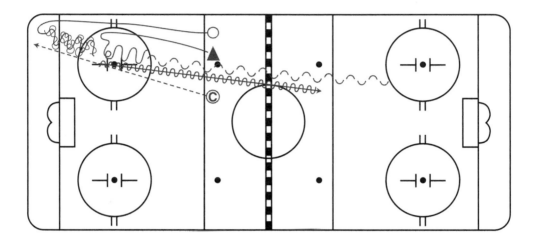

OLYMPIC 1V1

1. One puck is placed behind the net at each end of the rink.
2. On the whistle, forward 1 and forward 2 skate behind the nets diagonally opposite from one another, get the pucks, and go straight down the rink along the boards to the center line.
3. Defenseman 1 and defenseman 2 are near the hash marks of the face-off circles, facing the net.
4. As soon as forward 1 and forward 2 touch the pucks, defenseman 1 and defenseman 2 skate backward down the ice, and the players go 1v1.
5. Defenseman 1 and defenseman 2 cannot turn until the center line; forward 1 and forward 2 must skate straight down the boards until the center line before they can cut to the middle of the rink.

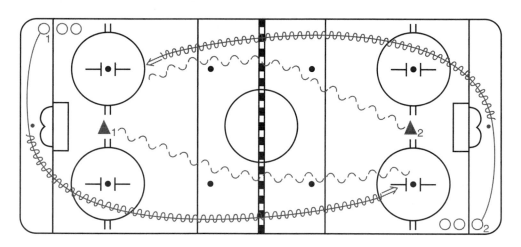

RIM, DEFLECT, 1V1

1. Forward 1 begins in the corner and rims the puck along the boards to defenseman 1 at the blue line.
2. Defenseman 1 skates along the blue line to the middle and shoots, then pivots and skates backward.
3. After rimming the puck, forward 1 goes to the front of the net for a deflection or screen on defenseman 1's shot.
4. Forward 1 then gets a puck at the top of the circle and goes 1v1 against defenseman 1.
5. Forward 2 and defenseman 2 complete the same pattern, and the drill goes in both directions.

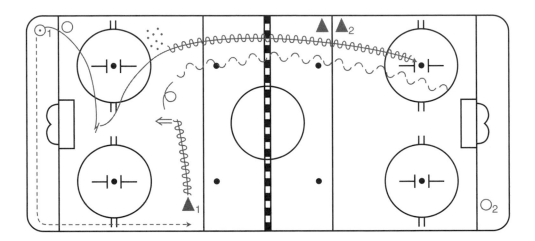

111

DEFENSEMAN IN THE MIDDLE, RIM 1V1

1. Forward 1 rims the puck along the boards to forward 2, who is positioned at the boards near the face-off circle.
2. Defenseman 1 skates forward, pivots, and skates backward.
3. Forward 2 goes 1v1 against defenseman 1.
4. Forward 3, forward 4, and defenseman 2 complete the same pattern on the other end, and the drill goes in both directions.

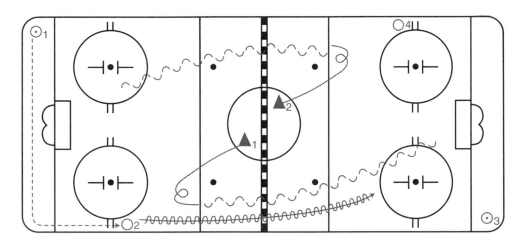

1. Forward 1 passes to defenseman 1.
2. Forward 1 goes to the front of the net for a tip-in or screen.
3. At the same time, defenseman 1 skates across to the middle of the blue line and shoots.
4. Offensive forward 1 then skates across and receives a pass from the coach.
5. Defenseman 1 pivots, skates backward, and defends against offensive forward 1 in a 1v1 going to the far end of the rink.
6. Forward 2 and defenseman 2 complete the same pattern at the other end, and the drill goes in both directions.

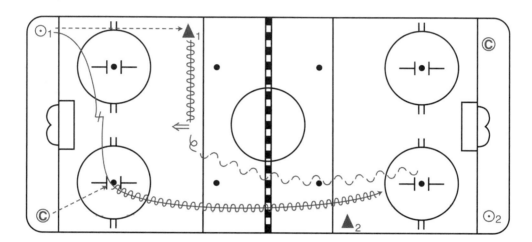

113   1V1 SWEDISH

1. Forward 1 skates with the puck from the blue line toward defenseman 1 in the opposite corner.
2. Forward 1 passes to defenseman 1 and then pivots.
3. Defenseman 1 gives a return pass to forward 1.
4. Defenseman 2 skates inside the blue line, pivots, and defends forward 1 in a 1v1 the length of the rink.
5. Forward 2, defenseman 3, and defenseman 4 perform the same pattern at the other end, and the drill goes in both directions.

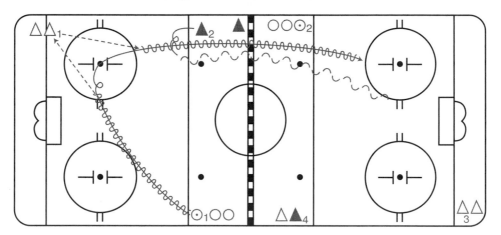

114   SHOOT 1V1

1. Forward 1 skates in from the blue line and shoots, then skates across and receives a pass from the coach.
2. Defenseman 1 skates over the blue line, pivots, and defends forward 1 in a 1v1 the length of the rink.
3. Forward 2 and defenseman 2 perform the same pattern at the other end, and the drill goes in both directions.

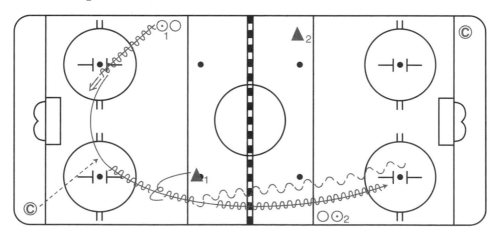

CROSS-ICE PASS 1V1

1. Defenseman 1 passes cross ice to forward 1.
2. Defenseman 2 passes cross ice to forward 2.
3. Defenseman 1 and defenseman 2 skate forward outside opposite blue lines, pivot, and skate backward.
4. Forward 2 then goes 1v1 against defenseman 1, and forward 1 goes 1v1 against defenseman 2.
5. The drill is continuous.

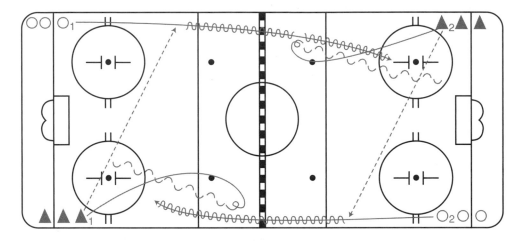

HALF-ICE 1V1

1. Defenseman 1 passes cross ice to forward 1 coming from the opposite corner.
2. Forward 1 skates outside the blue line to the center line.
3. Defenseman 1 skates to the blue line, pivots, and skates backward.
4. Forward 1 then goes 1v1 against defenseman 1.
5. Forward 2 and defenseman 2 perform the same pattern at the opposite end, and the drill is continuous at both ends.

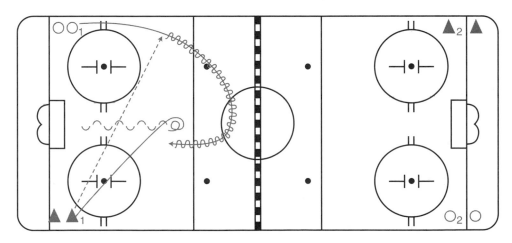

FINLAND THREE ONE-TOUCHES, 1V1

1. Forward 1 skates with the puck to the far blue line, loops across, and exchanges two one-touch passes with forward 2.
2. Defenseman 1 skates to the center line, pivots, and skates backward.
3. Forward 1 goes 1v1 against defenseman 1.
4. After passing, forward 2 goes to the other line in the corner.
5. The drill can alternate and goes in both directions.

Variation

Forward 2 can join the play with forward 1 and go 2v1 against defenseman 1.

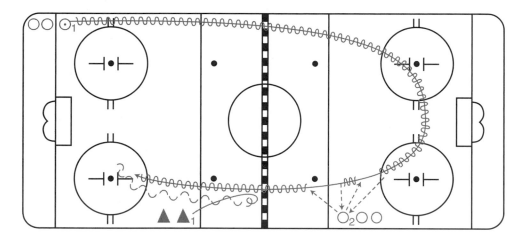

1V1 LOOP

1. Forward 1 skates over the far blue line, loops across, and takes a pass from forward 3.
2. Defenseman 1 skates to the center line, stops, and skates backward.
3. Forward 1 goes 1v1 against defenseman 1.
4. At the same time, forward 2 skates the same pattern in the opposite direction, receives a pass from forward 4, and goes 1v1 against defenseman 2.
5. The drill is continuous.

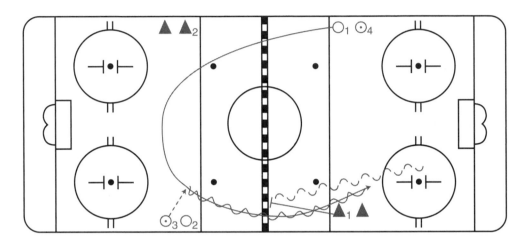

1V1 CIRCLE BACK

1. Defenseman 1 starts at the blue line and passes to forward 1 in the corner.
2. Forward 1 skates with the puck and turns and circles back two times.
3. Defenseman 1 reacts by skating backward and mirroring the movements of forward 1 and closes the gap when the forward circles back.
4. After circling back twice, forward 1 goes 1v1 against defenseman 1 to the other end of the rink.
5. At the same time, forward 2 and defenseman 2 perform the same pattern at the opposite corner, and they go 1v1 on the other side of the rink.
6. The drill is continuous.

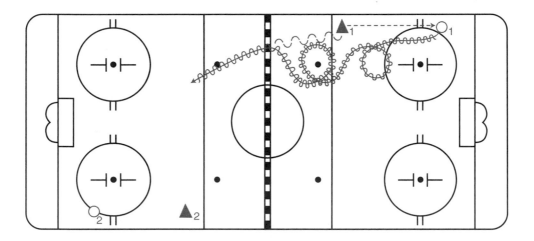

1. Defenseman 1 and defenseman 2 exchange one-touch passes.
2. Defenseman 3 and defenseman 4 exchange one-touch passes.
3. Forward 1 loops toward the far blue line and takes a pass from defenseman 1.
4. Forward 2 loops toward the other blue line and takes a pass from defenseman 4.
5. Defenseman 1 and defenseman 4 skate toward the center line, pivot, and skate backward.
6. Forward 1 goes 1v1 against defenseman 4, and forward 2 goes 1v1 against defenseman 1.
7. The drill is continuous.

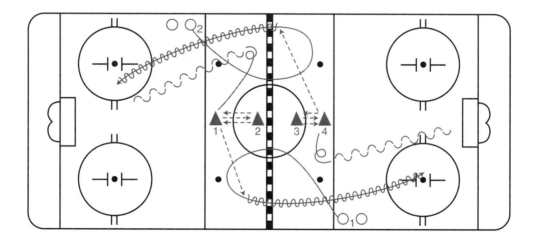

CROSS ICE, D CROSS STEPS, 1V1

1. Forward 1 passes cross ice to forward 2.
2. Defenseman 1 skates from the center circle diagonally to the blue line, moves along the blue line using cross steps, pivots, and skates backward.
3. Forward 2 skates with the puck the length of the ice and goes 1v1 against defenseman 1.
4. Forward 3, forward 4, and defenseman 2 perform the same pattern on the other end.
5. The drill goes in both directions at the same time.

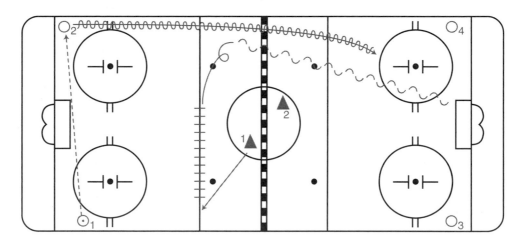

DEFENSE ONE TOUCH, 1V1

1. Forward 1 and defenseman 1 exchange one-touch passes while defenseman 1 skates backward.
2. Forward 2 and defenseman 2 exchange one-touch passes while defenseman 2 skates backward.
3. With the defensemen continuing to skate backward, forward 1 goes 1v1 against defenseman 2, and forward 2 goes 1v1 against defenseman 1.
4. The drill is continuous.

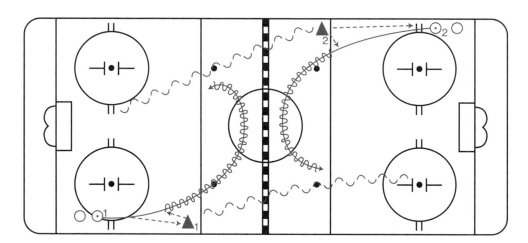

1V1 D PASS LOOP

1. Defenseman 1 and defenseman 2 skate backward with pucks from the center circle.
2. Forward 1 and forward 2 skate toward the defensemen, loop around, and take passes from defenseman 1 and defenseman 2.
3. After passing the pucks, defenseman 1 and defenseman 2 skate forward, pivot, and skate backward.
4. Forward 1 skates to the far blue line, loops back, and goes 1v1 against defenseman 1; forward 2 skates the same pattern and goes 1v1 against defenseman 2.

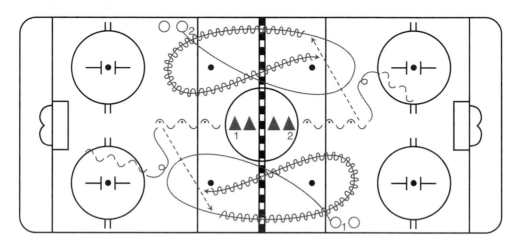

DEFENSIVE SHOOT, 1V1

1. Defenseman 1 and defenseman 2 shoot and then take a pass from the coach.
2. Forward 1 and forward 2 start at the top of the circle, skate around the cone, and take a pass from defenseman 1 and defenseman 2.
3. Defenseman 1 and defenseman 2 skate to the center line, pivot, and skate backward.
4. Forward 1 goes 1v1 against defenseman 1, and forward 2 goes 1v1 against defenseman 2.

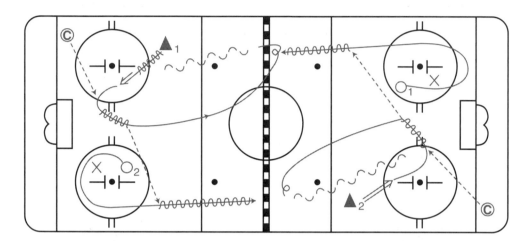

1V1, FORWARDS IN CENTER CIRCLE

1. Forward 1 passes the puck from the center circle to defenseman 1, who is positioned in the face-off circle.
2. Defenseman 1 skates backward with the puck to the goal line, skates forward, and passes the puck to forward 1, who has skated inside the face-off circle and looped back.
3. Forward 3 and defenseman 2 perform the same pattern from the opposite end.
4. Defenseman 1 and defenseman 2 skate over the blue line on the opposite side, pivot, and skate backward.
5. Forward 1 goes 1v1 against defenseman 2, and forward 3 goes 1v1 against defenseman 1.

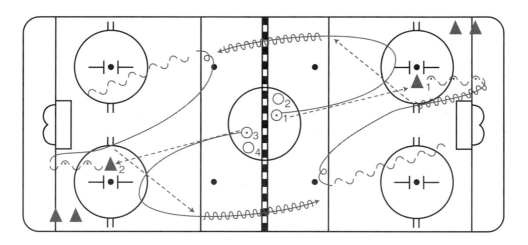

1V1, NEUTRAL ZONE LOOP BACK

1. Forward 1 skates over the blue line and across the ice.
2. Defenseman 1 passes to forward 1 and receives the return pass.
3. Defenseman 1 skates toward the blue line and passes again to forward 1.
4. Forward 1 skates over the far blue line with the puck and loops back.
5. Defenseman 1 skates around the center circle, pivots, and skates backward.
6. Forward 1 then goes 1v1 against defenseman 1.
7. Forward 2 and defenseman 2 perform the same drill simultaneously on the other end.

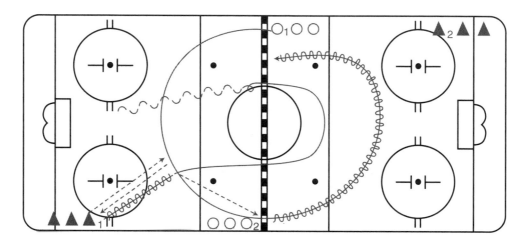

1V1, WIDE PASS

1. Defenseman 1 passes to forward 1.
2. Defenseman 1 skates backward diagonally along the blue line.
3. Forward 1 passes to forward 2, skates across the ice, and receives a return pass from forward 2.
4. Forward 1 goes 1v1 against defenseman 1.
5. Defenseman 2, forward 3, and forward 4 perform the same drill simultaneously on the other end.

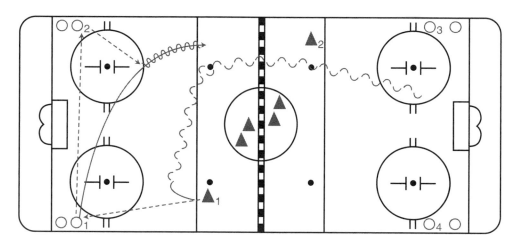

128

NET DRIVE, 1V1

1. Defenseman 1 skates around the far cone, pivots, and skates backward.
2. Forward 1 skates around the far cone and drives hard to the net, going 1v1 against defenseman 1.
3. Forward 2 and defenseman 2 perform the same drill from the opposite side.

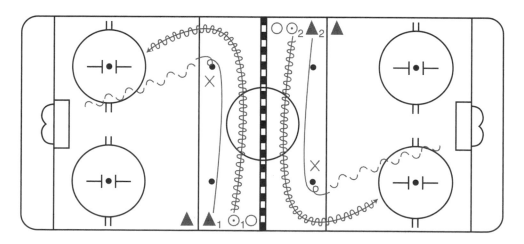

chapter 5

Two-on-One Drills

A two-on-one usually occurs in a game when one defenseman gets caught up ice. A two-on-one creates unique opportunities for the attacking players. It also creates challenges for the defensive player that gets caught alone. The drills in this chapter are designed to teach the offensive players to take advantage of a two-on-one. They also give defensive players the opportunity to practice defending two-on-one plays.

For the drills in this chapter, the attacking players should work on executing the two-on-one at full speed, because this gives the defenders less time to react. The attackers can cross in front of the defender and use a drop pass, stay wide with the player without the puck going to the net, or use a strategy where the player without the puck trails the play for a pass back. These techniques allow the attacking players the opportunity to get the defenseman to be moved away from the middle of the ice, to be blocked or picked, or to be used as a screen against the goalie. Cross-ice passes should be made early in the attack because they are more easily intercepted closer to the net where there is less space. A saucer pass over the defender's stick or a pass between the defender's stick and skates is risky but can be used close to the net. The biggest mistake on a two-on-one is not getting a shot on net—players should know that it is never wrong to shoot in these situations! If a player has room to take a shot, the player should take the shot, and the other player should go for a rebound.

Defensively in a two-on-one situation, the defender should close the gap as much as possible and should stay in the middle of the ice, favoring the side of the puck carrier. Generally, the goalie should have the puck carrier, and the defender should focus on preventing a pass across to the other offensive player in close. The defender should only pressure the puck carrier in close. Pressuring the puck carrier too early leaves too much opportunity for a pass to a wide open player for an easy shot. Leaving the feet and sliding to prevent a pass across on a two-on-one is a special skill and should not be used unless the defender is highly proficient with the move. If a defender slides and is not successful, it is difficult for the defender to return to his or her feet in time to get back in the play.

2V1 CAROUSEL

1. Forward 1 and forward 2 skate inside the far blue line and loop back (see figure 1).
2. Defenseman 1 skates around the center circle, pivots, and skates backward.
3. Defenseman 2 passes to forward 2.
4. Forward 1 and forward 2 go 2v1 with defenseman 1.
5. After defenseman 2 passes the puck, defenseman 2, forward 3, and forward 4 perform the same pattern in the other direction.
6. The drill is continuous.

Variation

After the 2v1 play is completed, the coach puts a second puck in the corner, and forward 1 and forward 2 go against defenseman 1 out of the corner (see figure 2).

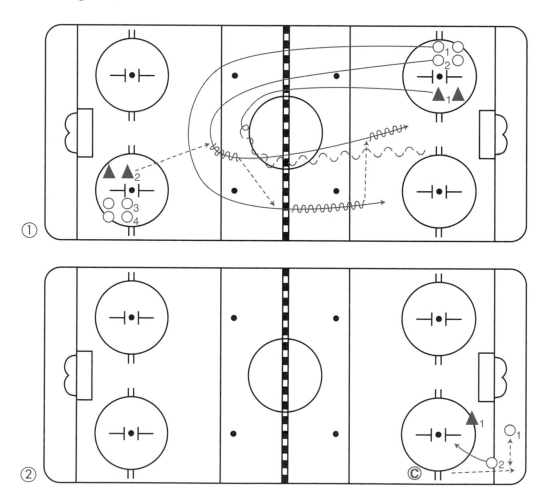

1. Forward 1 and forward 2 come out of the corners, take a pass from defenseman 1, and go outside the near blue line.
2. Forward 1 and forward 2 then come back 2v1 against defenseman 1.
3. At the same time, forward 3 and forward 4 perform the same pattern at the other end with defenseman 2.

Variation

Forward 1 and forward 2 can regroup with defenseman 1 before going 2v1.

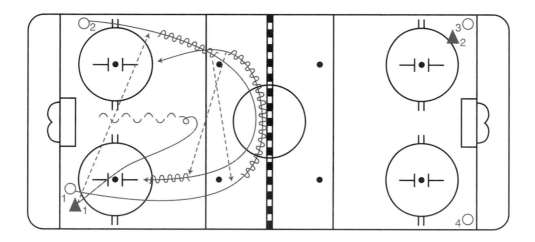

1. Forward 1 passes to defenseman 1.
2. Forward 1 and forward 2 skate across the ice from opposite sides.
3. Defenseman 1 pivots 360 degrees and passes to forward 2.
4. Either forward 1 or forward 2 pass the puck to defenseman 2.
5. Defenseman 2 returns the pass to either forward 1 or forward 2 as the two players loop back in the other direction.
6. Forward 1 and forward 2 go 2v1 against defenseman 1.
7. Forward 3 and forward 4 go next, repeating the same pattern and going 2v1 against defenseman 2 in the other direction.
8. The drill is continuous.

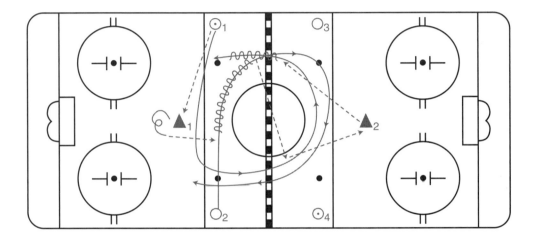

1. Defenseman 1 starts the drill by skating along the blue line with a puck and shooting.
2. After shooting, defenseman 1 pivots and skates backward.
3. Forward 1 starts from the corner with a puck and goes 2v1 with forward 2 against defenseman 1.
4. After the play on the net, the coach whistles.
5. Forward 1 and forward 2 stay in front of the net.
6. Defenseman 1 also stays in front and defensively takes either forward 1 or forward 2.
7. Defenseman 2 starts the next sequence by skating along the blue line and shooting, and then forward 3 and forward 4 go 2v1 to the other end against defenseman 2.

Variation

After defenseman 2 shoots, the coach can pass to either forward 1 or forward 2 in front of the net for another shot.

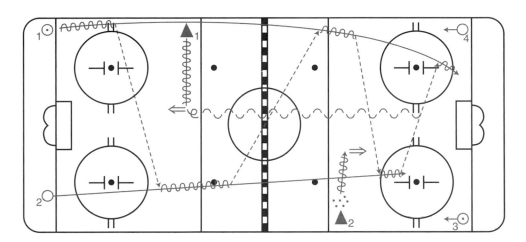

2V1 D AROUND THE NET

1. Defenseman 1 starts the drill by skating behind the net with the puck and passing to forward 1.

2. Forward 2 comes off the boards and joins forward 1 in a 2v1 against defenseman 2, who skates backward from the blue line.

3. After the play on the net, the coach passes another puck to defenseman 1, who has followed the play to the far blue line.

4. Defenseman 1 shoots, with forward 1 and forward 2 staying in front of the net to deflect or screen (defenseman 2 defends either forward 1 or forward 2).

5. Defenseman 3 starts the next sequence of the drill by skating behind the net and passing to forward 3.

6. Forward 3 and forward 4 go 2v1 against defenseman 3 in the other direction.

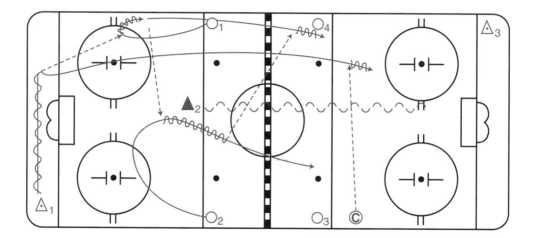

2V1 CHIP BACK

1. Defenseman 1 skates to the center line, stops, and skates backward.
2. The coach passes a puck off the boards (chips back) to defenseman 1.
3. Forward 1 and forward 2 skate across the ice from opposite sides, and one of them takes a pass from defenseman 1.
4. Defenseman 2 skates to the center line, stops, and skates backward.
5. Forward 1 and forward 2 go 2v1 against defenseman 2.

Variation

Forward 1 and forward 2 can come off the boards from the same side of the rink and take a pass from defenseman 1.

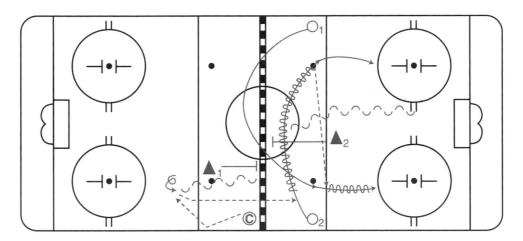

2V1 FROM A SHOOT-IN OR RIM

1. Forward 1 shoots the puck into the corner.
2. Defenseman 1 skates backward from the blue line, pivots, skates forward, and gets the puck.
3. Defenseman 1 then skates behind the net and passes to forward 1 or forward 2, who have skated across the ice from opposite sides.
4. Forward 1 and forward 2 go 2v1 against defenseman 2.
5. Forward 3 shoots the puck in to start the next play with forward 4 and defenseman 3, who is standing by the boards just inside the blue line.

Variation

Forward 1 can rim the puck along the boards—with the goalie stopping it behind the net—or forward 1 can shoot directly at the goalie to start the play.

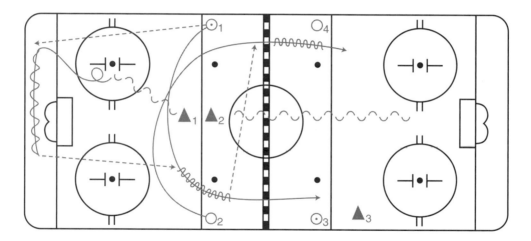

1. Forward 1 passes to defenseman 1.
2. Forward 1 and forward 2 skate across the ice from opposite sides.
3. Defenseman 1 pivots and passes the puck to either forward 1 or forward 2.
4. Forward 1 and forward 2 exchange passes and then pass to defenseman 2.
5. Defenseman 2 returns the pass, and forward 1 and forward 2 go 2v1 against defenseman 1.
6. Defenseman 2 then skates to the center line, stops, skates backward, goes to the corner at the near end of the rink, gets a puck, skates behind the net, and passes to forward 3 or forward 4 to start the next 2v1 with a new defenseman at the other blue line.

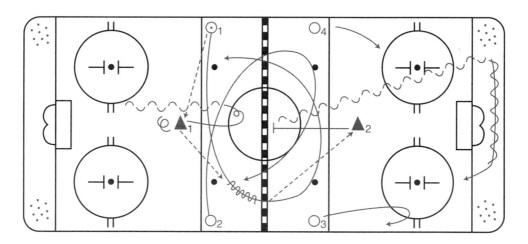

137   2V1 RIM

1. The coach starts the drill by rimming the puck to forward 1.
2. Forward 1 and forward 2 skate from opposite sides, cross, and go 2v1 against defenseman 1.
3. The coach at the other end starts the next play by rimming the puck to forward 4.
4. Forward 3 and forward 4 go 2v1 against defenseman 2.

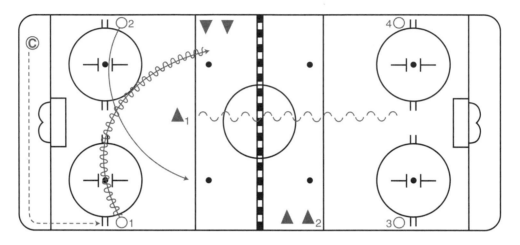

138   DYNAMO 2V1

1. Defenseman 1 skates backward, pivots, goes to the corner and gets a puck, and then passes to forward 1, who has skated from the far blue line to the near blue line.
2. Forward 2 skates from the near blue line across the center line.
3. Forward 1 and forward 2 go 2v1 against defenseman 2.
4. Defenseman 2 starts the next sequence by passing to forward 4 and forward 3, who start at the far blue line and go 2v1 against defenseman 1.

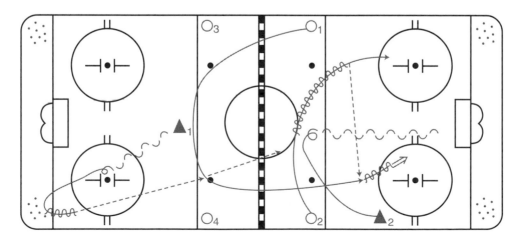

139   2V1 DOUBLE REGROUP

1. Forward 1 passes to defenseman 1.
2. Defenseman 1 passes to defenseman 2.
3. Forward 1 and forward 2 skate from opposite sides, cross, and take a pass from defenseman 2.
4. Forward 1 and forward 2 regroup by passing to defenseman 1 again.
5. Forward 1 and forward 2 take a return pass then go 2v1 against defenseman 2.

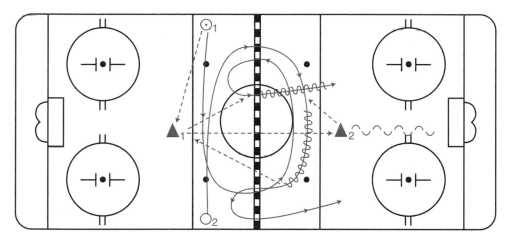

140   THREE SHOTS 2V1

1. Forward 1, forward 2, and defenseman 1 skate in from the blue line and shoot.
2. Forward 2 takes a pass from the coach.
3. Forward 1 and forward 2 then go 2v1 against defenseman 1, who has pivoted and skated backward.
4. When the 2v1 is done, forward 3, forward 4, and defenseman 2 perform the same pattern beginning on the opposite end.

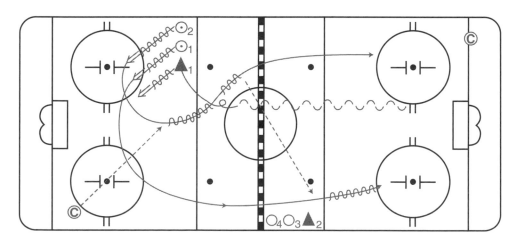

2V1 NEW JERSEY

1. Defenseman 1 passes across the ice to forward 1.
2. Forward 1 and forward 2 skate from opposite sides, cross, and go 2v1 against defenseman 1.
3. Defenseman 2 passes to forward 3, and forward 3 and forward 4 go 2v1 against defenseman 2 in the other direction.

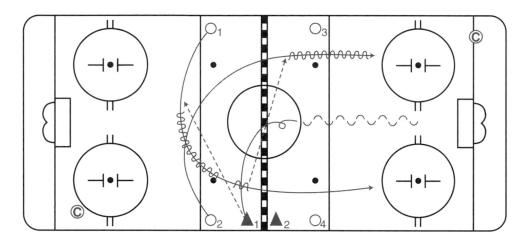

2V1 LOW, 2V1 FULL ICE

1. Defenseman 1 passes to forward 1 in the corner.
2. Forward 1 and forward 2 come out of the corner and go 2v1 against defenseman 2 at the near goal.
3. After shooting, forward 1 or forward 2 takes a pass from the coach.
4. Forward 1 and forward 2 then go 2v1 against defenseman 1 to the far goal.
5. Defenseman 3 starts the next play by passing to forward 3 in the corner at the other end.
6. Forward 3 and forward 4 go 2v1 against defenseman 1 at the near goal, then go 2v1 full ice against defenseman 3.

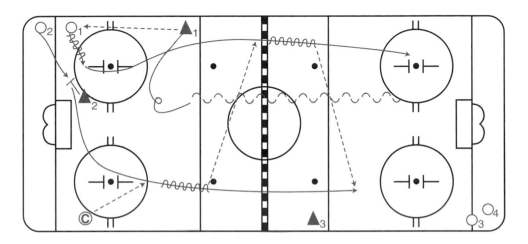

2V1 CZECH

1. Defenseman 1 goes to the corner, gets a puck, and passes to forward 1 or forward 2, who have come off the boards and looped at the top of the circles.
2. Forward 1 and forward 2 go 2v1 against defenseman 2.
3. Defenseman 2 goes to the corner, gets a puck, and passes to forward 3 or forward 4 to start the next 2v1 against defenseman 3.
4. After passing the puck, defenseman 1 goes to the side boards and defenseman 3 moves to the far blue line to take the next 2v1 with forwards 3 and 4.

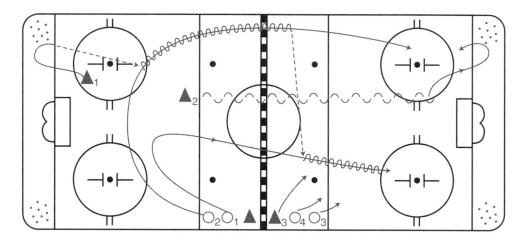

SWEDEN PUCK EXCHANGE 2V1

1. Forward 1 and forward 2 start on the same side, skate across the ice, and take a pass from defenseman 1.
2. Forward 1 or forward 2 passes to forward 3 at the opposite blue line.
3. Forward 3 passes back to forward 1 or forward 2, and forward 1 and forward 2 go 2v1 against defenseman 1.
4. Forwards 3 and 4 start the next play by receiving a pass from defenseman 2.

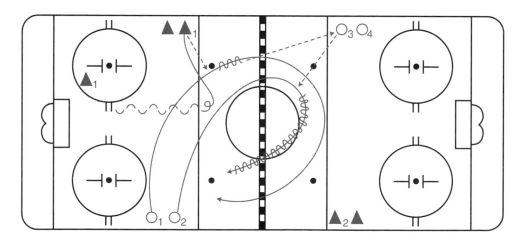

WINNIPEG 2V1

1. Forward 1 passes across to forward 2.
2. Forward 2 passes to forward 3.
3. Forward 3 passes to forward 4.
4. Forward 1 and forward 2 skate in from opposite sides, cross, regroup, and take a pass from forward 4.
5. Forward 1 and forward 2 go 2v1 against defenseman 1.
6. Forward 3 starts the next play by passing to forward 4.
7. Forward 3 and forward 4 go 2v1 against defenseman 2 in the other direction.

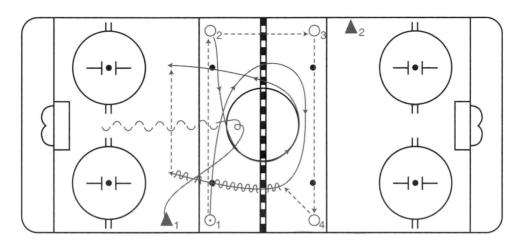

146   SHOTGUN 2V1

1. On the whistle, forward 1 and forward 2 go 2v1 against defenseman 1, and forward 3 and forward 4 go 2v1 against defenseman 2.
2. This drill is a half ice drill and the defenseman plays between the two forwards rather than in the middle of the ice on a normal 2v1.

Variation

A second puck can be placed in the corner. When the play is completed, the two forwards come out of the corner and go 2v1 against the defenseman again.

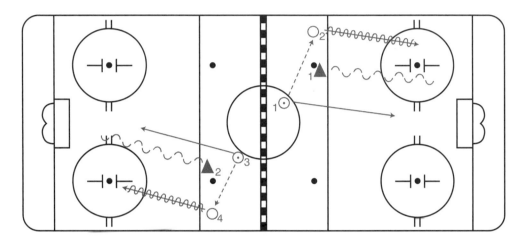

147   SWEDEN 2V1

1. Forward 1 and forward 2 pass to defenseman 1 and regroup twice with defenseman 1, then go 2v1 against defenseman 2.

   Note: The diagram shows only one regroup with defenseman 1 and does not show passing and receiving.

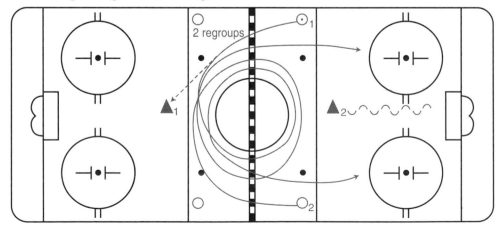

QUICK 2V1 D IN THE MIDDLE

1. Forward 1 passes to defenseman 1 in the center circle.
2. Forward 1 and forward 2 skate in from opposite sides, cross, and take a pass from defenseman 1.
3. Defenseman 1 pivots and skates backward.
4. Forward 1 and forward 2 go 2v1 against defenseman 1.
5. At the same time, forward 3 and forward 4 go 2v1 against defenseman 2 in the same pattern on the other end.

Variation

Forward 1 and forward 2 can regroup twice with defenseman 1.

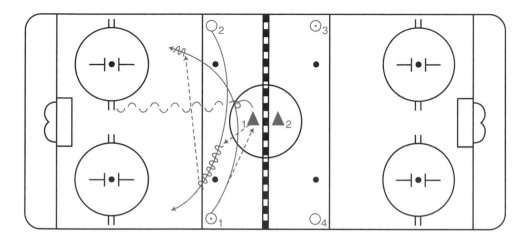

FINLAND 2V1 CONTINUOUS, ONE PUCK

1. Forward 1 and forward 2 go 2v1 against defenseman 1.
2. After the play passes the top of the circles, forward 3 and forward 4 go to the boards above the hash marks of the face-off circles.
3. When defenseman 1 gains control of the puck or the goalie holds the puck, defenseman 1 passes the puck to forward 3 or forward 4; forward 3 and forward 4 then break out against defenseman 2 for a 2v1 at the other end.
4. The drill is continuous with the next two forwards waiting at the blue line to move in and break out.

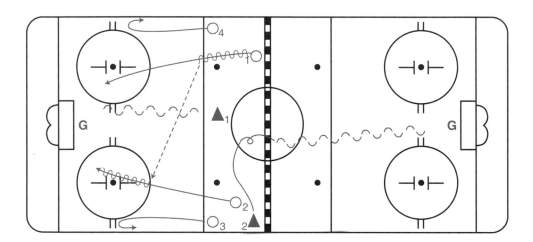

2V1 D CIRCLE SKATE

1. Defenseman 1 and defenseman 2 skate forward around the circles at opposite ends.
2. Defenseman 1 receives a pass from forward 1.
3. Defenseman 1 pivots, skates backward around the circle with the puck, pivots, skates forward, and passes to forward 1 coming off the boards.
4. Forward 1 passes to forward 2 coming diagonally off the far boards.
5. After skating forward, backward, and forward around the circle at the other end, defenseman 2 skates to the blue line, pivots, and skates backward.
6. Forward 1 and forward 2 go 2v1 against defenseman 2.

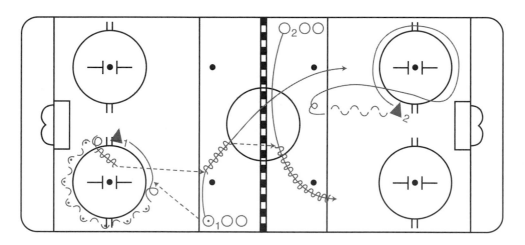

2V1 COUNTER

1. Forward 1 passes to forward 2.
2. Forward 1 and forward 2 skate in from opposite sides and cross; forward 2 passes the puck to defenseman 1.
3. Defenseman 1 passes to defenseman 2.
4. Forward 1 and forward 2 cross again and receive a pass from defenseman 2.
5. Forward 1 and forward 2 go 2v1 against defenseman 1.

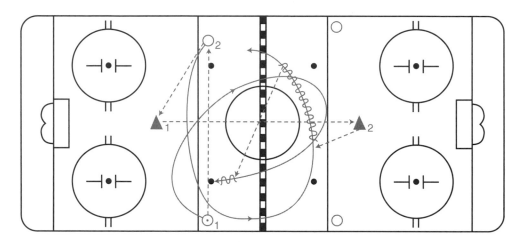

2V1, LOOP

1. Forward 1 and forward 2 loop across the far blue line and take a pass from the coach.
2. Defenseman 1 loops around the center circle, pivots, and skates backward.
3. Forward 1 and forward 2 go 2v1 against defenseman 1.
4. Forward 3 and forward 4 go next from the diagonally opposite end against defenseman 2.

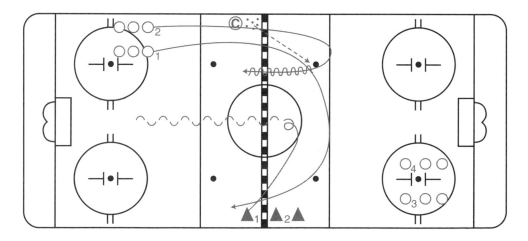

2V1, BEHIND AND IN FRONT

1. Forward 1 and forward 2 are at the blue line. Forward 1 starts with the puck.
2. Forward 1 passes to defenseman 1, then skates over and goes behind defenseman 1, exchanging a one-touch pass along the way.
3. Forward 2 comes off the boards at the same time and receives a pass from defenseman 1 while skating in front of defenseman 1.
4. Forward 2 then one-touch passes with defenseman 2 and goes behind.
5. Forward 1 skates in front of defenseman 2.
6. Forward 1 and forward 2 then go 2v1 against defenseman 1 toward the opposite goal.

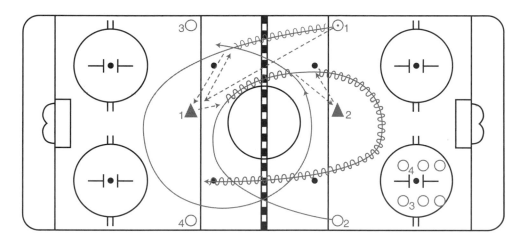

2V1, TWO TIMES OPPOSITE ENDS

1. Forward 1 and forward 2 skate to the neutral zone and go 2v1 against defenseman 1.
2. Forward 3 and forward 4 then go 2v1 at the opposite end against defenseman 2.
3. The coach passes the puck to start each 2v1.
4. For the first 2v1, the forwards stay wide; the forward without the puck goes to the net.
5. For the second 2v1 at the other end, the forwards cross or do a drop pass in front of the defenseman.

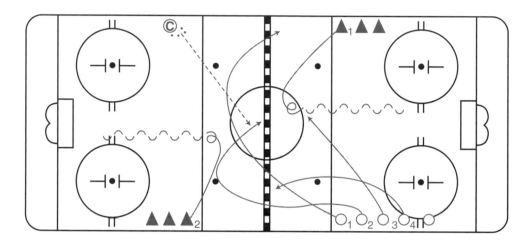

chapter 6

Two-on-Two Drills

Two-on-two situations occur frequently in a game, and players should work on these situations regularly in practices. Like two-on-ones, they create special concerns for both the attacking and defensive players. The drills in this chapter are designed to address those special concerns.

In the drills in this chapter, the two attacking players can use various techniques to beat the two defenders, such as attacking with speed, crossing, crossing with a drop pass, or changing speed, which are all effective techniques to beat the defense. The attackers can try to isolate one defender to create a two-on-one situation by attacking on half of the ice. If the defenders leave a large gap, the attacking players should shoot while using the defenders to screen the goalie.

Two-on-two drills are particularly important to allow defenders to work on gap control. In a two-on-two situation, the defenders should try to close the gap between the defenders and the attackers in order to give the offensive players less space. If the attackers cross before the top of the circles in the offensive zone, a general rule is that the defenders should play in their area and not cross. If the attackers cross below the circles, the general rule is that the defenders should play one on one and stay with the attacking players when they cross because the defenders do not have time to switch in close.

1. Defenseman 1 passes to forward 1.
2. Defensemen 1 and 2 skate over the blue line, pivot, and skate backward.
3. Forwards 1 and 2 go 2v2 against defensemen 1 and 2.
4. After the play is finished, defenseman 3 passes to forward 3 at the other end.
5. Forwards 3 and 4 go 2v2 against defensemen 3 and 4.

Variation

On the whistle, forwards 1 and 2 curl back, passing the puck, and defensemen 1 and 2 close the gap by mirroring the offensive players' movements. On the next whistle, forwards 1 and 2 go 2v2 again against defensemen 1 and 2.

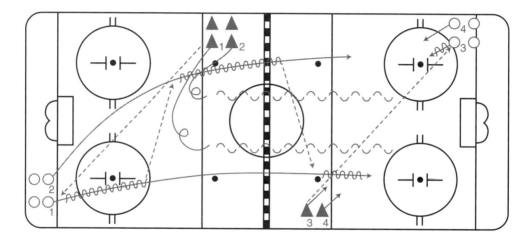

1. Forwards 1 and 2 skate the length of the rink and shoot, then loop back and take a pass from the coach.
2. Defensemen 1 and 2 skate to the center line, pivot, and skate backward.
3. Forwards 1 and 2 then go 2v2 against defensemen 1 and 2.

Variation

Forwards 1 and 2 begin by skating backward and exchanging one-touch passes with the next two forwards. Forwards 1 and 2 then pivot, skate the length of the ice, shoot, and come back 2v2.

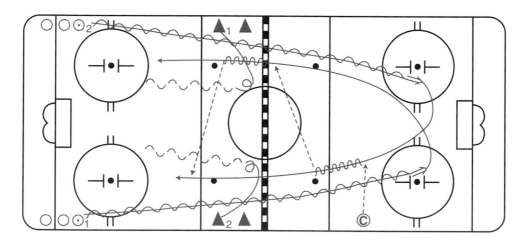

1. Forwards 1 and 2 skate in from opposite sides, cross, and take a pass from defenseman 1 in the corner.
2. Forwards 1 and 2 go 2v0 and shoot, then loop back and take a pass from defenseman 2.
3. Defensemen 3 and 4 come out from the side boards at the center line, pivot, and skate backward.
4. Forwards 1 and 2 go 2v2 against defensemen 3 and 4.
5. The defensemen should rotate after each sequence of the drill.

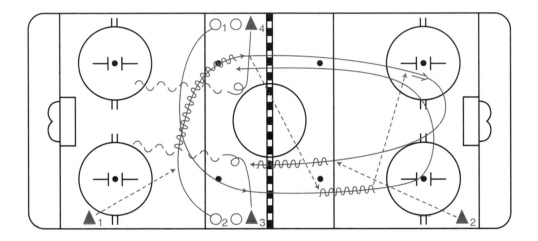

SHOOT, DEFLECT, 2V2

1. Forward 1 passes to defenseman 1 at the blue line.
2. Defenseman 1 skates along the blue line and shoots.
3. Forward 1 goes to the front of the net to deflect and screen.
4. Forward 2 performs the same pattern with defenseman 2.
5. After shooting, defensemen 1 and 2 pivot and skate backward.
6. Forward 3 passes to forward 1, and offensive forwards 1 and 2 go 2v2 against defensemen 1 and 2 to the other end.
7. Forwards 3 and 4 go next with defensemen 3 and 4.

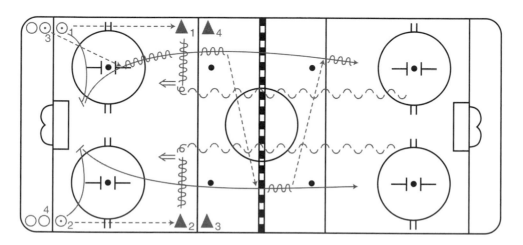

1. Defenseman 1 passes behind the net to defenseman 2.
2. Defenseman 2 passes to forward 2.
3. Forwards 1 and 2 go 2v0 to the far blue line, passing the puck.
4. Defensemen 1 and 2 skate forward outside the blue line, pivot, and skate backward.
5. Forwards 1 and 2 loop back and go 2v2 against defensemen 1 and 2.
6. The drill alternates from each end of the rink, and defensemen 3 and 4 go next with forwards 3 and 4.

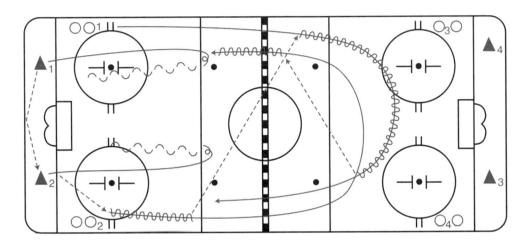

1. Defenseman 1 skates backward from the middle of the face-off circle, pivots, gets a puck from behind the goal line, and passes to forward 1.
2. Defenseman 2 performs the same pattern with forward 2.
3. Forwards 1 and 2 skate the length of the ice. Forward 1 shoots, then forward 2 shoots.
4. Forwards 1 and 2 loop back and take a pass from the coach.
5. Defensemen 1 and 2 skate to the center line, pivot, and skate backward.
6. Forwards 1 and 2 go 2v2 against defensemen 1 and 2.
7. The drill begins from one end of the rink. Switch goalies halfway through the drill.

Variation

Forward 1 can skate across the ice inside the blue line and receive a pass from defenseman 2, and forward 2 can cut across and receive a pass from defenseman 1.

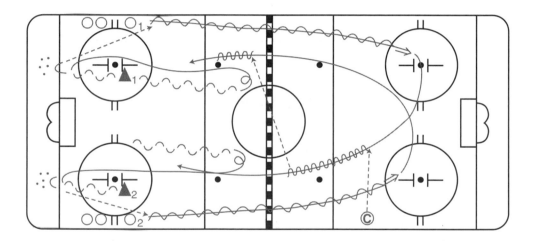

161   SWISS 2V2

1. Forwards 1 and 2 regroup with defensemen 1 and 2, then with defensemen 3 and 4.
2. Forwards 1 and 2 then go 2v2 against defensemen 1 and 2.
3. Forwards 3 and 4 repeat the same pattern with defensemen 3 and 4.

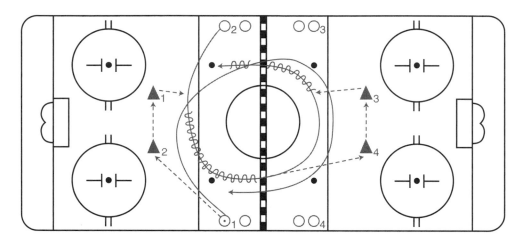

162   2V2 QUICK

1. Forwards 1 and 2 come off the boards, with forward 1 passing to forward 2.
2. At the same time, defensemen 1 and 2 come off the boards from the same side, pivot, and skate backward.
3. Forwards 1 and 2 go 2v2 against defensemen 1 and 2.
4. Forwards 3 and 4 start the drill going in the opposite direction with defensemen 3 and 4.

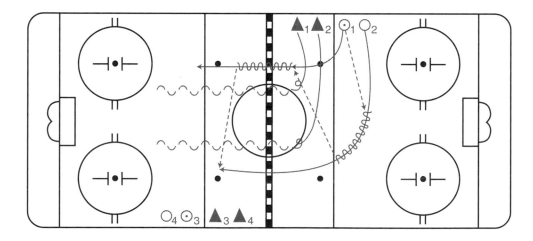

1. Forward 1 skates out of the corner and passes to forward 2.
2. Forward 1 and forward 2 exchange passes and loop over the center line.
3. Defenseman 1 and defenseman 2 skate to the center line from the boards at the near blue line, pivot, and skate backward.
4. Forward 1 and forward 2 go 2v2 against defenseman 1 and defenseman 2.
5. Forward 3 and forward 4 go next from the opposite end, repeating the same sequence and going 2v2 against defenseman 3 and defenseman 4.

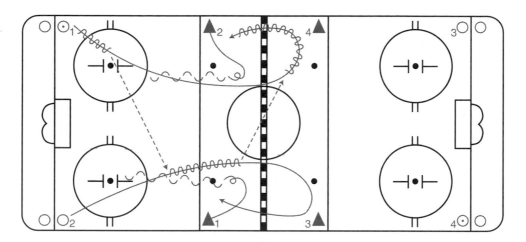

2V2 TO CYCLE 2V2

1. Forward 1 and forward 2 skate to the far blue line, cross, and take a pass from the coach.
2. Defenseman 1 and defenseman 2 skate to the center line, pivot, and skate backward.
3. Forward 1 and forward 2 go 2v2 against defenseman 1 and defenseman 2.
4. After the play is finished, forward 1 and forward 2 cycle in the same corner, receive a second pass from the coach, and go 2v2 low against defenseman 1 and defenseman 2.

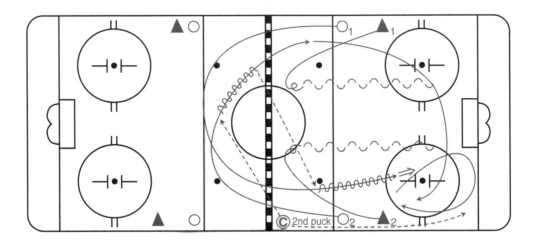

1. Defenseman 3 and defenseman 4 start a breakout with forward 1 and forward 2.
2. Forward 1 and forward 2 go 2v2 against defenseman 1 and defenseman 2.
3. When forward 1 and forward 2 cross the blue line in the offensive zone, forward 3 and forward 4 take positions on the boards inside the blue line.
4. When defenseman 1 and defenseman 2 gain possession of the puck or when a goal is scored, a breakout is started with forward 3 and forward 4.
5. Forward 3 and forward 4 go 2v2 against defenseman 3 and defenseman 4, who have moved up to the offensive blue line.
6. The drill is continuous with one puck.

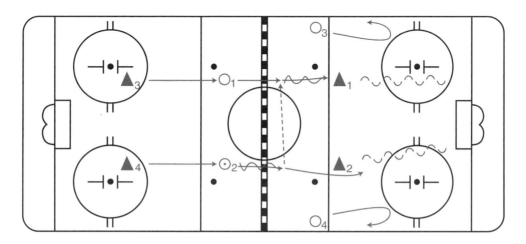

1. The drill begins with the coach shooting the puck in the corner. Forward 1 and forward 2 go 2v2 low against defenseman 1 and defenseman 2.

2. Defenseman 3 and defenseman 4 are waiting at the blue line, and forward 3 and forward 4 are behind them.

3. As soon as defenseman 1 and defenseman 2 gain possession, forward 3 and forward 4 enter the zone along the boards and break out 2v2 against defenseman 3 and defenseman 4.

4. After the play is finished, the coach passes in a second puck, and the 2v2 continues low until defenseman 3 and defenseman 4 gain possession and start the next 2v2 with two new forwards.

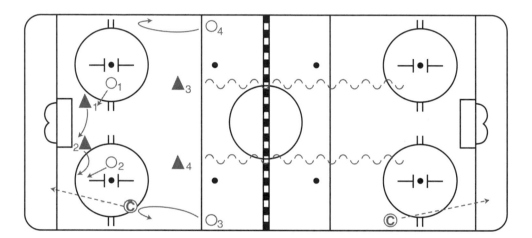

CZECH 2V0, 2V2

1. Forward 2 passes to defenseman 1.
2. Forward 1 and forward 2 skate wide to the far boards and go 2v0 to the far goal.
3. Defenseman 1 and defenseman 2 follow forward 1 and forward 2 to the far blue line.
4. After shooting, forward 1 and forward 2 circle back, receive a pass from the coach, and return 2v2 against defenseman 1 and defenseman 2 toward the other end.

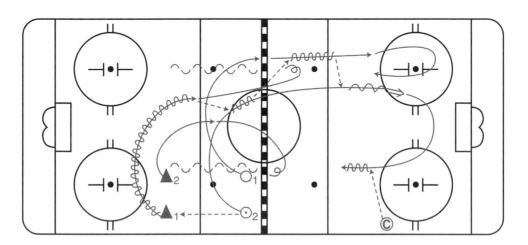

1. Forward 1 and forward 2 come off the side boards and receive a pass from the coach.
2. At the same time, defenseman 1 and defenseman 2 come off the side boards, pivot, and skate backward.
3. Forward 1 and forward 2 go 2v2 against defenseman 1 and defenseman 2.
4. After the play is finished, forward 3 and forward 4 come off the opposite side for the next 2v2 along with defenseman 3 and defenseman 4.

Variation

After the 2v2 is finished, the other coach chips back a puck in the neutral zone, and the same players go 2v2 again.

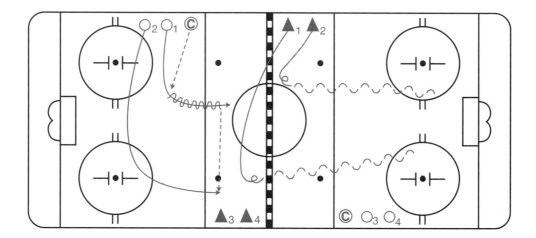

1. Forward 1 passes to defenseman 2.
2. Defenseman 2 shoots.
3. Forward 1 goes to the front of the net to screen and deflect.
4. Forward 2 repeats the same pattern with defenseman 1.
5. After both defensemen shoot, forward 1 receives a puck from the coach.
6. Forward 1 and forward 2 then go 2v2 against defenseman 1 and defenseman 2.

Variation

Forward 1 and forward 2 can first regroup with defenseman 1 and defenseman 2, circle back, and then go 2v2 against defenseman 1 and defenseman 2.

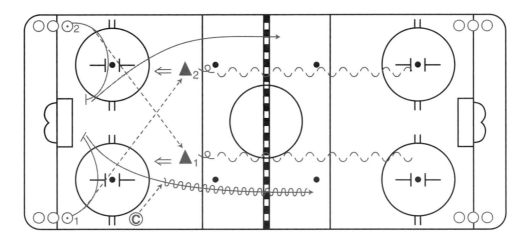

U.S.A. 2V2 CONTINUOUS

1. Defenseman 1 passes to forward 1.
2. Forward 1 goes 1v1 against defenseman 1.
3. After the 1v1 is finished, defenseman 2 passes to forward 2.
4. Forward 2 and defenseman 1 go 2v2 against defenseman 2 and forward 1, who now backchecks to make it 2v2.
5. The play is continuous with defenseman 1 going on offense with forward 2 in the corner who has taken a pass from the next defenseman.
6. The forward who starts in the corner after going offense always backchecks for the next 2v1. The defenseman always goes offense in the opposite direction after taking the 2v2.

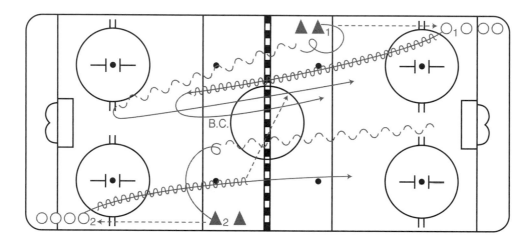

2V2 BOTH ENDS, ONE OR TWO PUCKS

1. Forward 1 and forward 2 go 2v2 against defenseman 1 and defenseman 2.
2. When defenseman 1 and defenseman 2 gain control of the puck, they pass to forward 3 in the neutral zone.
3. Forward 4 tries to check forward 3.
4. Forward 3 passes to forward 5 or forward 6, and they go 2v2 against defenseman 3 and defenseman 4.
5. When defenseman 3 and defenseman 4 gain control of the puck, they pass to forward 4 in the neutral zone.
6. Forward 3 tries to check forward 4.
7. Forward 4 passes to forward 1 or forward 2 for the next 2v2.
8. Play is continuous, with players changing every two minutes.

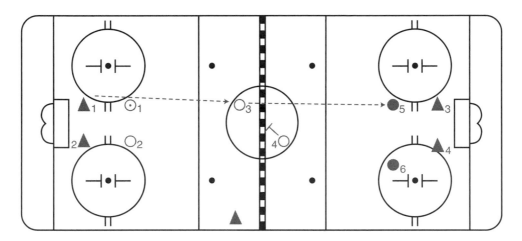

chapter 7

Three-on-One Drills

Three-on-one drills are not overly common in game situations, but they are an effective way for the forward lines to work on passing combinations. In these drills, the players have more space to execute the skills than they do in traditional three-on-two drills. This allows the players to really work on the techniques and skills involved. The drills in this chapter are designed to help players master the basic skills needed for the more common three-on-two. Three-on-two drills are covered in the next chapter.

Generally, in a three-on-one situation, the puck carrier attacks with speed, the second player goes to the net to disrupt the defender (the defender must go with a player who goes past the defender to the net), and the third player trails the play in the high slot. Crossing and drop passes are also used, usually with two of the three forwards executing these moves. Another option is for the middle attacker with the puck to slow up while both wide attackers go to the net to receive a pass on either side. A common mistake is for the attacking players to make too many passes and fail to get a shot on net. One or two passes inside the offensive blue line are usually adequate unless the defenseman is out of position.

Defensively on a three-on-one, if the puck carrier is in the middle, the defender has little choice but to stay in the middle of the ice. If the puck carrier is on the side, the defender should slightly favor the puck carrier's side of the ice. Staying in the middle enables the defender to cover the middle of the ice, which is the primary scoring area. The defender should try to prevent a shot from the middle of the ice and should not be tempted to chase a puck carrier and leave the middle area open. The goalie has responsibility for the shot from the side, with the defender preventing a pass through the middle. The defender should not allow a large gap between him- or herself and the attackers because a large gap screens the goalie, and most attackers will use this screen and shoot the puck.

1. Defenseman 1 gets a puck, skates behind the net with the puck, and passes to forward 1 for a breakout.
2. Defenseman 1 then skates over the near blue line, pivots, and skates backward.
3. Forwards 1, 2, and 3 pass the puck to defenseman 2, regroup, and go 3v1 against defenseman 1.
4. After passing for the regroup, defenseman 2 skates backward, pivots, gets a puck in the corner, and makes a pass to start the next 3v1 for forwards 4, 5, and 6 at the other end.

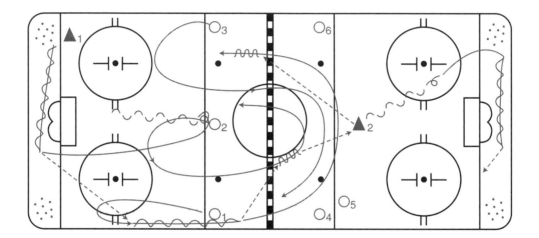

173   3V1 DOUBLE REGROUP

1. Forwards 1, 2, and 3 come off the side boards and regroup with defenseman 1, then with defenseman 2, and come back 3v1 against defenseman 1.
2. Forwards 4, 5, and 6 come off the boards next and regroup with defenseman 2, then with defenseman 1, and come back 3v1 against defenseman 2 toward the other end.
3. The drill continues with two other groups of three forwards repeating the same pattern.

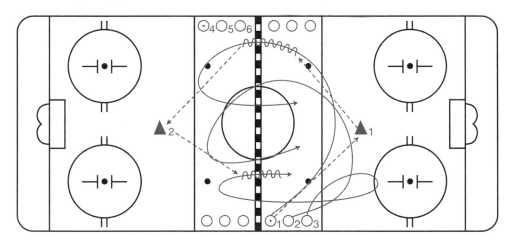

174   TWO REGROUPS, 3V1

1. Forward 1 comes off the boards with a puck and passes to defenseman 1.
2. Defenseman 1 passes to defenseman 2.
3. Defenseman 1 then skates to the center line, pivots, and skates backward.
4. Forwards 1, 2, and 3 receive a return pass from defenseman 2, regroup with defenseman 3 and defenseman 4, and then come back 3v1 against defenseman 1.

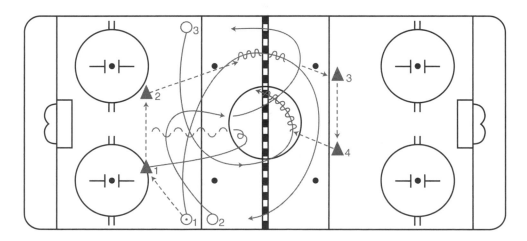

175   3V1, REGROUP

1. Forwards 1, 2, and 3 come off the boards and pass to defenseman 1.
2. Defenseman 1 passes back to the forwards.
3. Forwards 1, 2, and 3 regroup with defenseman 2 and come back 3v1 against defenseman 1.
4. Forwards 4, 5, and 6 start the next 3v1 with defenseman 1.

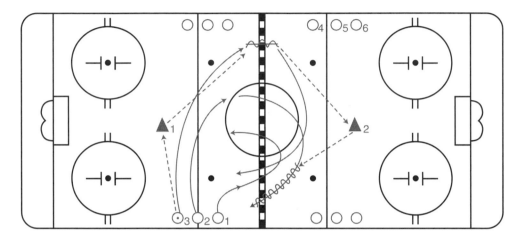

176   RIM, REGROUP, 3V1

1. Defenseman 1 rims the puck around the boards to forward 1.
2. Forwards 1, 2, and 3 pass the puck and regroup with defenseman 2.
3. Defenseman 1 skates to the center line, pivots, and skates backward.
4. Forwards 1, 2, and 3 go 3v1 against defenseman 1.

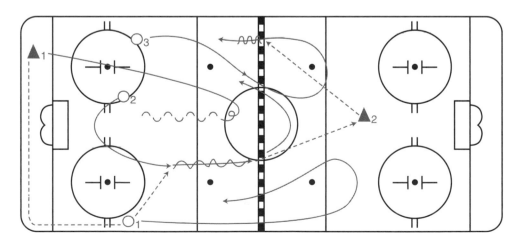

3V1 BREAKOUT, REGROUP

1. Forward 1 shoots the puck into the corner.
2. Defenseman 1 skates backward, pivots, gets the puck, and starts a breakout with forwards 1, 2, and 3.
3. Forwards 1, 2, and 3 regroup with defenseman 2 and come back 3v1 against defenseman 1, who has skated to the center line.
4. Defenseman 1 pivots and skates backward.
5. Forward 4 starts the next play from the other end by shooting the puck in the corner.
6. Defenseman 2 skates backward, pivots, gets the puck, and starts a breakout with forwards 4, 5, and 6.

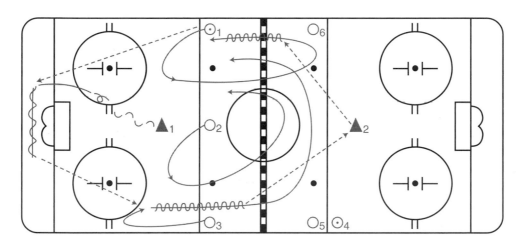

1. Forwards 1, 2, and 3 are on the center line. Forward 1 passes to defenseman 1.
2. Forwards 1, 2, and 3 regroup with defenseman 1, then with defenseman 2, then go 3v1 against defenseman 1.
3. Forwards 4, 5, and 6 repeat the drill, regrouping with defenseman 2 and defenseman 1, and then going 3v1 against defenseman 2.

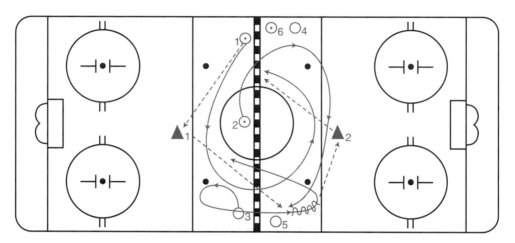

179   3V1 LOOP

1. Forward 1 passes to defenseman 1.
2. Defenseman 1 passes to forward 1, 2, or 3.
3. Forwards 1, 2, and 3 skate over the far blue line, passing the puck, and regroup with defenseman 2.
4. Defenseman 1 skates to the center line, pivots, and skates backward.
5. Forwards 1, 2, and 3 go 3v1 against defenseman 1.
6. Forward 4 starts the next play by passing to defenseman 2, and forwards 4, 5, and 6 repeat the same pattern at the other end.

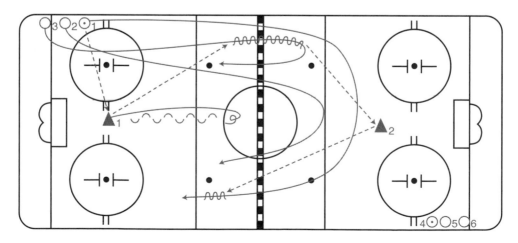

3V1 STRETCH

1. Defenseman 1 starts the play by skating behind the net with the puck and passing to forward 1 or 2; forwards 1 and 2 have come off the boards and crossed.
2. Forward 3 skates across at the far blue line and receives a pass from forward 1 or 2.
3. Forwards 1, 2, and 3 regroup with defenseman 2 and come back 3v1 against defenseman 1.

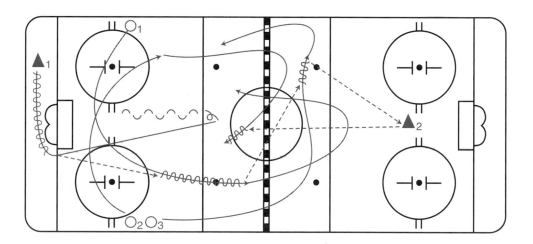

3V1 CHIP BACK

1. Defenseman 1 starts a breakout with forwards 1, 2, and 3 by skating behind the net with the puck and passing to forward 1 or 2 (see figure 1).
2. Forwards 1, 2, and 3 go 3v1 against defenseman 2.
3. After the play on net is finished, the coach blows the whistle. Forwards 1, 2, and 3 come outside the blue line.
4. The coach puts a second puck in the neutral zone (chip back)(see figure 2).
5. Defenseman 1 skates back, gets the puck, then passes to forward 1, 2, or 3.
6. Defenseman 2 comes outside the blue line, pivots, and skates backward.
7. Forwards 1, 2, and 3 then go for a second 3v1 against defenseman 2.

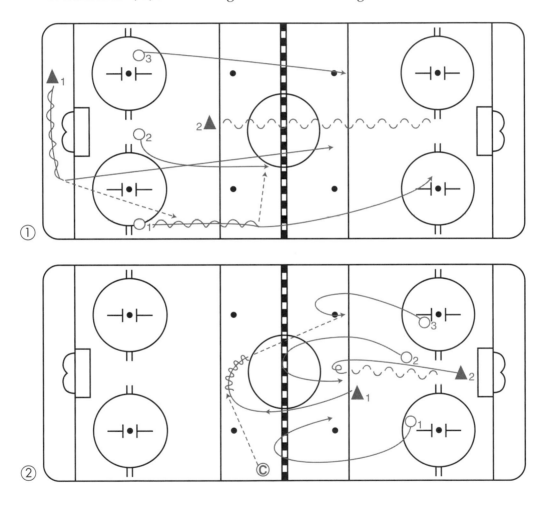

3V1 BOTH ENDS

1. Defenseman 1 skates behind the net and passes to forward 1.
2. Forwards 1, 2, and 3 come outside the blue line to the center line.
3. Defenseman 1 skates to the blue line, pivots, and skates backward.
4. Forwards 1, 2, and 3 go 3v1 against defenseman 1.
5. The drill is done at both ends of the rink at the same time with forwards 4, 5, and 6 going 3v1 against defenseman 2.

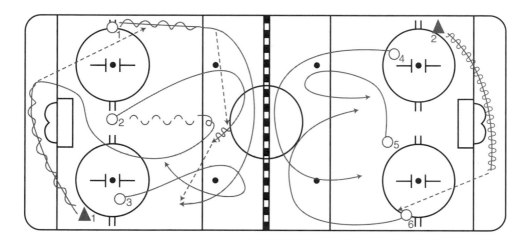

FINLAND 3V1, ONE PUCK

1. Forwards 1, 2, and 3 go 3v1 against defenseman 1.
2. As soon as forwards 1, 2, and 3 pass the top of the circles, forwards 4, 5, and 6 move into position at the top of the circles.
3. When defenseman 1 gains possession of the puck or when the goalie freezes the puck, defenseman 1 starts a breakout with forwards 4, 5, and 6 against defenseman 2.
4. The drill is continuous, using one puck.

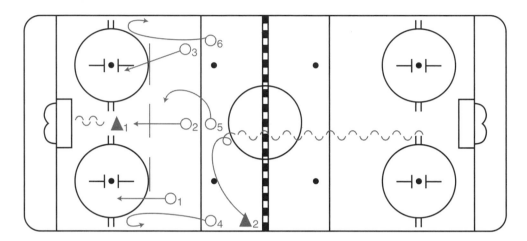

D PINCH 3V1

1. Forwards 1, 2, and 3 break out with defensemen 1 and 2, who pass the puck to forward 3.
2. Defenseman 3 pinches in at forward 3.
3. Forward 3 passes directly or off the boards to forward 2.
4. Forwards 1 and 2, with forward 3 trailing, go 3v1 against defenseman 4.

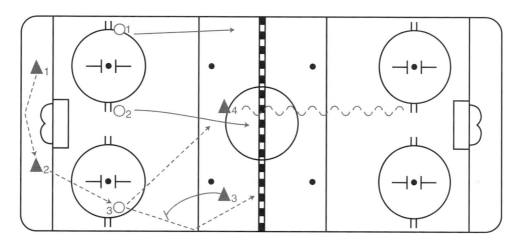

1. Defenseman 1 skates to the blue line, stops, pivots, skates backward, and receives a pass from the coach.
2. Defenseman 1 then skates forward and passes to forward 1 coming off the far blue line through the neutral zone.
3. Forward 1 skates in, shoots, and turns back.
4. Forwards 2 and 3 come off the side boards and join forward 1.
5. Forwards 1, 2, and 3 go 3v1 against defenseman 1, who has skated to the center line and pivoted backward.
6. Defenseman 2 follows the play to the center line and defends forwards 4, 5, and 6 in the next 3v1.

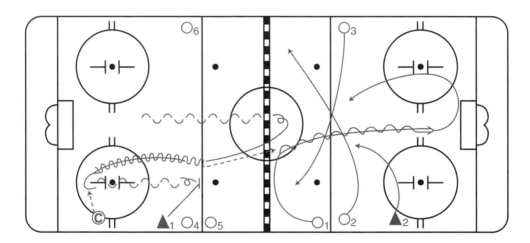

3V1 PASS BACK, STRETCH

1. Defenseman 1 carries the puck around behind the net and passes to forward 1 along the boards. Forward 2 comes off the far boards.
2. Forward 1 passes the puck back to defenseman 1.
3. Forward 3 comes off the boards at the center line.
4. Defenseman 1 passes to forward 3.
5. Forwards 1, 2, and 3 go 3v1 against defenseman 2.

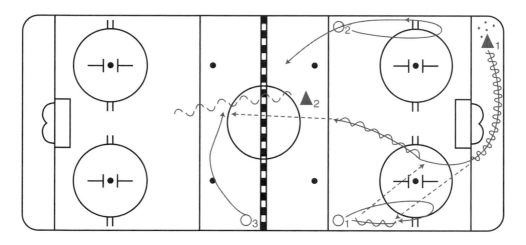

FORWARDS REGROUP TO 3V1

1. Forward 1 passes across the ice to defenseman 1.
2. Defenseman 1 skates to the middle of the ice and passes to forward 1, 2, or 3.
3. The forwards skate over the center line, regroup (without a defenseman), and come back 3v1 against defenseman 1.

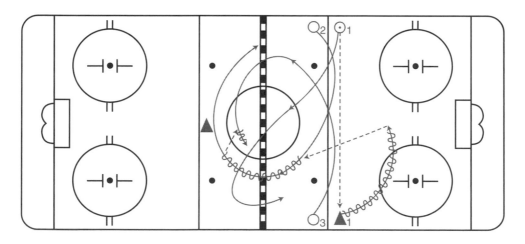

chapter 8

Three-on-Two, Five-on-Two, and Breakout Drills

This chapter includes breakout drills and drills for three-on-two and five-on-two situations. The breakout drills in this chapter offer a variety of common systems for moving the puck up the ice quickly and transition in the neutral zone. Three-on-twos are common in game situations and the drills in this chapter will help both offensive and defensive players to develop the skills needed to execute them properly. The five-on-two drills included in this chapter enable the team to practice situations in which two defensemen break out of the defensive zone with three forwards, which makes a five-on-two. Five-on-twos are basically the same as three-on-twos with the exception that two defensemen trail the play. Therefore, the five-on-two drills here also include working on neutral zone regroups as regroups usually result in a three-on-two situation moving from the neutral zone to the defensive zone.

The general rules used in a three-on-one also apply to three-on-two situations. The puck carrier attacks with speed, the second attacker goes to the net to disrupt the two defenders, and the third player trails the play in the high slot, which opens up after the defender goes to the net. Other offensive plays include the player with the puck going wide and passing back to a trailing player, or the player with the puck in the middle slowing up at the blue line while the two wide players go to the net. In each case, at least one player without the puck goes to the net to force one defender to turn. If the three-on-two starts with a breakout, the puck should be passed by the defensemen to the forwards. Short passes are best in this situation because there is less risk of interception. However, a long pass can occasionally be made either up the middle or up the boards to the neutral zone in order to force the defensemen to retreat from the blue line.

In a three-on-two situation, the defenders should play on the middle two-thirds of the ice, protecting the middle. They should be positioned with slightly more space to the middle in order to protect the main scoring area. Each defender should play on half the ice toward the middle between two of the three attackers but not allowing the attacker to beat the defender wide. The defender should try not to get turned by an attacker going wide. The defenders should try to keep as tight a gap as possible and not leave too much space because this screens the goalie for the shot.

5V0 BACK 3V2

1. The coach shoots the puck into the corner to start the drill.
2. Defenseman 1 takes the puck and passes behind the net to defenseman 2, who then passes to forward 1.
3. Defensemen 1 and 2 break out with forwards 1, 2, and 3 (going 5v0).
4. When forwards 1, 2, and 3 get to the far blue line, they loop back and go 3v2 against defensemen 1 and 2.

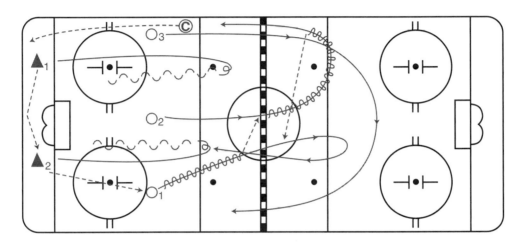

The following sequences are basic breakout systems that should be practiced with the 5v2 to break out of the defensive 2v2.

Sequence 1: D to D Behind the Net

1. Defenseman 1 passes the puck behind the net to defenseman 2.
2. Defenseman 2 passes to forward 2.
3. Forwards 1, 2, and 3 break out of the zone.

Sequence 2: Quick Up

1. Defenseman 1 turns quickly with the puck and passes to forward 1.
2. Forwards 1, 2, and 3 break out of the zone.

Sequence 3: D to D in the Corner

1. Defenseman 1 stops behind the net.
2. Defenseman 2 goes to the corner.
3. Defenseman 1 passes to defenseman 2.
4. Defenseman 2 passes to forward 2.
5. Forwards 1, 2, and 3 break out of the zone.

Sequence 4: Double Swing

1. Defenseman 1 stops behind the net.
2. Forward 2 swings to one corner.
3. Defenseman 1 passes to forward 3.
4. Forward 3 skates straight ahead, and forward 1 skates to the middle of the ice.
5. Forwards 1, 2, and 3 break out of the zone.

Sequence 5: Rim

1. The coach passes the puck to defenseman 1 in the corner.
2. Defenseman 1 receives the puck and then rims the puck around the boards to forward 1.
3. Forwards 1, 2, and 3 break out of the zone.

Sequence 6: Reverse

1. Defenseman 1 skates behind the net with the puck and back passes the puck off the boards.
2. Defenseman 2 comes from the front of the net, gets the puck, goes in the opposite direction, and then passes the puck to forward 1.
3. Forwards 1, 2, and 3 break out of the zone

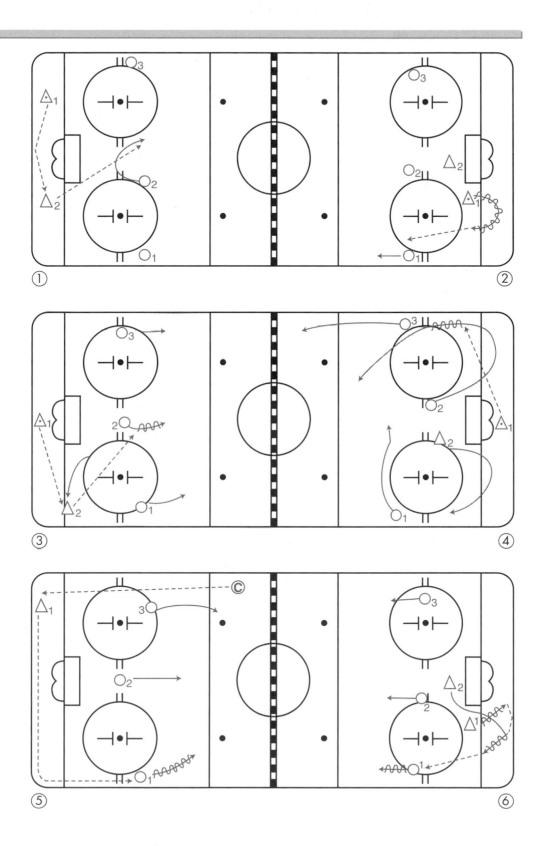

1. The coach shoots the puck into the corner to start the play (see figure 1).
2. Defensemen 1 and 2 use different breakouts each time with forwards 1, 2, and 3.
3. Forwards 1, 2, and 3 go 3v2 against defensemen 3 and 4 toward the other end.

Variations

- After the play is finished, the coach passes a second puck to defenseman 1. Defenseman 1 passes to defenseman 2, and defenseman 2 shoots. Forwards 1, 2, and 3 stay in front of the net with defensemen 3 and 4 (see figure 2).
- After the play is finished, the coach shoots a second puck into the corner. Forwards 1, 2, and 3 play 3v2 against defensemen 3 and 4 down low (see figure 3).

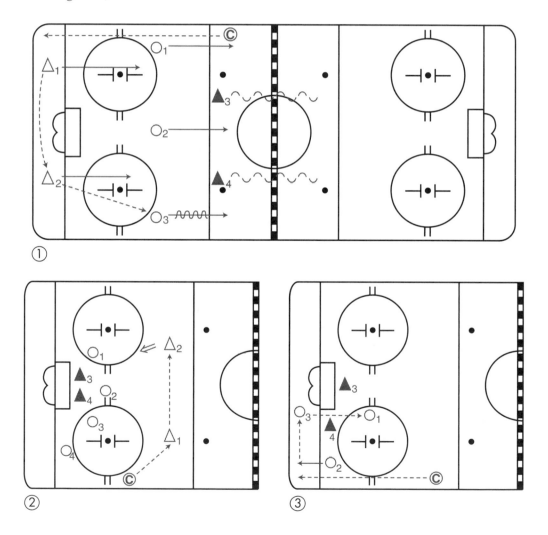

CHIP BACK 5V2

1. The coach shoots the puck in to start the drill.
2. Defensemen 1 and 2 break out with forwards 1, 2, and 3, going 5v2 against defensemen 3 and 4 (see figure 1).
3. When the play is finished at the far end, the coach passes a puck (chips back) to the far blue line.
4. Forwards 1, 2, and 3 clear the offensive zone by skating over the blue line to the neutral zone.
5. The defenseman that retrieves the puck passes the puck to the other defenseman or to forward 1, 2, or 3 and the three forwards go 3v2 again against defensemen 3 and 4 (see figure 2).

Variation

After the last 3v2 the coach can pass a puck to defenseman 1 or 2 for a second shot or put a puck in the corner for a low 3v2.

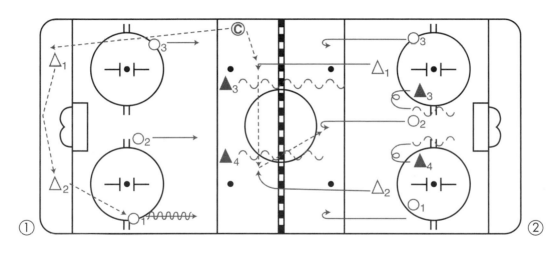

3V2 CONTINUOUS ONE PUCK

1. Forwards 1, 2, and 3 go 3v2 against defensemen 1 and 2.
2. As soon as forwards 1, 2, and 3 pass the top of the face-off circles, forwards 4, 5, and 6 go inside the blue line to the top of the face-off circles.
3. When defensemen 1 and 2 gain possession of the puck or when the goalie freezes the puck, defensemen 1 and 2 start a breakout with forwards 4, 5, and 6 toward the other end.
4. Defensemen 3 and 4 skate to the blue line, pivot, and skate backward.
5. Forwards 4, 5, and 6 go 3v2 against defensemen 3 and 4.
6. Only one puck is used. If the puck is shot over the glass and boards, the goalie retrieves a puck from the net to start the next rush.
7. The drill is continuous.

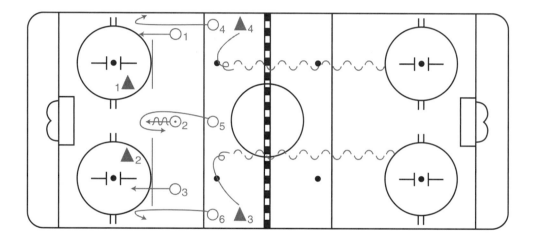

TWO REGROUPS, 5V2 FROM THE CENTER LINE

1. Forward 1 passes to defenseman 2.
2. Defenseman 2 passes to defenseman 1.
3. Forwards 1, 2, and 3 regroup with defensemen 1 and 2, regroup with defensemen 3 and 4, then go 5v2 against defensemen 1 and 2.
4. Forwards 4, 5, and 6 go next, regrouping with defensemen 3 and 4, then with defensemen 1 and 2, and finally going 5v2 against defensemen 3 and 4.

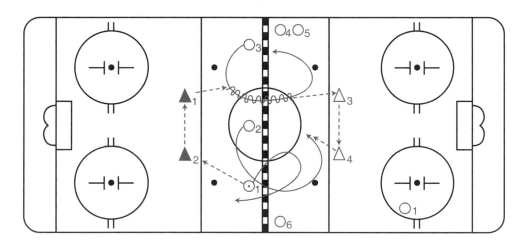

CHICAGO 5V2, TWO REGROUPS, 5V2, TWO REGROUPS, REPEAT

1. Defensemen 1 and 2 break out with forwards 1, 2, and 3.
2. Forwards 1, 2, and 3 regroup with defensemen 3 and 4 first, then regroup with defenseman 1 and 2 (see figure 1).
3. Forwards 1, 2, and 3 and defensemen 1 and 2 go 5v0, with defensemen 3 and 4 going to the side boards.
4. Defensemen 1 and 2 skate to the end boards after the 5v2 and start the next breakout with forwards 1, 2, and 3 (see figure 2).
5. Defensemen 3 and 4 go to the opposite blue line.
6. Forwards 1, 2, and 3 regroup with defensemen 3 and 4 and then with defensemen 1 and 2, who are now at opposite blue lines (see figure 3).
7. Forwards 1, 2, and 3 go 5v0 to finish the drill with defensemen 1 and 2.
8. Defensemen 3 and 4 move to the side boards.
9. The next part of the drill starts at the opposite end, with forwards 4, 5, and 6 breaking out.

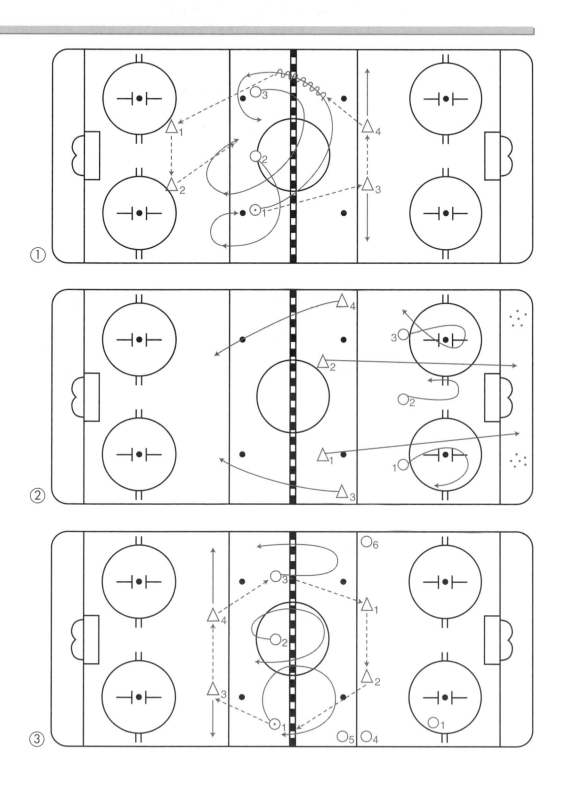

TWO REGROUPS,
3V2 FROM THE SIDE BOARDS

1. Forwards 1, 2, and 3 come off the side boards and regroup with defensemen 1 and 2, and then with defensemen 3 and 4.

2. Forwards 1, 2, and 3 then go 3v2 against defensemen 1 and 2.

3. Forwards 4, 5, and 6 go next, regrouping with defensemen 3 and 4, then with defensemen 1 and 2, before going 3v2 against defensemen 3 and 4.

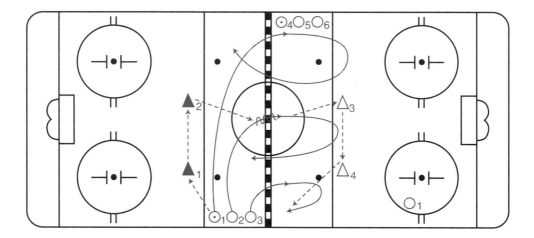

1. Forwards 1, 2, and 3 start at the center line. Defensemen 1 and 2 start at the blue line.
2. On the whistle from the coach, forwards 1, 2, and 3 skate to the far blue line, stop, and skate back toward the center line.
3. Defensemen 1 and 2 skate to the center line, stop, pivot, and skate backward.
4. The coach then passes a puck to forward 1, 2, or 3, and the forwards go 3v2 against defensemen 1 and 2.
5. The next three forwards and two defensemen go in the opposite direction for the 3v2.

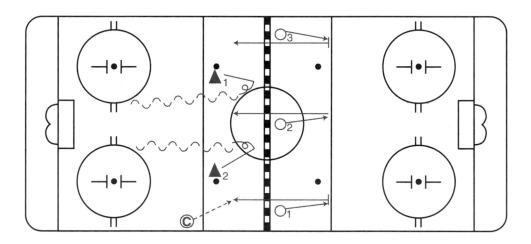

1. Forwards 1, 2, and 3 come off the side boards and take a pass from the coach (see figure 1).
2. Defensemen 1 and 2 skate from the side boards, pivot, and skate backward.
3. Forwards 1, 2, and 3 go 3v2 against defensemen 1 and 2.
4. Forwards 4, 5, and 6 go next against defensemen 3 and 4, repeating the same pattern from the opposite side boards and toward the opposite goal.

Variations

- Forwards 1, 2, and 3 go behind the net, receive a pass from the coach, and go 3v2 against defensemen 1 and 2 (see figure 2).
- After the 3v2 play is finished, the coach shoots a second puck into the corner. Forwards 1, 2, and 3 go 3v2 against defensemen 1 and 2 by cycling in the corner.

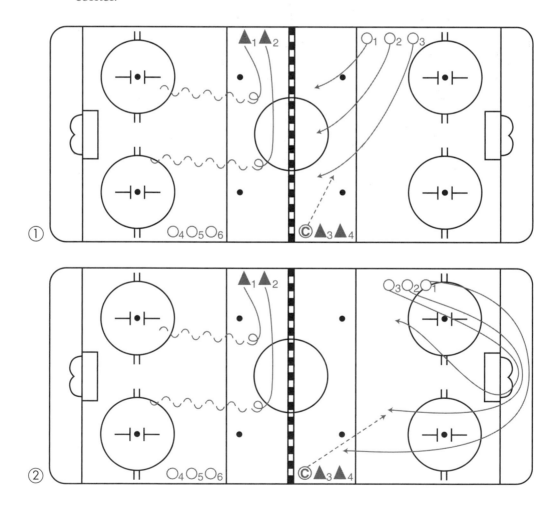

BREAKOUT REGROUP:
START THE NEXT REGROUP

1. Defensemen 1 and 2 break out with forwards 1, 2, and 3.
2. After reaching the first blue line, defensemen 1 and 2 pivot and skate backward.
3. Forwards 1, 2, and 3 regroup with defensemen 3 and 4, and then go 3v2 against defensemen 1 and 2.
4. After the regroup with forwards 1, 2, and 3, defensemen 3 and 4 skate to the corner, get a puck, and break out with forwards 4, 5, and 6 to start the next breakout from the opposite end of the rink.

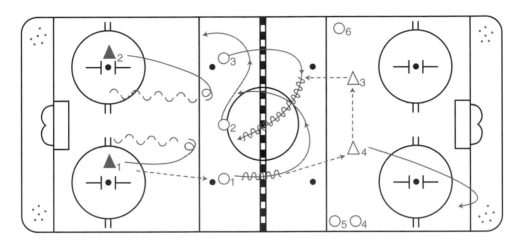

chapter 9

Defensive Drills

This chapter contains drills for working on individual and team defensive skills, including drills that can be used to practice forechecking, backchecking, and defensive zone play. Good teams in ice hockey play well defensively, and the drills in this chapter will improve defensive play if done regularly and executed properly. The defensive part of the game is very important, and defensive drills should be included in most practices.

Since defensemen are constantly working in the corners and in front of the net during one-on-one battles for the puck, many of the drills provided here are designed to work in those areas. All the drills in the chapter should be run with game intensity to simulate game situations. If a skill is not being executed properly, the coach should stop the drill and make sure the players know how to perform the skill. Checking should also be incorporated into these drills when appropriate, as it is an important defensive skill. To prevent injuries, checking should be monitored so that it is not done too hard. The coach should also be sure when practicing checking that in a game situation, with a referee, no penalties would be called.

Goalies should also be used to further simulate game situations whenever the drill calls for a shot to be taken. Because defense is such an important aspect of the game, these drills should be incorporated into practices frequently.

1V1 FOUR CORNERS

1. Four offensive players go 1v1 against four defensive players simultaneously in the four corners of the rink.
2. The drill goes for 20 to 30 seconds, beginning with a whistle from the coach.
3. The offensive and defensive players then switch positions and go 1v1 at the whistle for the next 20 to 30 seconds.

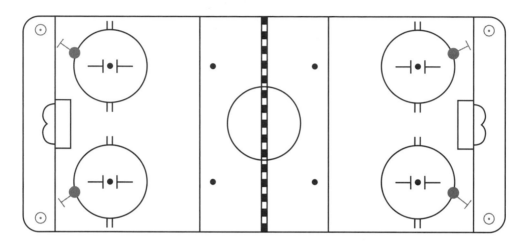

ONE AGAINST ONE PLUS ONE

1. On the whistle, offensive player 1 comes out of the corner with the puck, going against defensive player 1.
2. On the next whistle, offensive player 2 joins the play for a 2v1 against defensive player 1.

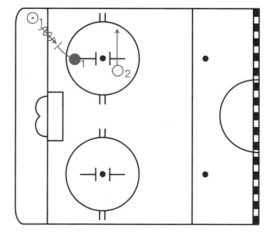

201 ANGLING

1. Offensive player 1 carries the puck behind the net.
2. Defensive player 2 mirrors offensive player 1 by skating in front of the net.
3. Defensive player 2 angles the puck carrier, makes body contact, and allows offensive player 3 to retrieve the puck, come out of the corner, and shoot.
4. The three forwards rotate to different lines.
5. This drill can be done from both sides of the rink.

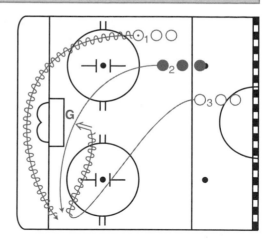

202 2V2 IN THE CORNER

1. On the whistle, the coach shoots a puck in the corner, and offensive forwards 1 and 2 go against defensive forwards 1 and 2.
2. The four players wait on their knees until the whistle starts the drill.

Variation

When the defensive players gain possession of the puck, they go 2v0 to the opposite end, with offensive forwards 1 and 2 chasing.

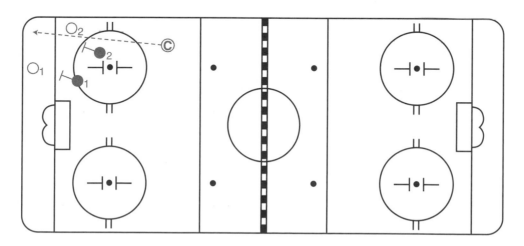

On a pass from the coach, offensive forwards 1, 2, and 3 go 3v3 against defensive forward 1, defensive defenseman 1, and defensive defenseman 2, who try to stop the offense from scoring.

Variation

When the defensive players gain control of the puck, they go 3v0 to the opposite end, with the offensive players chasing.

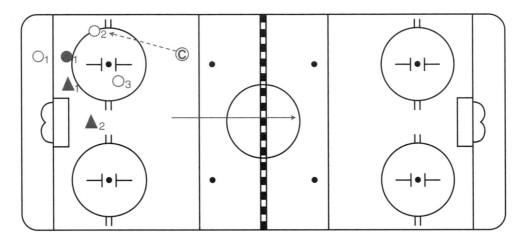

1. The slot area is marked by two lines using rope, rubber tubing, or spray paint.
2. Offensive players 1 and 2 go 2v2 against defensive players 1 and 2, who must protect the slot.

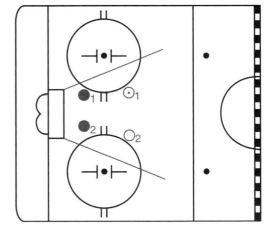

205   2V2 BEHIND THE NET

1. Forwards 1 and 2 are behind and beside the net.
2. Defensemen 1 and 2 are in front of the net. Forward 1 passes the puck behind the net to forward 2.
3. Forward 2 comes out in front of the net and either passes to forward 1, who has come out in front, or shoots.
4. Defensemen 1 and 2 try to block the shot or break up the play.

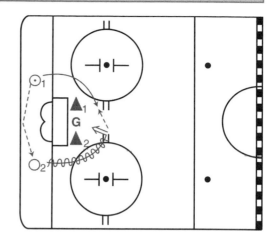

206   DEFENSIVE 2V2 LOW

1. Defenseman 1 skates across to the middle of the blue line and shoots.
2. Then defenseman 2 shoots.
3. Defenseman 1 and defenseman 2 go to the front of the net.
4. Forward 1 and forward 2 cross behind the net and exchange a puck.
5. Forward 1 and forward 2 go 2v2 against defenseman 1 and defenseman 2.

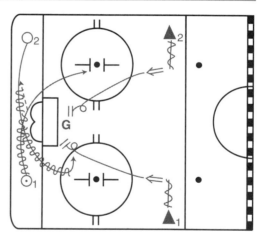

1V1 SMALL-AREA PLAY
WITH NETS IN THE CORNER

1. The net is moved to the corner of the face-off circle and turned toward the corner.
2. Players go 1v1 for 20 to 30 seconds. If a goal is scored or the puck goes outside the small area, the coach provides another puck. Players rotate from offense to defense.

Variation

The drill is the same but with four players going 2v2.

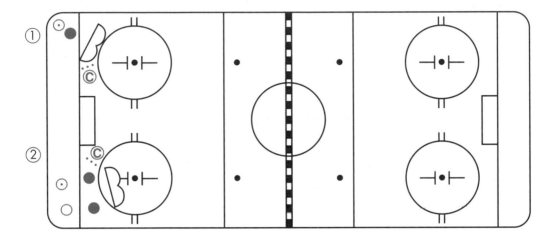

208   2V2 RUSSIAN

1. Offensive players 1 and 2 go 2v2 against defensive players 1 and 2, who try to get the puck.
2. When defensive players 1 and 2 gain possession of the puck, they pass to offensive players 3 and 4 at the blue line.
3. Offensive players 1 and 2 then go defensively against offensive players 3 and 4.
4. The drill is continuous.

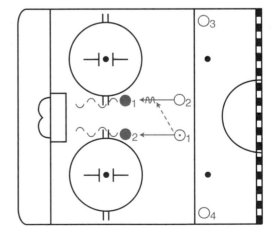

2V2 × 2, 3V2 × 1

1. The coach passes to forward 1 behind the net.
2. Forward 1 passes to either forward 2 or 3.
3. Forwards 2 and 3 go 2v2 against defensemen 1 and 2 in front of the net.
4. When that play is finished, the coach passes a second puck to forward 1, who again passes to forward 2 or 3 for a 2v2.
5. When that play is finished, the coach passes again to forward 1, who passes yet again to forward 2 or 3. Forwards 1, 2, and 3 then go 3v2 against defensemen 1 and 2.

1V1 BACKCHECK

1. Both defensive forward 1 and offensive forward 1 skate to the blue line and stop, then skate to the net at the end where they started.
2. The coach passes to offensive forward 1 on the outside.
3. Defensive forward 1 takes an inside position and backchecks to the net to prevent offensive forward 1 from making a shot or a play on the goalie.

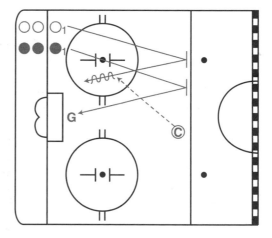

211   2V0 BACKCHECK

1. Forwards 1 and 2 go 2v0 the length of the ice.
2. As soon as forward 1 or 2 shoots, forwards 3 and 4 go 2v0 in the opposite direction with another puck.
3. After forward 1 or 2 shoots, both players backcheck against forwards 3 and 4.
4. The drill is continuous.

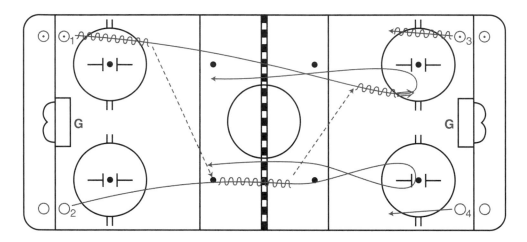

212   2V1 WITH BACKCHECKER

1. Forward 1 and forward 2 go 2v1 against defenseman 1.
2. Defensive forward 1 backchecks to the net.

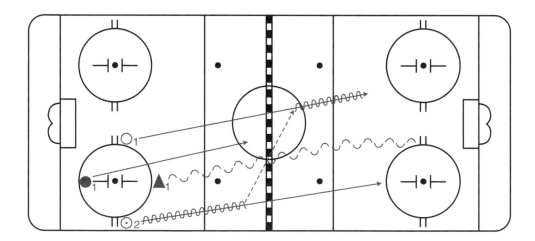

213   2V1 WITH BACKCHECKER, CONTINUOUS

1. Forwards 1 and 2 come off the boards from the same side and take a pass from the coach.
2. Defensive forward 1 comes from the opposite corner and backchecks the length of the ice as forwards 1 and 2 go 2v1 against defenseman 1.
3. After a play on the net, defensive forward 1 swings to one side and takes a pass from forward 3.
4. Offensive forward 3 then goes on offense with defensive forward 1, the original backchecker.
5. Defensive forward 2 comes from the opposite corner as the backchecker.
6. The drill is continuous, with the backchecker going on offense each time with the player in the corner that the backchecker swings to. The forward in the other corner that the backchecker doesn't swing to is always the next backchecker.

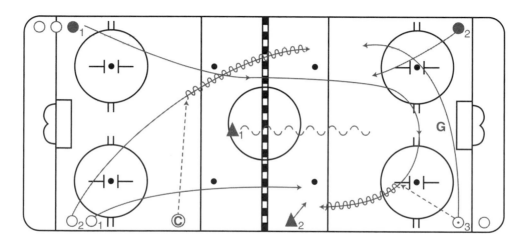

1. Offensive forward 1 and offensive forward 2 skate into the defensive zone and then backcheck.
2. On the whistle, offensive defenseman 1 (in front of the net) releases to the corner and receives a pass from offensive defenseman 2 behind the net.
3. Offensive defenseman 1 passes to start a 2v1 for offensive forward 3 and offensive forward 4 against defensive defenseman 1.
4. Offensive defenseman 1 follows the play down the ice and will play defense in the next 2v1.
5. After the play, defensive defenseman 1 passes behind the net to defensive defenseman 2, who starts the next 2v1 for offensive forwards 5 and 6.
6. Offensive forward 3 and offensive forward 4 now backcheck against forward 5 and 6.
7. The drill is continuous.

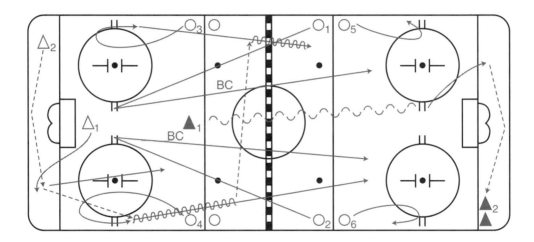

MINNESOTA 3V3, ONE PUCK

1. Forwards 1, 2, and 3 go offensively against defensemen 1 and 2 and defensive forward 4 on the next forward lineup at the far end of the rink.
2. When forwards 1, 2, and 3 pass the top of the circles in the opposite end, forwards 5 and 6 from the next line up skate to the boards at the face-off circles.
3. When defensemen 1 and 2 gain possession, they pass the puck to forward 5 or 6.
4. Forwards 4, 5, and 6 go 3v3 against defensemen 3 and 4 and forward 7, who have taken positions on the blue line after offensive forwards 1, 2, and 3 passed the top of the circles.
5. Forwards 8 and 9 wait at the far blue line to go offensively with forward 7, who is playing 3v3 with defensemen 3 and 4.
6. The drill is continuous, and the three forwards up next should alternate taking the one defensive far position on the far blue line with the two defensive defensemen for the next 3v3.

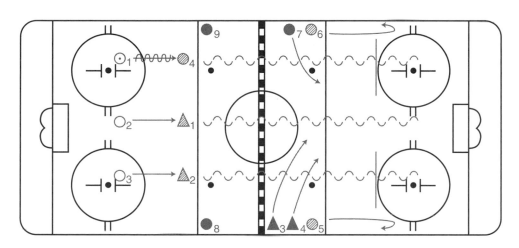

1. Offensive forward 1 passes to defenseman 3.
2. Defenseman 3 passes to defenseman 4.
3. Forwards 1, 2, and 3 regroup with defensemen 3 and 4 and then go 3v2 against defensemen 1 and 2.
4. At the same time, defensive forward 1 skates in from the blue line and shoots, skates across the rink over the center line, pivots, and backchecks against forwards 1, 2, and 3 as they are going 3v2 against defensemen 1 and 2.

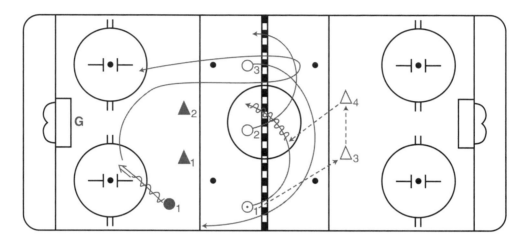

READ THE RUSH 1

1. Offensive forwards 1, 2, and 3 break out with offensive defensemen 1 and 2 against defensive defensemen 1 and 2.
2. Defensive forwards 1, 2, and 3 are in front of the net at the end of the rink where the breakout starts.
3. The coach signals for a backcheck with defensive forwards 1, 2, or 3.
4. The coach can send one, two, or three backcheckers early or have one or two of them trail the play into the offensive zone depending on what he signals.
5. The players should rotate so that all forwards take a turn at backchecking.

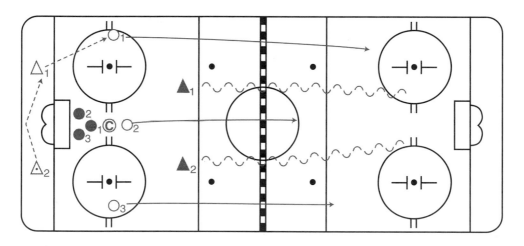

218 **READ THE RUSH 2**

1. Offensive forwards 1, 2, and 3 exchange passes; on the whistle, they go 3v3 against defensive forward 1 and defensive defensemen 1 and 2.
2. Defensive forward 1 goes on the command "Go" and either forechecks or trails the play.

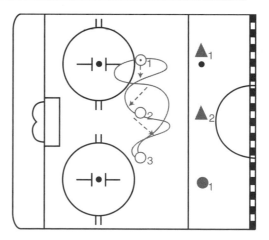

5V2, LATE BACKCHECKER, ONE PUCK

1. Offensive forwards 1, 2, and 3 go 3v2 against third-unit defensemen 1 and 2 with forward 6 coming into the zone as a late backchecker.

2. After forwards 1, 2, and 3 pass the top of the circles, forwards 4 and 5 go to the side boards by the face-off circles.

3. When defensemen 1 and 2 gain possession of the puck, they pass to forward 4 or 5.

4. Forwards 4, 5, and 6 go 3v2 against defensive defensemen 3 and 4, who have taken positions on the blue line after offensive forwards 1, 2, and 3 passed the top of the circles.

5. Forward 1 (the high offensive forward) now becomes the late backchecker against forwards 4, 5, and 6.

6. Forwards 7, 8, and 9 wait at the far blue line to start the drill again.

7. The high forward on each rush is the backchecker against the next forward line.

8. The drill is continuous, using one puck.

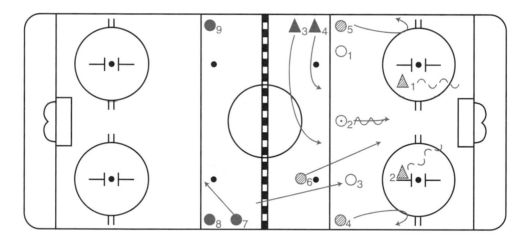

220 THREE FORECHECKERS

1. Offensive defenseman 1 and offensive defenseman 2 exchange passes in a staggered position inside the blue line.
2. Defensive forwards 1, 2, and 3 forecheck by exchanging positions as the first forechecker.
3. The coach whistles every 15 seconds, and players become active or pause at his whistle.

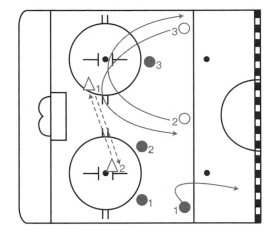

221 OTTAWA 5V3, 2V2

1. Forward 4 goes 1v1 in the corner against offensive defenseman 1.
2. When offensive defenseman 1 gains possession of the puck, forwards 1, 2, and 3 and offensive defensemen 1 and 2 break out 5v2 against defensive defensemen 1 and 2.
3. Forward 4 then backchecks to make the play 5v3.
4. When the players clear the zone, team forwards 5 and 6 cross with a puck at the center line and come back 2v2 against defensemen 1 and 2, who have skated to the blue line, pivoted, and are skating backward.

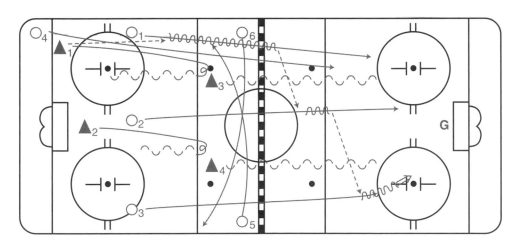

5V3, 2V0

1. Offensive forwards 1, 2, and 3 and offensive defensemen 1 and 2 go 5v3 into the offensive zone against defensive forward 4 and defensive defensemen 1 and 2.
2. The play continues 5v3 in the offensive zone until defensive defensemen 1 and 2 and defensive forward 4 gain possession and make a long pass to defensive forwards 5 and 6 over the center line.
3. Defensive forwards 5 and 6 go 2v0 at the far end of the rink.
4. Defensive forwards change positions as the defensive forward on the 5v3.

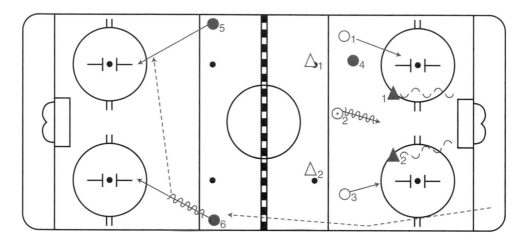

223   5V4 TO 5V5

1. Offensive forwards 1, 2, and 3 break out with offensive defensemen 1 and 2 against defensive defensemen 1 and 2; defensive forwards 1 and 2 are backchecking.
2. After offensive forwards 1, 2, and 3 cross the offensive blue line, defensive forward 3 joins the play. Play continues 5v5 until the defensive team gains control of the puck and breaks out.

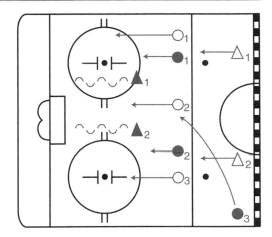

224   5V3 PLUS 2, 5V5

1. Offensive forwards 1, 2, and 3 and offensive defensemen 1 and 2 break out against defensive defensemen 1 and 2 and defensive forward 1.
2. Defensive forwards 2 and 3 are at the center line.
3. After the play enters the offensive zone, defensive forwards 2 and 3 join the play for a 5v5.
4. The play ends when the defensive team gains possession and clears the zone.

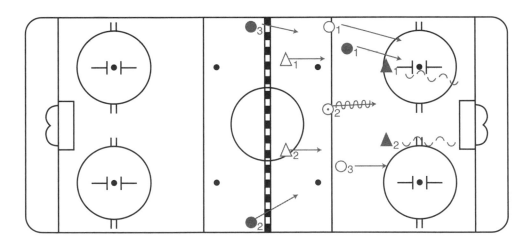

1. Offensive defensemen 1 and 2 break out with offensive forwards 1, 2, and 3 against defensive defensemen 1 and 2.
2. Defensive forwards 1, 2, and 3 trail the play to the far zone and then join the play to make it a 5v5 in the zone.
3. Play continues until the defensive team gains possession of the puck and clears the zone.

Variation

One or two early backcheckers are used to make it 5v3 to 5v5 or 5v4 to 5v5.

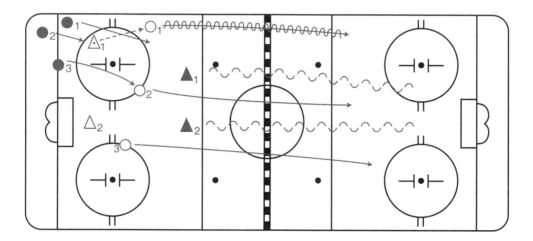

226   ONE FORECHECK, ONE BACKCHECK, ONE LATE BACKCHECK

1. The coach shoots the puck into the corner, and offensive defensemen 1 and 2 break out with offensive forwards 1, 2, and 3.
2. Defensive forwards 1 and 2 are at the blue line with defensive defensemen 1 and 2.
3. Defensive forward 1 forechecks, defensive forward 2 backchecks, and defensive forward 3 comes late back to the zone.
4. The play continues 5v5 until the defensive team gains possession of the puck and clears the zone.

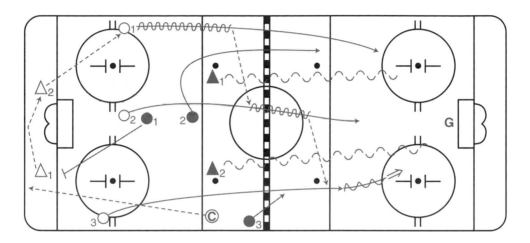

227   5V5, THREE PUCKS, DEFENSIVE ZONE

1. The coach passes a puck to the offensive team (offensive forwards 1, 2, and 3 and offensive defensemen 1 and 2), and they play against the defensive team (defensive defensemen 1 and 2 and defensive forwards 1, 2, and 3).

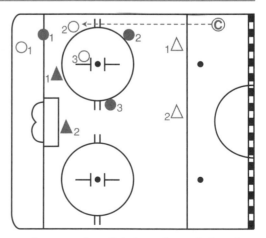

2. When the defensive team gains possession and clears the zone, the coach passes a second puck to the offensive team for another 5v5.
3. When the puck is cleared again, the coach passes in a third puck, and the play continues after the defensive team gains possession of the puck.

5V5 TURN STICKS

1. The coach passes to the offensive team (offensive forwards 1, 2, and 3 and offensive defensemen 1 and 2).

2. The players on the defensive team (defensive forwards 1, 2, and 3 and defensive defensemen 1 and 2) turn their sticks upside down.

3. After 10 to 15 seconds, the coach blows the whistle, and the players turn their sticks right side up and play 5v5 for another 30 to 40 seconds.

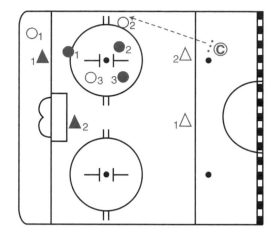

4. If the puck is cleared by the defensive team, the coach passes another puck to the offensive team, and the 5v5 continues.

1. Offensive defensemen 1 and 2 and offensive forwards 1, 2, and 3 go 5v5 against defensive defensemen 1 and 2 and defensive forwards 1, 2, and 3.
2. When the defensive team gains possession, they clear the puck to defensemen 3 and 4 and forwards 4, 5, and 6, who are waiting at the blue line.
3. The five players go into the offensive zone with the puck.
4. Defensemen 5 and 6 and forwards 7, 8, and 9 are in the slot and play defense 5v5 after the offensive team makes two passes.
5. The five players playing offense go back to the neutral zone when the puck is cleared and wait at the far blue line for the next puck.
6. After two or three sequences, offensive teams switch to playing defense and vice versa.

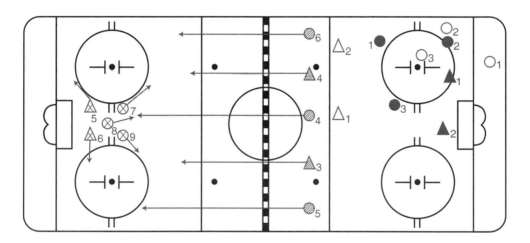

chapter 10

Combination Drills

Combination drills usually include offensive and defensive skills or combine a number of different offensive or defensive skills. Many of these drills are team-oriented drills such as those involving breakouts with forechecking and backchecking. Others are continuous drills that move from a one-on-one to a two-on-one or a two-on-one with a backchecker, and so forth.

Combination drills are often used with older or more advanced players to combine a number of individual or team skills. All of these drills are designed to simulate game situations and should be executed with high intensity to further simulate game situations. These are drills that don't fit into just one category like the other chapters of the book. They are, however, some of the best drills used by experienced coaches to combine a number of different skills into one drill. Because they combine so many different skills, sometimes they take more time than simpler drills. It's worth taking the extra time to run these drills, and coaches should try to work them into practice. They will get players used to game speed and intensity. They will also help players work on executing many skills at once.

1. Defenseman 1 passes across to forward 1.
2. Forward 1 skates outside the blue line.
3. Defenseman 1 skates toward the blue line, pivots, and skates backward.
4. Forward 1 goes 1v1 against defenseman 1 (see figure 1).
5. When the play is finished, forward 1 skates outside the blue line again.
6. Forward 2 comes off the boards at the blue line and takes a pass from the coach.
7. Defenseman 1 skates to the blue line again, pivots, and skates backward.
8. Forwards 1 and 2 go 2v1 against defenseman 1 (see figure 2).

Variation

The drill sequence can be repeated a third time by adding forward 3 and having forwards 1, 2, and 3 go 3v1 against defenseman 1.

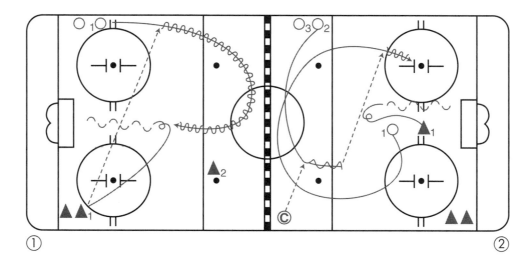

231 2V1 OUT OF THE CORNER, 2V1 HALF ICE

1. Forwards 1 and 2 are in the corner.
2. The coach passes the puck to forward 1 or 2. Forwards 1 and 2 then go 2v1 against defenseman 1 from the corner (see figure 1).
3. After the play is finished, the coach blows the whistle, and forwards 1 and 2 come outside the blue line and take another pass from the coach.
4. Defenseman 1 comes to the blue line, pivots, and skates backward.
5. Forwards 1 and 2 go 2v1 against defenseman 1 from outside the blue line (see figure 2).

Variation

The drill can be done with an additional forward, making the play 3v1.

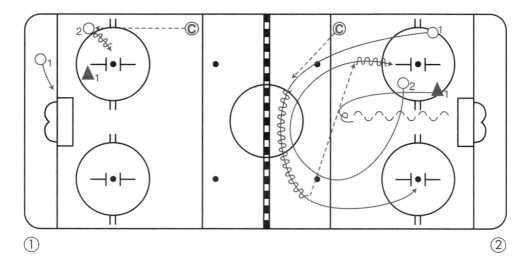

MAINE 1V1, 2V1 BACKCHECK

1. Defenseman 1 passes to forward 1 (see figure 1).
2. Forward 1 skates outside the blue line.
3. Defenseman 1 skates to the blue line, pivots, and skates backward.
4. Forward 1 goes 1v1 against defenseman 1.
5. When the 1v1 is completed, the coach blows the whistle, and defenseman 2 and forward 2 repeat the same sequence at the opposite end of the rink.
6. Forward 2 and defenseman 1 go 2v1 against defenseman 2, who skates to the blue line, pivots, and skates backward. Forward 1 goes on defense and skates to the other end as a backchecker (see figure 2).
7. The drill is continuous with the next 1v1 starting at the end where the 2v1 with the backchecker ended.

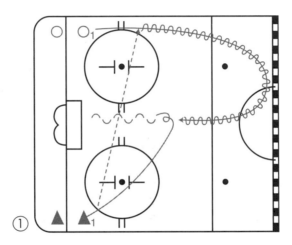

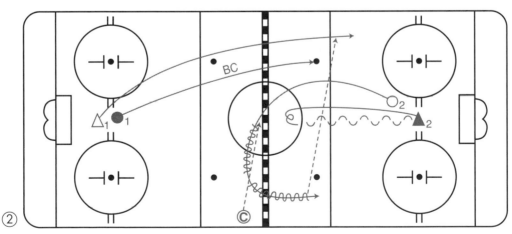

KAZAKHSTAN 1V1, 2V1, 3V2

1. The coach passes to forward 1 (see figure 1).
2. Forward 1 goes 1v1 against defenseman 1.
3. The coach then passes to forward 2.
4. Forward 2 and forward 3 go 2v1 against defenseman 2.
5. Next, the coach passes to forward 1, 2, or 3 (see figure 2).
6. Forwards 1, 2, and 3 go 3v2 against defensemen 1 and 2.

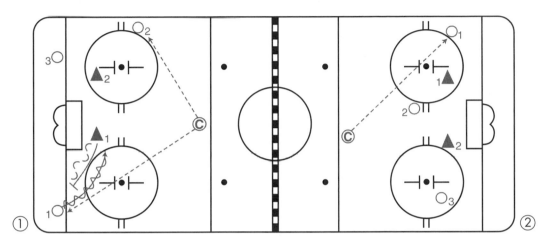

1. Defenseman 1 passes to forward 1.
2. Forwards 1 and 2 skate outside the blue line.
3. Defenseman 1 skates to the blue line, pivots, and skates backward.
4. Forwards 1 and 2 go 2v1 against defenseman 1 (see figure 1).
5. After the 2v1 is completed, the coach blows the whistle.
6. Defenseman 1 skates to the blue line, pivots, and skates backward.
7. Defenseman 2 joins defenseman 1 at the blue line, pivots, and skates backward.
8. Forwards 1 and 2 skate outside the blue line.
9. Forward 3 comes off the boards at the center line and takes a pass from the coach.
10. Forwards 1, 2, and 3 go 3v2 against defensemen 1 and 2 (see figure 2).

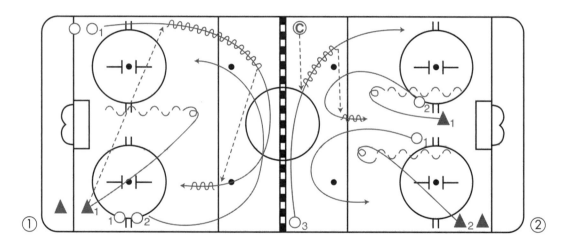

3V1, 3V2

1. Forwards 1, 2, and 3 break out with offensive defensemen 1 and 2 and then forwards 1,2 and 3 go 3v1 against defenseman 1 (see figure 1).
2. When the 3v1 is completed, the coach blows the whistle.
3. Forwards 1, 2, and 3 and offensive defensemen 1 and 2 come outside the offensive blue line into the neutral zone.
4. The coach passes a puck to the far blue line (see figure 2).
5. Offensive defensemen 1 and 2 go back and get the puck and pass to forward 1, 2, or 3.
6. Defensive defenseman 1 skates to the blue line, pivots, and skates backward.
7. Defensive defenseman 2 comes off the side boards, pivots, and skates backward, joining with defenseman 1 to defend against forwards 1, 2, and 3 in a 3v2.

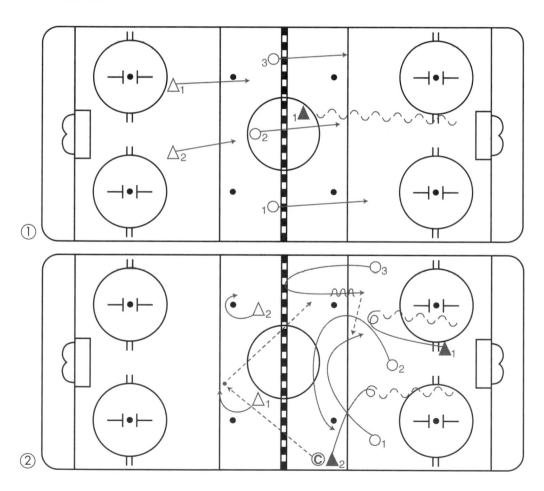

1. Offensive forwards 1, 2, and 3 and offensive defensemen 1 and 2 break out and go 5v2 against defensemen 1 and 2 (see figure 1).
2. When the 5v2 is completed, the coach blows the whistle.
3. Forwards 1, 2, and 3 skate back to the center line, and the coach passes to one of them (see figure 2). (The coach passes to a different forward each time.)
4. The player who receives the puck shoots it into the corner where the break-out started.
5. Offensive defensemen 3 and 4 and forwards 4, 5, and 6 are at the blue line, and they break out while the player who shot the puck in forechecks.
6. The other two offensive forwards who did not receive the puck for the shoot-in go to the side boards.
7. Defensive defensemen 3 and 4 take the 5v2 with offensive forwards 4, 5, and 6 and offensive defensemen 3 and 4 going toward the same end.
8. The breakouts are from the same end each time, so the goalies should be alternated halfway through the drill.

Variations

- The coach passes to forward 1, 2, or 3. The player with the puck shoots it into the corner to initiate the breakout, and the other two players forecheck.
- The player who shoots the puck into the corner to initiate the breakout back-checks from the blue line instead of forechecking.

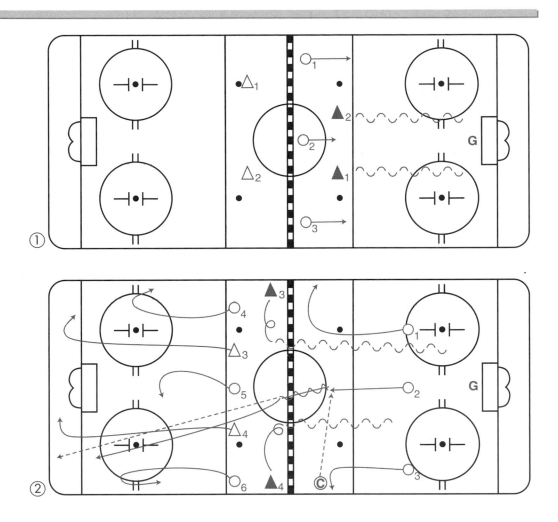

1. Forwards 1 and 2 come off the side boards to start the drill. One of them takes a pass from defenseman 1 in the corner (see figure 1).
2. Forwards 1 and 2 go 2v1 against defenseman 2.
3. After the 2v1 is completed, defenseman 2 goes to the corner and gets a puck.
4. Defenseman 2 starts the next 2v1 with a pass to forwards 3 and 4, who have come off the side boards.
5. Defenseman 2 comes to the side boards.
6. Defenseman 3 follows the play to the far blue line and takes the next 2v1.

Variations

• The drill is the same except that an additional offensive forward comes off the boards to start each sequence, making the play 3v1 (see figure 2).
• Play is the same as in the previous variation except that two offensive defensemen are used to make it 3v2.

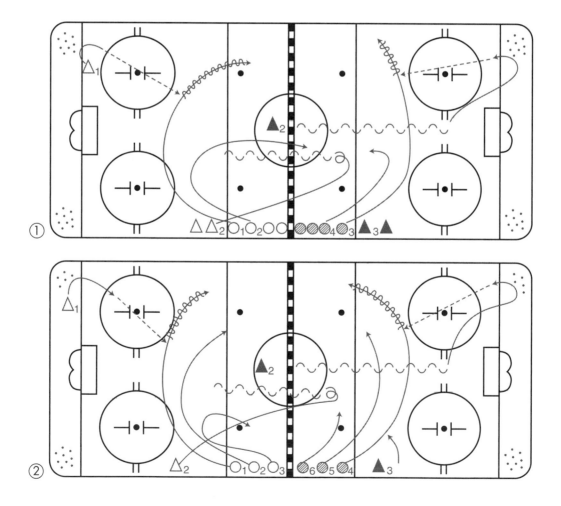

1. Offensive forwards 1, 2, and 3 break out with offensive defensemen 1 and 2 to go 5v3 against defensive defensemen 1 and 2 and defensive forward 1 (see figure 1).
2. After the 5v3, the coach blows the whistle. Offensive defensemen 1 and 2 and offensive forwards 1, 2, and 3 go back to the far blue line and take a pass from the coach (see figure 2).
3. Defensive defensemen 1 and 2 and defensive forward 1 come out to the center line, and defensive forward 2 joins the play as a backchecker.
4. Offensive forwards 1, 2, and 3 and offensive defensemen 1 and 2 then go 5v4 against the defensive team.

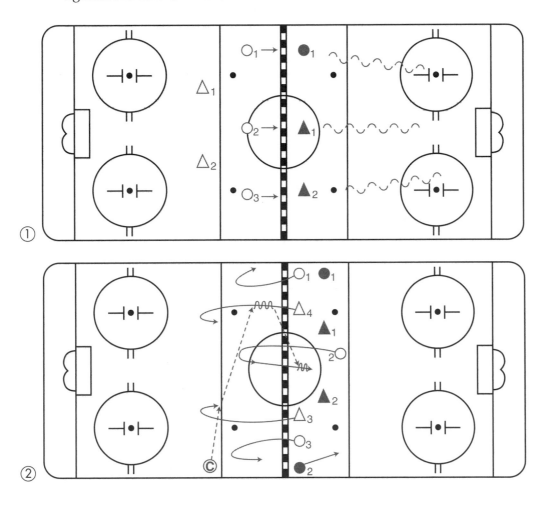

1. The coach shoots a puck into the corner. Forward 1 goes to the corner and gets the puck (see figure 1).
2. Defenseman 1 skates backward from the blue line and pivots.
3. Forward 1 comes out of the corner and goes 1v1 against defenseman 1.
4. On the whistle, forward 1 comes outside the blue line (see figure 2).
5. Defenseman 1 skates to the blue line, pivots, and skates backward.
6. Forward 2 comes off the side boards and takes a pass from the coach.
7. Forwards 1 and 2 then go 2v1 against defenseman 1.

Variation

The drill is the same except that a second defenseman is added. After the 1v1, defenseman 2 comes off the boards, and forwards 1 and 2 take a pass from the coach and go 2v2 against defensemen 1 and 2 (see figure 3).

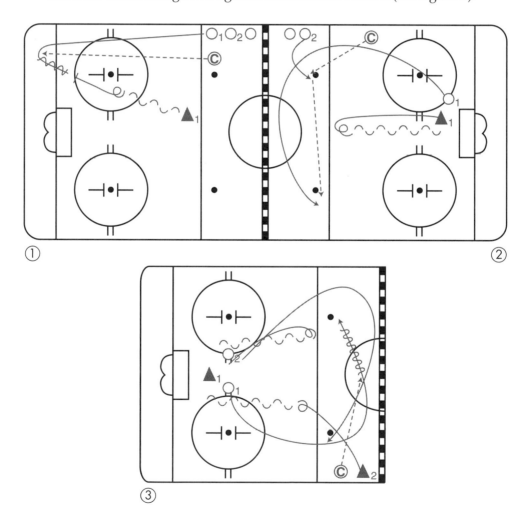

1. Forward 1 skates around the face-off circle and shoots, then one-touch passes with forward 2 in the corner, who has a puck.
2. Defenseman 1 takes a pass at the blue line from forward 3.
3. Defenseman 1 skates to the middle of the blue line, shoots, pivots, and skates backward.
4. Forward 1 skates outside the blue line, loops back, and goes 1v1 against defenseman 1.
5. This drill can be done at both ends of the rink at the same time.

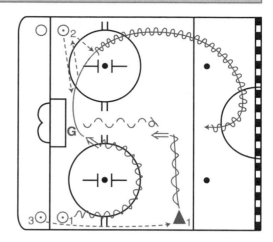

2V1, 2V2

1. Forwards 1 and 2 come off the opposite side boards and go 2v1 against defenseman 1 (see figure 1).

2. When the play is completed, the coach blows the whistle, and forwards 1 and 2 take a pass from the coach.

3. Forwards 1 and 2 then go 2v2 in the opposite direction against defensemen 2 and 3, who come off the opposite side boards (see figure 2).

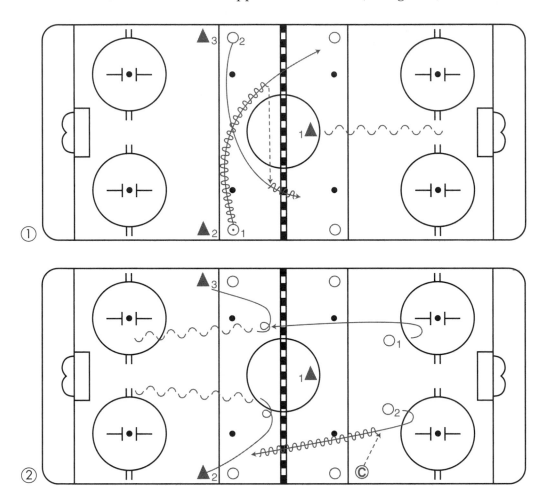

1. Forwards 1 and 2 skate to the far blue line, loop and cross, take a pass from the coach, go 2v0 back to the other end, and shoot (see figure 1).
2. After shooting, forwards 1 and 2 skate again to the far blue line, get a pass from the coach, and come back 2v1 against defenseman 1, who comes off the side boards, pivots, and skates backward (see figure 2).

Variation

The drill is the same except that a second defenseman is added. After the 2v0, defenseman 2 joins defenseman 1 by skating in from the opposite side boards, pivoting, and skating backward—making the play 2v2 (see figure 3).

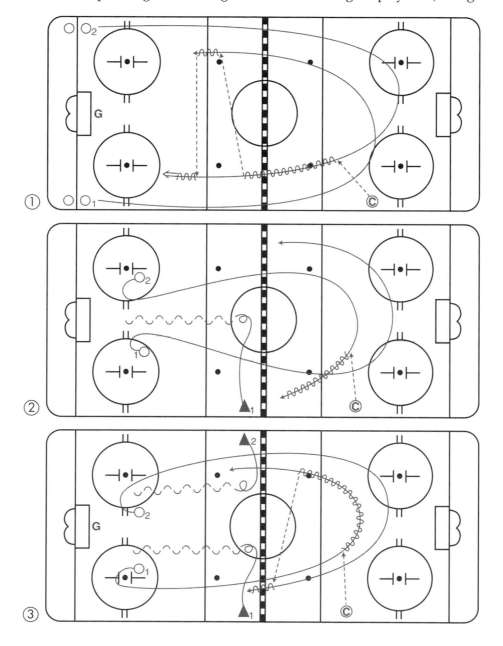

2V0, LONG PASS, 2V1

1. Defenseman 1 skates forward to the center line, stops, and receives a pass from forward 1 (see figure 1).
2. Forward 1 and forward 2 loop inside the center line.
3. Defenseman 1 skates backward with the puck and passes to forward 1 or forward 2.
4. Forward 1 and forward 2 go 2v0.
5. Defenseman 2, forward 3, and forward 4 perform the same pattern simultaneously from the other side of the rink.
6. After going 2v0 and shooting, forward 1 and forward 2 circle back and take a long pass from defenseman 1. Defenseman 2 also makes a long pass to forwards 3 and 4 (see figure 2).
7. After making the long pass, defenseman 2 skates forward to the blue line, pivots, and skates backward. Defenseman 1 skates the same pattern on the other end of the rink.
8. Forward 1 and forward 2 then go 2v1 against defenseman 2.
9. Forward 3 and forward 4 go 2v1 against defenseman 1 on the other end.

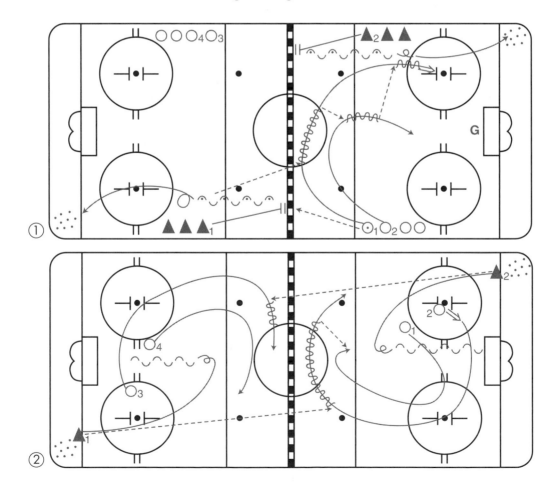

TWO FORWARDS CROSS 2V1 TO 3V2

1. Forward 1 and forward 2 cross at the blue line and go 2v1 against defenseman 1.
2. Forward 3 skates around the face-off circle and shoots, then skates to the neutral zone.
3. After the 2v1 is completed, the coach passes to forward 1 or forward 2.
4. Defenseman 2 and defenseman 3 come off the boards, pivot, and skate backward.
5. Forwards 1, 2, and 3 go 3v2 toward the other end against defensemen 2 and 3.
6. The drill is continuous from both ends.

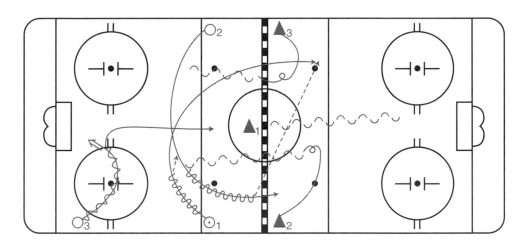

Players can perform the following sequences for either a 2v0 or 2v1.

Sequence 1

1. Forward 1 and forward 2 skate backward from the side boards, pivot, and skate forward.
2. Forward 1 one-touch passes with forward 3, and forward 3 then passes to forward 2.
3. Forward 1 and forward 2 go 2v0 over the far blue line and shoot.
4. Simultaneously, forward 4 and forward 5 perform the same drill, exchanging passes with forward 6 and then going 2v0 in the opposite direction.
5. The drill is continuous with the diagonally opposite groups going next.

Sequence 2

1. The drill is similar to the 2v0 version except that three players come off the boards, with forward 1 taking an exchange pass with forward 4, then pivoting, skating backward, and being the defenseman on the 2v1.
2. Forward 4 then exchanges passes with either forward 2 or forward 3.
3. Forward 2 and forward 3 go 2v1 against forward 1 acting as a defenseman.
4. The drill alternates sides, with forwards 5, 6, and 7 going next and exchanging passes with forward 8.

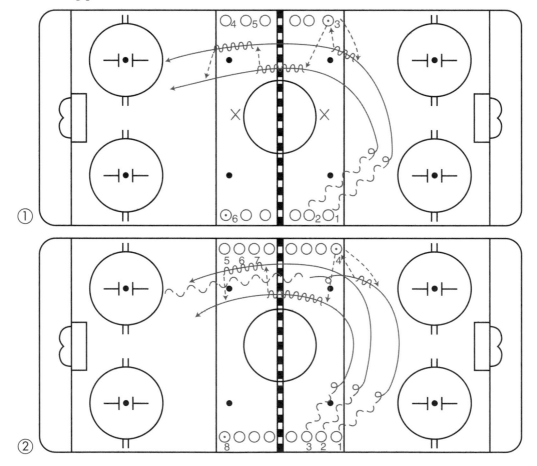

1. Player 1 passes to player 2 to start the play (see figure 1).
2. Player 1 skates to the center line, pivots, and skates backward.
3. Player 2 goes 1v1 against player 1.
4. As soon as players 1 and 2 go past the blue line, player 3 passes to player 4.
5. Player 3 skates to the center line, pivots, and skates backward.
6. Player 1 then goes on offense with player 4, and they go 2v1 against player 3 playing defense, with player 2 backchecking.
7. After the 2v1 with a backchecker passes the blue line, player 5 passes to player 6 (see figure 2).
8. Players 6, 3, and 1 then go 3v3 against players 5, 2, and 4 playing defense.

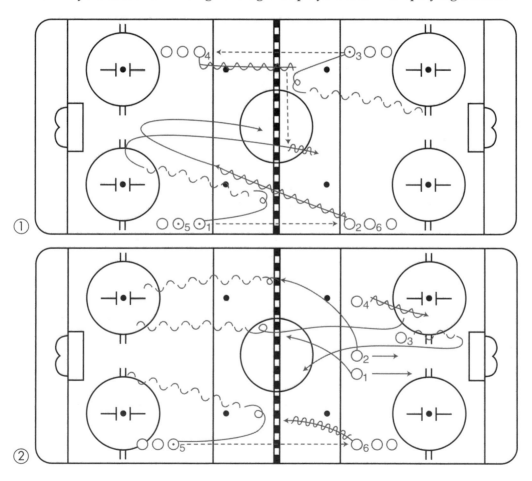

Alternate the following sequences on different ends of the ice, or run them simultaneously to use the entire rink at once.

Sequence 1

1. Forward 1 passes to defenseman 1.
2. Defenseman 1 moves laterally and returns a pass to forward 1.
3. Forward 1 skates through the center circle.
4. Defenseman 1 skates to the blue line, pivots, and skates backward.
5. Forward 1 goes 1v1 against defenseman 1.

Sequence 2

1. Forward 3 passes to defenseman 3.
2. Defenseman 3 passes to defenseman 2.
3. Defenseman 2 passes to forward 3, who has looped across inside the blue line.
4. Forward 3 skates outside the blue line and curls.
5. Forward 2 skates across the center line and takes a pass from forward 3.
6. Defenseman 2 and defenseman 3 skate to the blue line, pivot, and skate backward.
7. Forward 2 and forward 3 then go 2v2 against defenseman 2 and defenseman 3.

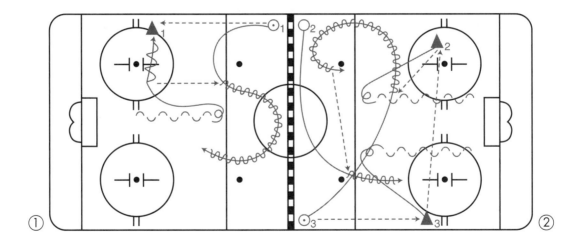

chapter 11

Shooting Drills

These drills are usually performed at each end of the rink simultaneously, and some of the drills are specific to forwards and defensemen. The shooting drills can be inserted at any time during the practice. In many cases, only half the rink is used for these drills, so less skating is involved; therefore, the shooting drills may be used after a high-intensity drill. Quick release, one timers (shooting the puck without stopping the puck first) and getting into position to score are keys to scoring goals. These drills are excellent for both forwards and defensemen working on shooting.

Goalies should be used in all of these drills to help players learn the skills they will need to beat the goalie, like shot placement and deking. He should be positioned, as usual, just outside the line at the top of the crease. Including the goalie will also give him a chance to face a good number of shots in a fast paced environment, as in a game situation. Also, keep in mind that although the drills in this chapter should be high intensity for the shooters as well as for the goalies and are intended for use when the goalies are already warmed up to prevent injury. More goalie specific drills can be found in chapter 15. And, in the same way that the drills in this chapter work both shooting and goalie skills, many of the drills in chapter 15 can also be used to work on shooting.

BLUE LINE SHOOT

1. The players are lined up on the blue line.
2. The first player skates in, receives a pass from the coach, and shoots.
3. The players skate in and shoot in succession.

Variation

The coach randomly passes to players on the blue line, and they go in and shoot.

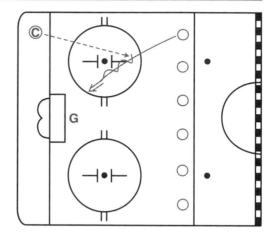

SEMICIRCLE SHOOT

1. The players are in a semicircle, and they shoot in succession starting from one side.

Variation

The players alternate, with a player shooting from one side, and then a player shooting from the other side.

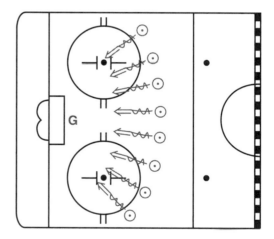

250 BLUE LINE, BACKWARD, ONE-TOUCH, SHOOT

1. The players are lined up on the blue line.
2. The first player skates backward with the puck to the center line, passes to the next player on the blue line, skates forward, takes a return pass, and shoots.
3. The players shoot in succession.

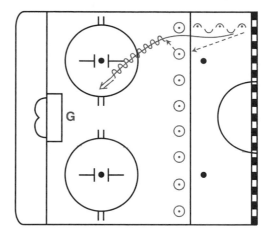

251 THREE SHOTS, FIVE TIMES

1. Five players are positioned on the ice as shown. Each player has three pucks.
2. The players take turns shooting their three pucks, going in the following order: forward 1, forward 3, forward 2, defenseman 1, and defenseman 2.

Variation

Players shoot one puck each time, going in the same order, until each player has shot three pucks.

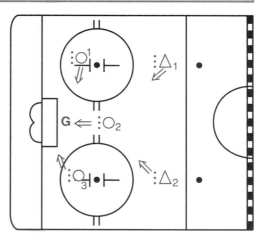

TWO PASSES AND SHOOT

1. The players are in three lines at the center line.
2. Player 1 passes to player 2.
3. Player 2 shoots.
4. Player 1 passes to player 3.
5. Player 3 shoots.
6. Player 1 skates in with the puck and shoots from the high slot.
7. After shooting, the players return to the center line and go to a different line.

Variation

Before shooting, each player does a curl (tight turn).

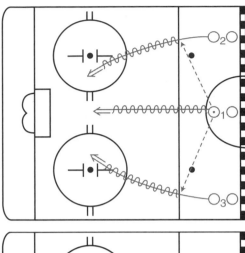

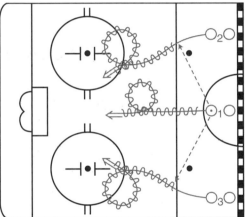

1. The players are in two lines at the blue line.
2. Forward 1 skates in, receives a pass from the opposite corner from forward 2, and then shoots (see figure 1).
3. Forward 1 takes the position of forward 2 in the corner, and forward 2 goes to the line on the same side.
4. Forward 3 then skates in, takes a pass from the opposite corner from forward 4, and shoots.
5. Forward 3 takes the position of forward 4, and forward 4 goes to the line on the same side.

Variation

1. Forward 1 skates in, takes a pass from forward 2, and shoots (see figure 2).
2. Forward 3 follows forward 1 in and goes for a rebound.
3. Forward 1 takes the position of forward 2. Forward 3 (the rebounder) goes back to the shooting line.

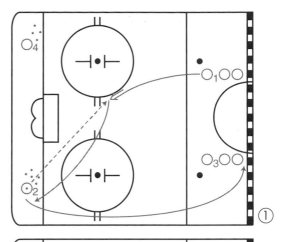

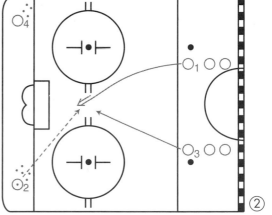

1. Several pucks are placed on the ice.
2. Forward 1 stickhandles around the pucks and shoots.
3. Forward 2 stickhandles around the pucks, pivots 360 degrees, and shoots.

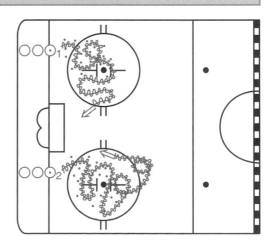

255   SHOOT, CURL, SHOOT

1. The players are in two lines at the blue line.
2. Forward 1 starts with the puck, skates in, and shoots.
3. Forward 1 then skates around the face-off circle, receives a pass from forward 2, and shoots again.
4. Forward 1 takes the position of forward 2 in the corner, and forward 2 goes to the line on the same side.
5. Forward 3 then skates in, shoots, skates around the circle, takes a pass from forward 4, and shoots again.
6. The drill is continuous.

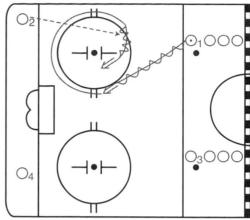

256   TWO PASS-OUT OPTIONS

1. Forward 1 skates with the puck beside and behind the net.
2. Forward 1 passes to forward 2 in the high slot either from the side of the net or after skating behind the net.
3. Forward 2 shoots.
4. Forward 3 then skates with the puck and does the same pattern with forward 4.
5. The drill is continuous.

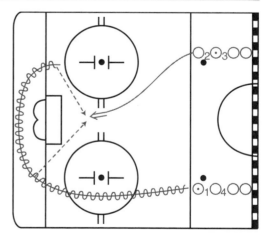

257 SHOOT, PASS TO D, SECOND SHOT

1. Forward 1 skates with the puck around the face-off circle, shoots, and then stays in front of the net to screen, deflect, or rebound for the next shot.
2. Forward 2 passes to defenseman 1.
3. Defenseman 1 skates across the blue line and shoots, with forward 1 screening and deflecting in front of the net.
4. The drill alternates from each side.

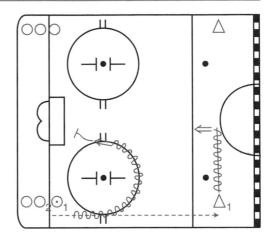

258 FIGURE EIGHT SHOOT, TWO OR THREE SHOTS

1. Forward 1 skates out of one corner, skates around the face-off circle, receives a pass from forward 2, and shoots.
2. Forward 1 continues on and skates around the opposite face-off circle in a figure eight pattern, takes a pass from forward 3, and shoots.
3. The drill is continuous, alternating from each side.

Variation

After shooting the second shot, forward 1 backs up to the high slot and receives another pass from forward 2 for a third shot.

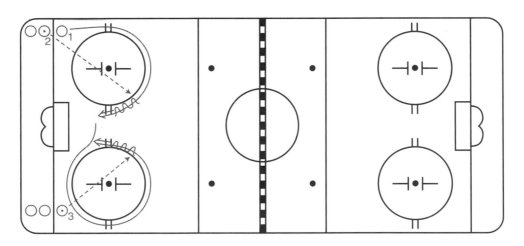

PASS-OUT, SLOT SHOT

1. Forward 1 skates with the puck around the cone at the lower side of the face-off circle and passes to forward 2, who has skated to the high slot.
2. Forward 2 shoots.
3. Forwards 3 and 4 then perform the same pattern from the other side.
4. The two players change lines after finishing the drill.
5. The drill is continuous, alternating from each side.

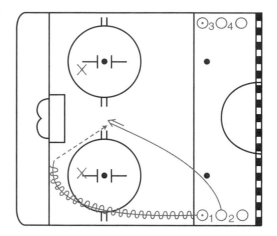

AROUND THE CONE, SHOOT

1. Forward 1 skates around the cone and comes back to the slot for a pass from forward 2.
2. Forward 1 shoots.
3. Forward 2 then performs the same pattern from the other side, taking a pass from forward 3.
4. The drill is continuous, alternating from each side.

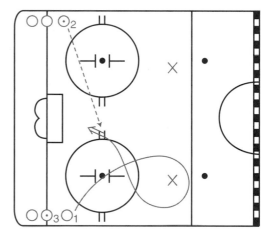

261 TWO ONE-TOUCH PASSES GIVE AND GO, SHOOT

1. Forward 1 skates with the puck, one-touch passes with forward 2 and forward 3, and then shoots.

2. The two players receiving the one-touch passes (forward 2 and forward 3) should rotate every five shots.

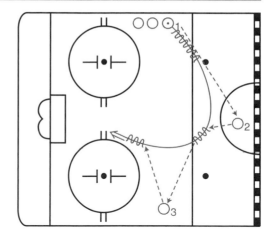

262 FIGURE EIGHT, BACKWARD, PIVOT, SHOOT

1. Forward 1 skates backward out of the corner and around the face-off circle, pivots, takes a pass from forward 2, and shoots.

2. Forward 1 then one-touch passes with forward 3, skates backward around the opposite face-off circle, pivots, takes another pass from forward 3, and shoots.

3. The drill is continuous, alternating from each side.

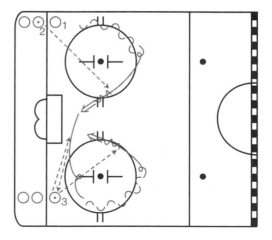

263   PASS, WALKOUT, SHOOT

1. Forward 1 passes behind the net to forward 2.
2. Forward 2 skates out from the side of the net and either shoots or passes to forward 1, who has come out of the corner for a pass or a rebound.
3. The drill is continuous, alternating from each side.

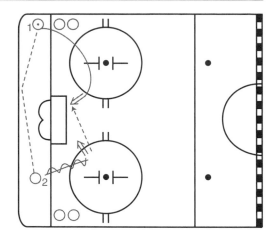

264   PASS BEHIND THE NET, SHOOT

1. Forward 1 and forward 2 skate from the blue line to behind the goal line.
2. Forward 1 passes behind the net to forward 2.
3. Forward 1 goes to the slot.
4. Forward 2 passes to forward 1.
5. Forward 1 shoots.
6. The drill is continuous, with the shooter alternating from each side.

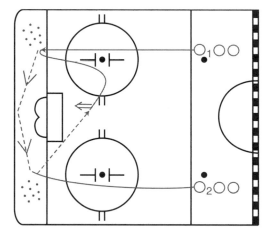

265   CROSS ICE, REDIRECT, SHOOT

1. Forward 1 skates toward the net and around the cone.
2. Forward 2 passes the puck just after forward 1 passes the cone.
3. Forward 1 redirects or one-times the shot (shoots without stopping the puck).

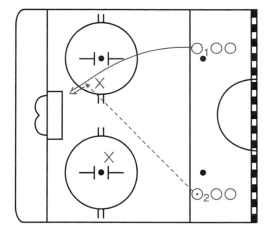

266   HIGH, LOW, SHOOT

1. Forward 1 skates to the high cone at the top of the circle, cuts toward the middle, and shoots.
2. Forward 2 skates around the low cone at the bottom of the circle and shoots.
3. The players change lines after shooting.

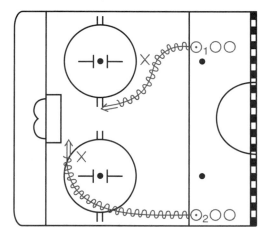

267   ONE-TOUCH, PIVOT, PASS, SHOOT

1. Forward 1 skates backward, one-touch passes with forward 2, then pivots, skates forward, receives another pass from forward 2, and shoots.
2. The players change lines after shooting.

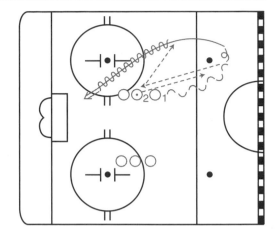

268   THREE PASSES, SHOOT

1. Forward 1 skates from the corner with the puck and passes to forward 2 at the blue line.
2. Forward 1 pivots, skates backward, one-touch passes with forward 2, pivots, takes another pass from forward 2, and shoots.
3. The drill alternates from each side.

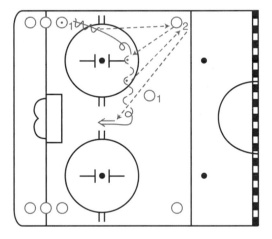

TWO PASSES TO D, SHOOT

1. Forward 1 passes to defenseman 1 at the center line.
2. Forward 1 skates around the face-off circle and receives a return pass from defenseman 1.
3. Forward 1 shoots, then goes to the corner and gets a puck.
4. Defenseman 1 moves to the blue line.
5. Forward 1 passes to defenseman 1.
6. Forward 1 goes to the front of the net to screen or deflect.
7. Defenseman 1 shoots.
8. Forward 2 goes next, passing with defenseman 2.

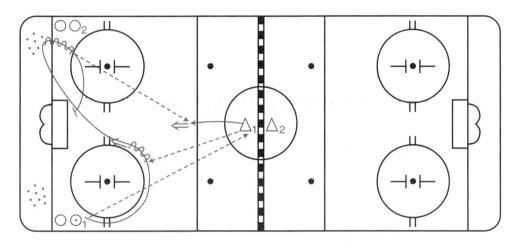

D TO D PASS, SHOOT

1. Forward 1 passes the puck from the corner to defenseman 2.
2. Defenseman 2 passes to defenseman 1.
3. Forward 1 skates around behind defenseman 1 and defenseman 2.
4. Defenseman 1 passes to forward 1.
5. Forward 1 shoots.
6. The drill alternates from each side.

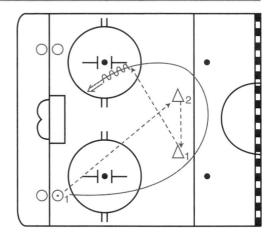

TWO ONE-TOUCHES, SHOOT

1. Forward 1 starts with the puck, skates toward forward 2 in the corner, and one-touch passes with forward 2.
2. Forward 1 then skates toward forward 3 at the center line, one-touch passes with forward 3, and shoots.
3. The drill alternates from each side.

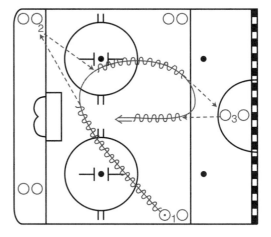

272   FIVE SHOTS

1. Each position starts with a puck.
2. Forward 1 skates out of the corner, skates around the face-off circle, shoots, and stays in front for a screen or deflection.
3. Forward 2 skates around the opposite face-off circle, shoots, and stays in front for a screen or deflection.
4. Defenseman 1 passes to offensive defenseman 2.
5. Defenseman 2 shoots.
6. Defenseman 2 passes to defenseman 1.
7. Defenseman 1 shoots.
8. Forward 3 starts at the blue line, skates in, and shoots.
9. Forward 1, forward 2, and forward 3 rotate with forward 1 becoming forward 2, forward 2 becoming forward 3, and forward 3 becoming forward 1.

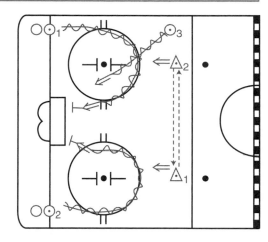

273   TWO RIMS, SHOOT

1. Forward 1 rims the puck along the boards to forward 2.
2. Forward 2 takes the puck off the boards, skates around the face-off circle, and shoots.
3. Forward 2 goes to the front of the net to deflect or screen.
4. Forward 1 rims a second puck to defenseman 1.
5. Defenseman 1 skates along the blue line and shoots.
6. Forward 1 goes to the front of the net to screen or deflect.

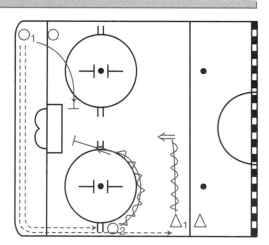

274 D TO MIDDLE, THREE SHOTS, FORWARDS SCREEN

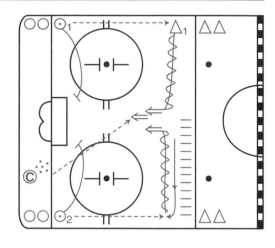

1. Forward 1 passes to defenseman 1 at the blue line.
2. Forward 1 goes to the front of the net and screens.
3. Defenseman 1 skates to the middle of the blue line and shoots.
4. Defenseman 1 cross steps laterally across the blue line to the far boards and takes a pass from forward 2.
5. Forward 2 skates in front of the goalie and screens with forward 1.
6. Defenseman 1 skates to the middle of the blue line again and shoots.
7. The coach passes to defenseman 1, who shoots a third shot from the blue line, with forward 1 and forward 2 screening and deflecting.

chapter 12

Defenseman Drills

This chapter includes individual skating, passing, and shooting drills designed specifically for defensemen. Defensemen need exceptional skating speed both forward and backward, must be able to start and stop on a dime, must have great agility, accurate passing and puck handling, and must be able to shoot quickly with both wrist shots and slap shots. Agility, balance, and strength are essential as the defenseman is constantly working in the corners and in front of the net during one-on-one battles for the puck. The drills included in this chapter have been used by experienced coaches to develop these important skills needed by the modern day defenseman.

During the execution of the drills in this chapter, players should be going near game intensity to simulate game situations. The coach should watch for proper technique in the players' shooting, skating, and passing. Additional defensive drills can be found in chapter 9.

1. The defenseman starts in the corner and skates forward to the blue line.
2. He then skates using chop steps along the blue line to the middle.
3. He skates backward to the face-off circle.
4. He then pivots, skates forward to the corner, and stops.
5. Then he skates to the front of the net, stops, and goes to the opposite corner.
6. The defenseman will then come out of that corner for his or her next turn.
7. The drill can be done from both corners simultaneously.

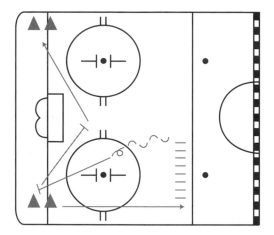

1. Defenseman 1 skates forward in a zigzag motion across the ice.
2. Defenseman 2 skates backward, head up, mirroring the movement of defenseman 1.
3. Defensemen 1 and 2 come back the other way, changing positions so that defenseman 2 skates forward and defenseman 1 skates backward, mirroring defenseman 2.
4. The offensive player being mirrored can skate with or without a puck.

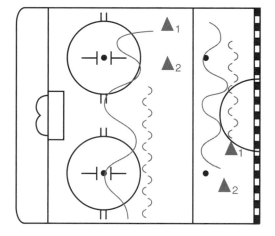

277   CONE TRIANGLE AGILITY

Players can perform either sequence to work on skating.

Sequence 1
1. Cones (or pucks) are arranged in a triangle.
2. The player skates around the cones, alternating between skating forward and backward at each cone.

Sequence 2
1. Two cones are placed about 5 to 10 feet apart.
2. The player alternately skates forward and backward in a figure eight pattern around the cones while exchanging passes with the coach or another player.

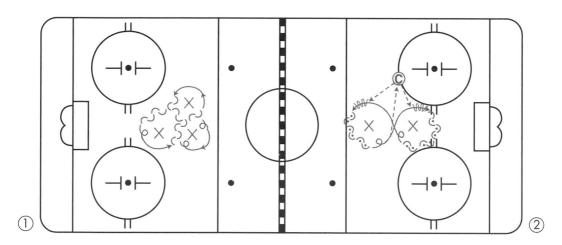

278   CONE ROW AGILITY

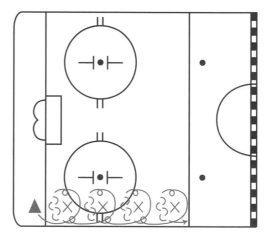

1. Several cones are placed in a row, approximately 7 to 10 feet apart, from the goal line to the blue line. The offensive defenseman skates forward around each cone, then pivots and skates backward halfway around it.
2. The player repeats this pattern all the way to the blue line.

1. Defenseman 1 skates forward with the puck. Defenseman 2 skates backward (see figure 1).
2. Defenseman 1 passes the puck to defenseman 2.
3. Defenseman 2 then skates forward, and defenseman 1 skates backward.
4. Defenseman 2 passes to defenseman 1, and they repeat the pattern.

Variations

- Defenseman 3 passes to defenseman 4, who pivots 360 degrees, skates forward, and passes to defenseman 1. Defenseman 1 then repeats the pattern (see figure 2).
- Defenseman 5 flips the puck in the air to defenseman 6, who knocks it down with a glove and passes it back to defenseman 1. Defenseman 1 then repeats the pattern (see figure 3).

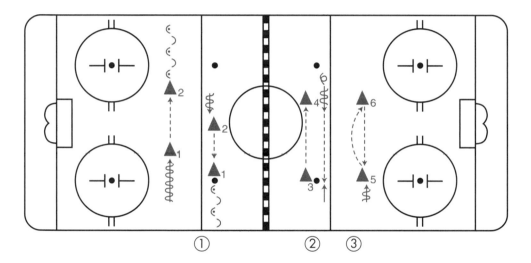

Players can perform these sequences consecutively, or they may form two separate groups and perform them simultaneously.

Sequence 1

1. Defenseman 1 starts from the side boards at the center line and skates laterally backward to the middle of the blue line.
2. Defenseman 2 passes the puck to defenseman 1, who pivots, skates forward to the center line at the boards, and passes the puck to defenseman 3.
3. Defenseman 1 then repeats the sequence going the other way, skating laterally backward from the center line to the middle of the blue line.
4. Defenseman 1 receives a pass from defenseman 3, pivots, skates forward, passes the puck to defenseman 2, and skates to the center line at the boards.

Sequence 2

1. Defenseman 1 skates laterally backward from the center line to the middle of the blue line and skates backward to the center line at the far boards, exchanging passes with defenseman 2.
2. Defenseman 1 repeats the pattern back to the starting position, skating laterally backward to the middle of the blue line and back to the center line at the boards, exchanging passes with defenseman 3.

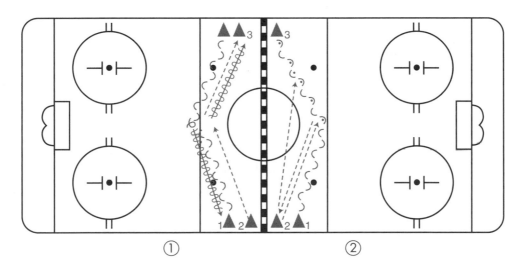

BACKWARD, PIVOT, SHOOT

1. Defenseman 1 skates backward with the puck along the blue line and exchanges passes with defenseman 2.

2. Defenseman 1 pivots, skates forward, and shoots the puck just inside the blue line.

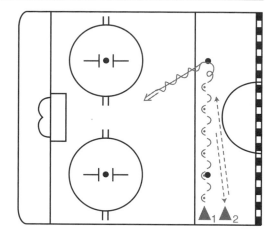

AGILITY AND SHOOTING

1. Defenseman 1 skates backward from the goal line and one-touch passes with defenseman 2 (see figure 1).

2. Defenseman 1 skates with the puck to the middle of the blue line and shoots.

3. Defenseman 1 then one-touch passes with defenseman 3, skates backward with the puck to the blue line, skates laterally along the blue line, and shoots a quick wrist shot.

4. The next player repeats the same pattern from the opposite corner. Players change lines after completing the drill.

Variation

The drill is the same, but on the second shot, defenseman 1 does a give-and-go with defenseman 3 and then shoots at the face-off circle (see figure 2).

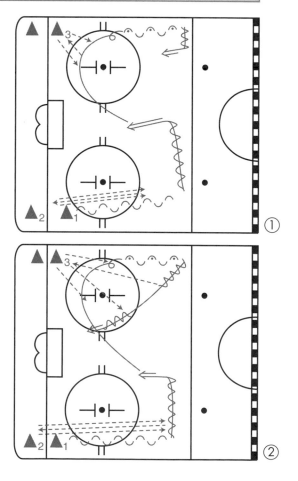

1. Defenseman 1 skates backward from the corner with the puck and one-touch passes with defenseman 2 (see figure 1).
2. After reaching the blue line with the puck, defenseman 1 stops, then moves to the outside (right), the inside (left), and quickly shoots.

Variations

- The drill is the same except that when defenseman 1 gets to the blue line, he or she pivots with the puck and quickly shoots (see figure 2).
- The drill is the same except that when defenseman 1 gets to the blue line, he or she fakes a shot and then moves right or left and shoots (see figure 3).

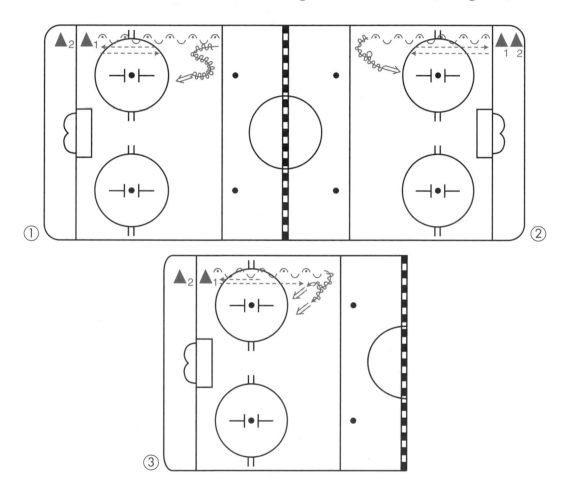

1. Defenseman 1 is at the boards, and defenseman 2 is at the middle of the blue line.
2. Defenseman 1 skates with the puck along the blue line to the middle of the ice.
3. Defenseman 2 moves to the top of the far circle.
4. Defenseman 1 passes to offensive defenseman 2 for a one-timer shot.
5. Defenseman 2 then skates to the blue line at the boards and gets a second puck.

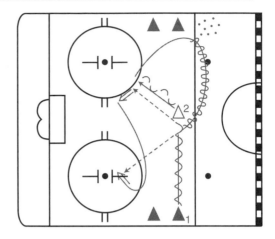

6. Defenseman 2 skates to the middle of the blue line.
7. Defenseman 1 skates to the top of the near circle.
8. Defenseman 2 passes to defenseman 1 for a one-timer shot.
9. The right shots are on the left side, and the left shots are on the right side.

1. The defenseman skates in from the blue line and gets a puck at the hash marks of the face-off circle near the boards.
2. The defenseman skates backward with the puck to the blue line, skates along the blue line, and shoots at the middle.
3. The defenseman then skates to the hash marks of the far face-off circle, gets a second puck, skates backward to the blue line with the puck, skates to the middle of the blue line, and takes a second shot.

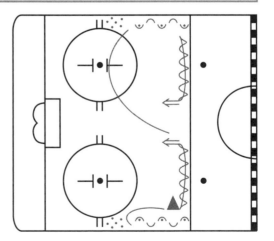

286 BACKWARD, FORWARD PASSING

1. Defenseman 1 or 2 receives a pass from the coach to start the drill.
2. Defensemen 1 and 2 skate backward from the center line, passing the puck, until they are behind the net.
3. Defensemen 1 and 2 then skate forward to the center line and pass the puck to the coach, who passes it to the next two defensemen to repeat the drill.

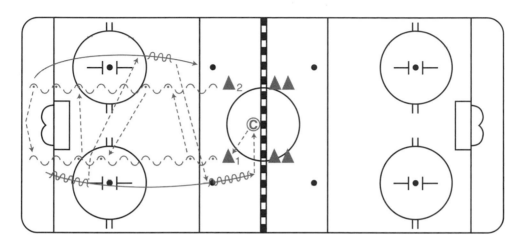

287 AGILITY WITH THE PUCK, SHOOT

1. Defenseman 1 one-touch passes with defenseman 2 in the corner while skating backward to the blue line.
2. Defenseman 1 then skates laterally along the blue line to the far boards, pivots, skates forward around the cone, skates to the middle of the ice, and shoots.

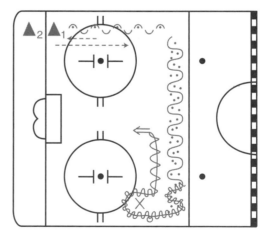

1. The coach shoots the puck in the corner to start the drill.
2. Defenseman 1 skates backward, pivots, skates forward, and gets the puck.
3. Defenseman 1, after giving a head fake in the opposite direction, skates around behind the net and starts up ice, does a tight turn, goes back behind the net, stops, passes to defenseman 2 at the boards, and skates toward the blue line.

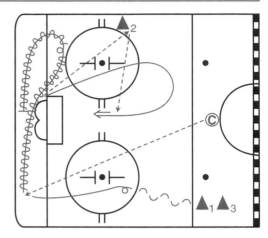

4. Defenseman 1 then loops back, takes a return pass from defenseman 2, and shoots.
5. Defenseman 1 then takes the position of defenseman 2 at the boards, and defenseman 3 starts the next sequence of the drill when the coach shoots the puck in the other corner (on the same half of the rink).

Variation

Defenseman 1 takes the return pass from defenseman 2 at the blue line, skates to the middle of the blue line, and shoots.

289 THREE BREAKOUT PASSES

1. Defenseman 1 skates backward, pivots, gets a puck in the corner, skates behind the net, and passes to forward 1 at the boards.
2. Defenseman 1 skates to the other corner, gets a puck, skates behind the net, and passes to forward 2 at the boards.
3. Defenseman 1 then skates to the corner, gets a puck, and passes to forward 3 up the middle of the ice.

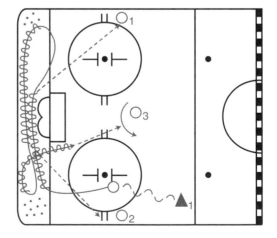

290 SKATING LATERALLY, PASSING, SHOOTING

1. Defenseman 1 skates backward from the blue line, pivots, gets a puck at the hash marks of the face-off circle near the boards, skates laterally with the puck, and passes to defenseman 2.
2. Defenseman 2 passes to defenseman 3.
3. Defenseman 3 shoots.
4. Defenseman 1 continues skating laterally, gets a puck at the hash marks near the opposite boards, and passes to defenseman 3.

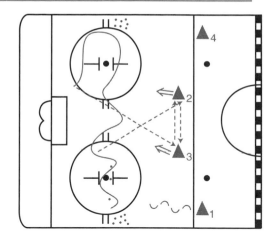

5. Defenseman 3 passes to defenseman 2, who shoots.
6. Defenseman 4 starts the next round of the drill from the opposite side.
7. The two players shooting at the blue line should rotate after they shoot with then next two defensemen.

291 RIM, PASS, SHOOT

1. The coach starts the drill by shooting the puck in the corner.
2. Defenseman 1 skates backward from the blue line, pivots, skates forward, gets the puck, and rims it around the boards to the far blue line.
3. Defenseman 2 moves in and stops the puck and then passes it to defenseman 3, who shoots.
4. The players should rotate after each shot.

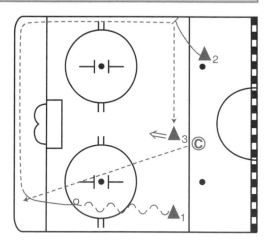

1. The coach passes to forward 1.
2. Forward 1 goes 1v1 against the defenseman.
3. After the 1v1 is finished, the coach passes to forward 2, and forward 2 goes 1v1 against the defenseman.
4. The coach then passes to forward 3, and forward 3 goes 1v1 against the defenseman.
5. After the third 1v1, the next defenseman repeats the same drill.

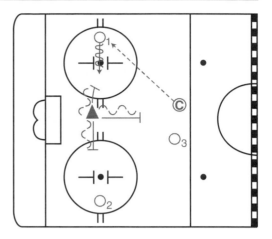

The defenseman starts on the outside of the circle and skates the following sequence:

1. Skates forward to the dot, backward to the outside, and then forward again to the dot (see figure 1).
2. Skates using chop steps right to the outside, then skates using chop steps back in to the dot.
3. Skates forward to the outside, then skates backward to the dot.
4. Skates using chop steps left to the outside, then skates using chop steps back in to the dot.
5. Skates backward to the outside, backward around the outside of the circle, stops, and skates backward in the other direction around the outside of the circle.

Variation

The defenseman starts in the middle of the circle, skates forward out to the outside, and skates backward back to the middle, moving around the circle in a pattern that resembles the spokes in a wheel (see figure 2).

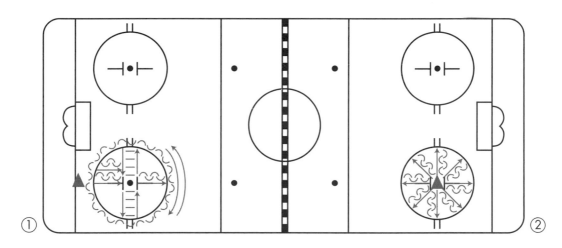

1. Defenseman 2 skates backward from the corner with the puck and passes to defenseman 1.
2. Defenseman 2 skates forward around the cone, gets a puck in the face-off circle, skates backward with the puck to the blue line, and shoots.
3. Defenseman 2 skates around the next cone at the top of the opposite circle, gets a puck in the circle, pivots, skates backward to the blue line, skates along the blue line, and shoots.
4. Defenseman 3 goes next from the opposite corner.

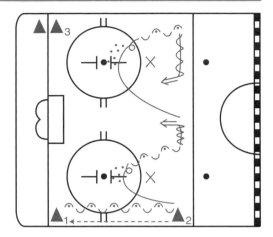

chapter 13

Forward Drills

This chapter includes drills that are designed specifically for forwards to work on skating, puck handling, shooting, and defensive play. Skating maneuvers such as change of pace, quick starts and stops, and tight turns, as well as all stickhandling and passing skills, including cycling and shooting with quick release and one timers should be included for the development of forward skills. Most of the drills included in other chapters develop these skills for all players. The drills in this chapter, however, are specifically for forwards. Checking drills, which forwards also need to develop, are included in chapter 9.

The drills in this chapter should be performed at game intensity to simulate game situations. The coach should watch that skills are performed using the proper technique and can stop the drill to correct players, or he can instruct players after the drill is complete. Goalies should also be used when the drill requires a shot be taken to simulate game situations and to help forwards work on skills such as shot placement and deking.

1. Forward 1 skates out of the center circle.
2. Forward 2 starts with the puck and passes to forward 1.
3. Forward 1 skates over the blue line and does a curl at the top of the face-off circle.
4. After passing to forward 1, forward 2 delays and then skates over the blue line.
5. Forward 1 passes to offensive forward 2.
6. Forward 2 shoots.
7. This drill can be done in both directions from the center circle.

Variation

The curl is done lower at the hash marks of the face-off circle or near the goal line.

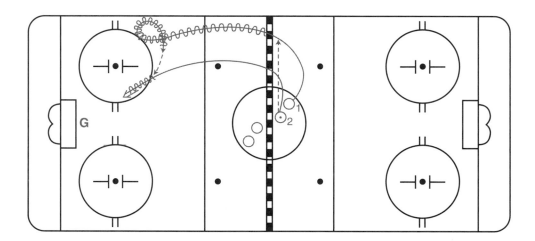

3V0 CURL

1. Forward 2 starts with the puck and passes to forward 1.
2. Forward 2 goes to the net.
3. Forward 1 skates over the blue line with the puck and curls toward the boards.
4. Forward 3 delays, then skates over the blue line.
5. Forward 1 passes to forward 3.
6. Forward 3 skates in and shoots.
7. The drill is done in both directions.
8. The players rotate and change lines for the next sequence of the drill.

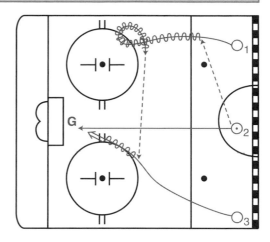

297 **CROSS, DROP PASS**

1. Forward 1 skates out of the center circle.
2. Forward 2 starts with the puck and passes to forward 1.
3. Forward 1 skates over the blue line and cuts to the middle of the ice.
4. Forward 2 delays, then skates over the blue line.
5. Forward 1 drop passes to forward 2.
6. Forward 2 cuts to the outside and shoots.
7. This drill is done in both directions from the center circle.

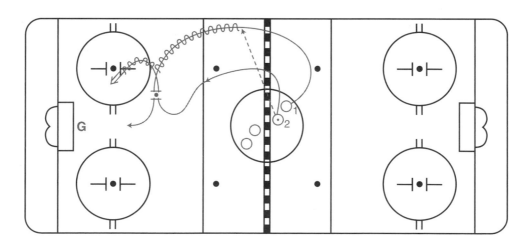

BOARD PASS

1. Forward 1 skates out of the center circle.
2. Forward 2 passes to forward 1.
3. Forward 1 skates over the blue line near the boards.
4. Forward 2 delays, then skates over the blue line behind forward 1.
5. Forward 1 passes the puck backward off the boards to forward 2.
6. Forward 2 skates in with the puck and shoots.
7. This drill is done in both directions from the center circle.

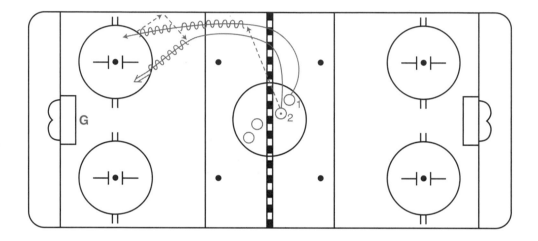

3V0 BOARD PASS

1. Forward 2 starts with the puck and passes to forward 1.
2. Forward 1 skates over the blue line and passes the puck backward off the boards to forward 2, who has followed forward 1 over the blue line.
3. Forward 3 delays and then skates over the blue line.
4. Forward 2 passes to forward 3.
5. Forward 3 shoots.
6. The drill is done in both directions.
7. Players rotate and change lines for the next sequence of the drill.

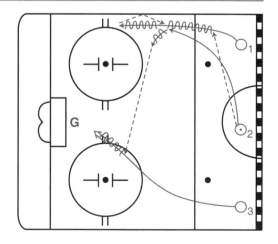

300   CYCLE

1. Forwards 1, 2, and 3 skate clockwise around the face-off circle and pass the puck back off the boards three times.
2. After the third pass, the player with the puck shoots.

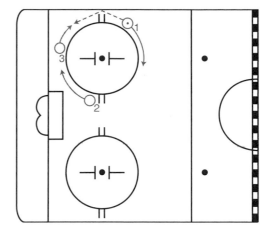

301   3V0 CYCLE

1. Forward 2 starts with the puck and shoots it into the corner.
2. Forwards 1, 2, and 3 skate clockwise around the face-off circle, with the first player to the corner getting the puck.
3. Forwards 1, 2, and 3 cycle around the circle and make board passes back to the player behind them.
4. After three passes, the player with the puck shoots.
5. The puck is shot into the opposite corner to start the drill each time so the cycle can be done around both face-off circles.
6. The drill is done in both directions.

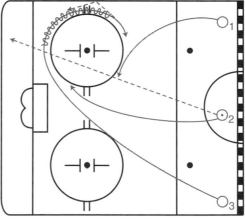

1. The coach shoots the puck into the corner to start the play (see figure 1).
2. Forward 1 and forward 2 skate clockwise around the face-off circle.
3. After two backward board passes, forward 2 shoots.
4. Forward 1 goes to the opposite face-off circle.
5. The coach shoots another puck into that corner.
6. Forward 3 joins forward 1, and they skate counter-clockwise around the circle.
7. After two backward board passes, forward 1 shoots.
8. The drill is continuous, with the player who does not shoot going to the opposite face-off circle, cycling, and then shooting.

Variation

A defenseman is added at both face-off circles to give resistance during the cycle, making it 2v1 (see figure 2).

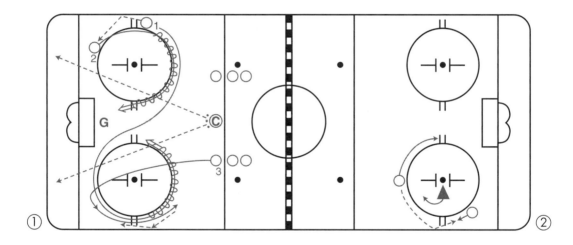

303   BACK NET PASS

1. Forward 1 skates out of the center circle.
2. Forward 2 starts with the puck and passes to forward 1.
3. Forward 2 delays, then skates behind forward 1.
4. Forward 1 starts to skate behind the net.
5. Forward 1 passes the puck back on the same side to forward 2.
6. Forward 2 shoots.
7. This drill is done in both directions from the center circle.

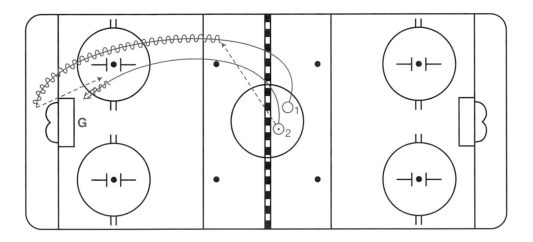

304   3VO, PASS-BACK BEHIND THE NET

1. Forward 2 starts with the puck and passes to forward 1.
2. Forward 1 skates over the blue line and starts to skate behind the net with the puck.
3. Forward 2 follows forward 1 over the blue line.
4. Forward 1 passes back to forward 2.
5. Forward 2 shoots or passes to forward 3 who goes to the net.
6. The drill is done on both side of the rink.

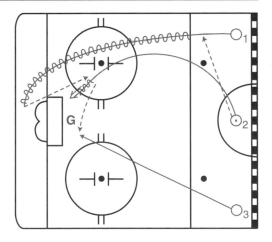

7. Players rotate and change lines for the next sequence of the drill.

305   3V0, PASS BEHIND THE NET

1. Forward 2 starts with the puck and shoots it into the corner.
2. Forward 1 goes to the corner and gets the puck.
3. Forward 3 goes to the opposite corner, and forward 1 passes behind the net to forward 3.
4. Forward 2 goes to the high slot.
5. Forward 3 passes to forward 2, and forward 2 shoots.
6. Players rotate and change lines for the next sequence of the drill.
7. The drill is done in both directions.

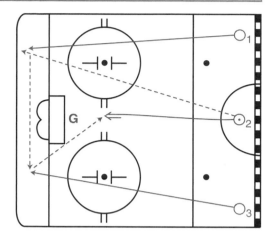

306   3V0 DROP PASS

1. Forward 2 starts with the puck and passes to forward 1.
2. Forward 1 skates over the blue line and cuts to the middle of the ice.
3. Forward 2 skates over the blue line.
4. Forward 1 drop passes to forward 2.
5. Forward 2 cuts toward the boards.
6. Forward 3 skates wide to the net.
7. Forward 2 passes to forward 3.
8. Forward 3 shoots.
9. The drill is done in both directions.
10. The players rotate and change lines for the next sequence of the drill.

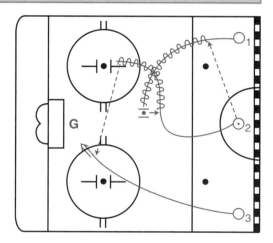

307   3VO DRIVE FOR THE NET

1. Forward 2 starts with the puck and passes to forward 1.
2. Forward 1 skates over the blue line.
3. Forward 2 skates to the net.
4. Forward 3 skates wide over the blue line.
5. Forward 1 passes across to forward 3.
6. Forward 3 shoots.
7. Forward 2 is in front of the net for a screen or rebound.
8. The drill is done in both directions.
9. The players rotate and change lines for the next sequence of the drill.

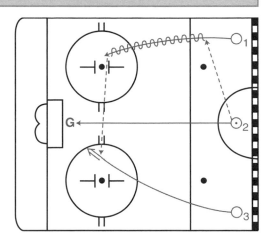

308   3VO HIGH-SLOT SHOT

1. Forward 2 starts with the puck and passes to forward 1.
2. Forward 1 skates over the blue line and skates wide to the face-off circle.
3. Forward 2 trails forward 1 in the high slot.
4. Forward 1 passes back to forward 2.
5. Forward 2 shoots.
6. Forward 3 skates wide to the net.
7. The drill is done in both directions.
8. The players rotate and change lines for the next sequence of the drill.

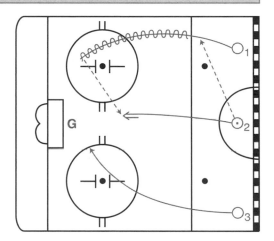

1. Forward 1 starts with the puck and passes behind the net to forward 2.
2. Forward 2 skates from the corner with the puck, going inside or outside the cone, and either shoots or passes to forward 1, who has skated to the front of the net.

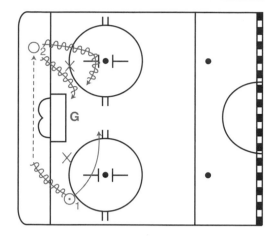

1. Forward 1 skates around the face-off circle, receives a pass from forward 2, and shoots.
2. Forward 1 goes to the opposite corner and gets a puck.
3. Forward 1 comes out in front of the net from the corner, skating on either side of the cone, and shoots.

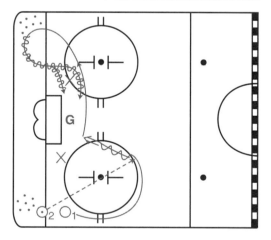

311   SHOOT, PASS, SHOOT

1. The players are in two lines at the blue line.
2. Forward 1 starts with the puck, shoots, goes to the corner on the same side, gets a puck, and passes to forward 2, who shoots and repeats the same pattern.
3. The drill is continuous. The forward should attempt to shoot quickly with one timers during this drill.

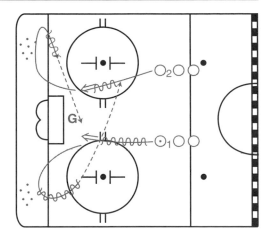

312   ONE PASS OR SHOOT

1. The players are in two lines at center ice.
2. Two players, one with the puck, skate 2v0 past the cones, and the player with the puck either shoots or passes to the other player, who shoots.
3. This is a quick drill. If there is a pass, there is only one.

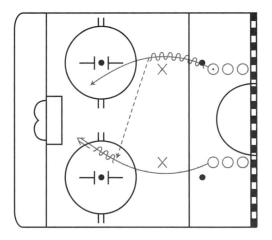

313   HIGH, LOW, SHOOT

1. Forward 1 skates to the high cone at the top of the circle, cuts toward the middle, and shoots.
2. Forward 2 skates around the low cone at the bottom of the circle and shoots.
3. The players change lines after shooting.

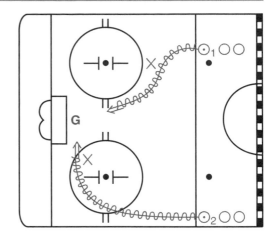

314   SHOOT AND SCREEN

1. Forward 1 skates out of the corner with a puck, skates around the face-off circle, shoots, and stays in front of the net for a screen, deflection, or rebound on the next shot.
2. Forward 2 skates with a puck out of the opposite corner, skates around the face-off circle, shoots, and then stays in front of the net for a screen, deflection, or rebound on the next shot.

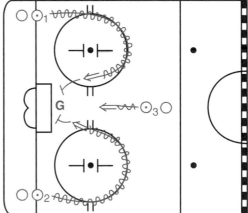

3. Forward 3 then skates in with a puck and shoots, with forward 1 and forward 2 in front of the net to screen, deflect, or rebound.
4. Forwards 1, 2, and 3 change lines.
5. The drill is continuous with three players each time.

QUICK SHOOT, PASS, SHOOT IN CLOSE

Players can perform the following patterns on both ends simultaneously to utilize the full rink.

Sequence 1

1. Forward 1 shoots, gets a puck at the goal line, and passes to forward 2, who shoots quickly.
2. Forward 3 then shoots, gets a puck on the other side of the goal, and passes to forward 4, who shoots quickly.

Sequence 2

Forward 5 shoots, gets a puck at the goal line, skates behind the net, and passes to forward 6, who shoots quickly.

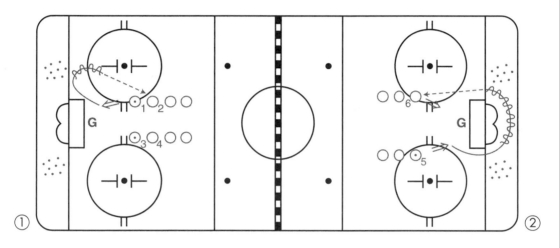

chapter 14

Goalie Drills

This chapter includes drills designed to help goalies develop the skills they need, such as the ability to react to various types of shots, agility movements, the use of the stick, and the use of the blocker and catcher glove.

These drills emphasize goalie skating movements such as moving side to side, in and out, and down and up. Movements such as skate save, half splits, full splits, double-leg slide, and use of the blocker and catching gloves are covered. Stopping the puck behind the net, passing and handling the puck, and the use of the poke check are incorporated in the drills in this chapter. Most shooting drills are also excellent for forwards.

1. Each player has three pucks.
2. Forward 1 shoots three pucks, then forward 2 shoots three pucks, followed by forward 3, defenseman 1, and then defenseman 2.
3. The goalie reacts to the different directions and change of position in the shots.

Variation

Players shoot one puck each time, going in the same order, until each player has shot three pucks.

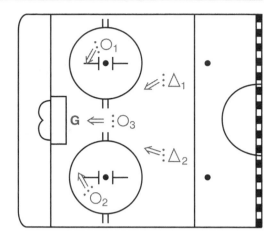

1. The players are in a semicircle inside the blue line, and they shoot in succession starting from one side.
2. Next, the players alternate, with a player shooting from one side, and then a player shooting from the other side.
3. The players then move in six feet and repeat the same sequence.
4. After shooting, the players move in the same distance again and repeat the sequence.

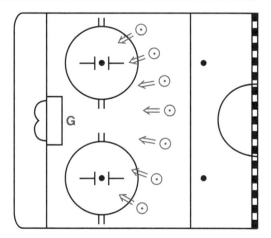

318   PASS OR SHOOT

1. Forward 1 starts with the puck and either shoots or passes to forward 2, who then shoots.
2. The goalie starts on the side of forward 1.
3. Forward 1 and forward 2 are stationary when the drill starts.

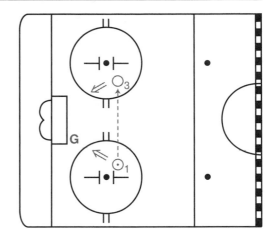

319   2V0 PASS OR SHOOT

Forward 1 and forward 2 go 2v0, with the puck carrier either shooting or making one pass for the shot.

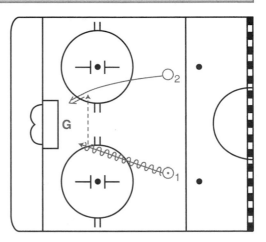

TRIANGLE SHOOT

1. Forwards 1, 2, and 3 form a stationary triangle in front of the net. Forward 1 starts with the puck.
2. Forwards 1, 2, and 3 make three quick passes and then shoot.

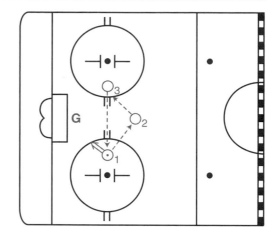

REBOUND OR SCREEN SHOOTING

Have players perform either sequence to work on goalie skills. Sequence 2 can be used to increase difficulty level.

Sequence 1

1. Forward 1 shoots.
2. Forward 2 and forward 3 are at the sides of the net and go for rebounds.
3. If they get a rebound, they shoot again.

Sequence 2

1. Forward 1 shoots.
2. Forward 2 and forward 3 are standing in front of the net to screen and go for rebounds.
3. If they get a rebound, they shoot again.

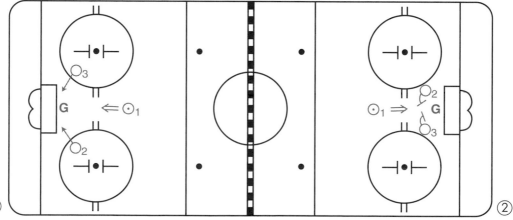

322   THREE SHOTS, IN CLOSE

1. Forward 1 shoots low to the side of forward 2.
2. Forward 2 shoots immediately after forward 1 has shot.
3. On the other side of the crease, forward 3 shoots after forward 2 has shot.

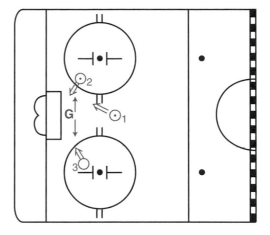

323   AGILITY

1. The goalie starts at the top of the circle, and the coach is positioned inside the blue line with pucks.
2. The goalie skates backward while the coach shoots a number of pucks in succession until the goalie reaches the net.
3. The drill should be done from both sides and the middle.

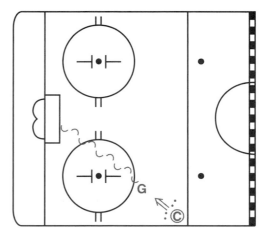

SQUARE AND TRIANGLE SHOOT

Have players perform either of these sequences to work on goalie skills. Also, to add difficulty to either of them, instead of passing to the front of the net, forward 1 or 2 can come out from behind the net and try to score.

Sequence 1: Square Shoot

1. Forward 1 and forward 2 are behind the net.
2. Forward 3 and forward 4 are at the top of the circles.
3. Forward 1 and forward 2 pass the puck behind the net three times, and then pass to forward 3 or forward 4.
4. After receiving the pass from behind the net, forward 3 or forward 4 makes one pass to the other player out in front, who shoots.
5. The goalie moves with the pass each time.

Sequence 2: Triangle Shoot

Setup is the same as in Square Shoot, except only one forward is in front of the net.

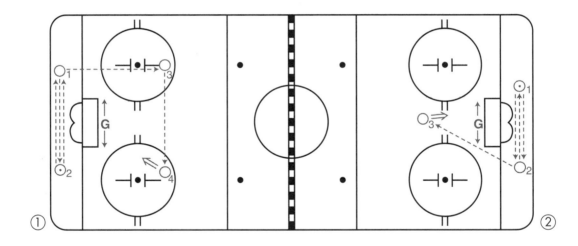

325   SHOOT, WALK OUT, EITHER SIDE

The forward shoots, then gets another puck in the corner and skates around the cone on the short side—or skates behind the net and around the cone on the other side—and shoots again.

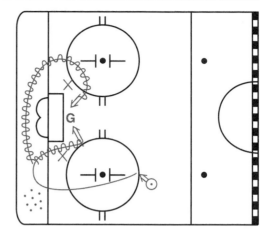

326   TIP IN, CURL, WALK OUT

1. Forward 1 passes the puck to forward 2 at the side of the net for a tip-in.
2. Forward 1 then skates in, does a curl, and receives a pass from the coach.
3. Forward 1 skates around the cone and goes in front of the net to try to score.
4. Forward 2 stays in front of the net for a pass or a rebound. If he gets a rebound, he shoots.

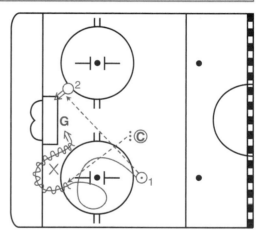

1. Forward 1 starts with the puck and skates to the net for a shot.
2. Forward 2 then skates to the net.
3. Forward 3 passes to forward 2 for a tip-in.

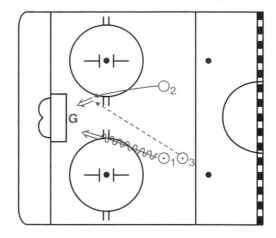

328   BEHIND NET, WALKOUT, PASS OR SHOOT

1. Forward 1 shoots the puck beside the net over the goal line.
2. Forward 2 goes behind the net on the other side.
3. Forward 1 retrieves the puck shot in and passes it behind the net to forward 2.
4. Forward 1 goes to the front of the net.
5. Forward 2 comes from behind the net and either shoots or passes to forward 1 for a shot.

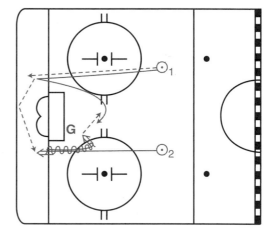

Variation

Forward 1 shoots the puck against the boards or glass to start the drill.

329   CIRCLE, BLUE LINE, CORNER, SHOOT

1. Forward 1 starts with the puck, skates around the face-off circle, shoots, and stays in front of the net to screen or deflect.
2. Forward 2 passes to defenseman 1 at the blue line.
3. Defenseman 1 skates to the middle of the blue line and shoots.
4. Forward 1 screens or deflects.
5. Forward 3 then skates from the opposite corner with a puck and skates out in front of the net from either side for a shot.

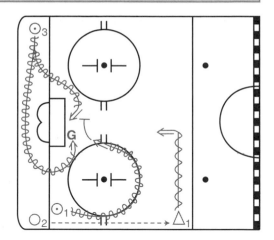

330   BOARD SHOT, TIP-IN, SLOT SHOT

1. Forward 2 and forward 3 skate from the opposite boards outside the blue line.
2. Forward 1 passes to forward 2 inside the blue line.
3. Forward 2 shoots.
4. Forward 1 then passes to forward 3 near the goal crease for a tip-in.
5. Forward 2 goes to the corner, gets a puck, and passes to forward 1, who has skated to the high slot.
6. Forward 1 shoots.

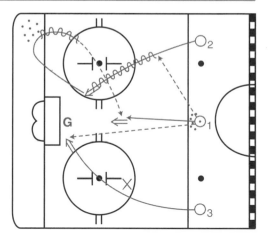

RAPID SHOOT

The forward rapidly shoots a number of pucks set up in a semicircle.

Variation

After the initial series of shots, the goalie stays on the knees for another sequence of rapid shots.

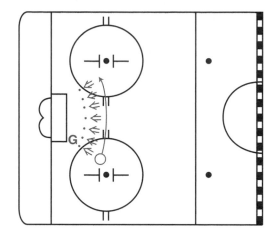

DROP PASS, SHOOT

1. Forward 1 skates over the blue line with the puck, then skates toward the middle of the ice and drop passes the puck to forward 2.
2. Forward 2 shoots immediately.
3. Forward 3 goes to the net for a rebound, then shoots.
4. The drill should be done from both sides.

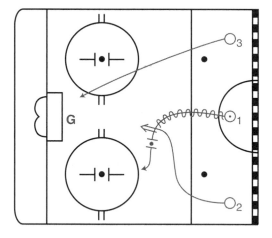

333   SHOT, DELAY, SECOND SHOT

1. Forward 1 passes to forward 2.
2. Forward 2 skates in, shoots, and stays in front of the net.
3. Forward 1 delays, then skates toward the boards and in on the net.
4. The coach passes to forward 1.
5. Forward 1 either shoots or passes to forward 2 for a shot.

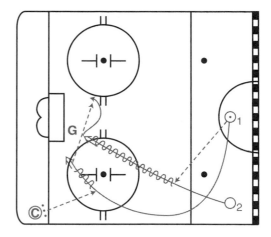

334   CREASE SHUFFLE, AGILITY

1. The goalie moves side to side, in and out with an X-movement or a Y-movement (see figure for examples of possible movements).
2. Goalie can perform either movement individually or consecutively to work on agility.

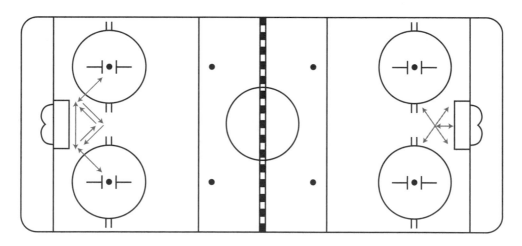

CUT ACROSS, SHOOT

1. The forward skates in from the blue line, cuts across at the top of the circles, and shoots at the first, second, or third position where pucks have been placed.
2. The goalie moves across the crease with the shooter.

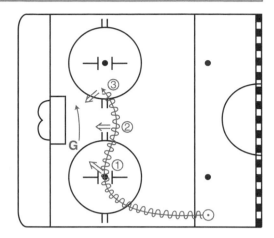

D TO D THREE TIMES, SHOOT

1. Defenseman 1 and defenseman 2 pass the puck two or three times and then shoot.
2. Forward 1 and forward 2 are in front of the net to screen or deflect the puck and to go for rebounds, then shoot.

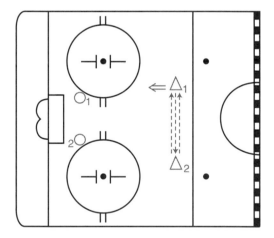

TWO QUICK SHOTS

Have players perform one of the two sequences to work on goalie skills.

Sequence 1

1. Forward 1 skates from the center circle and shoots at the hash marks.
2. Forward 2 leaves just after forward 1 and shoots at the hash marks (or shoots sooner, before forward 1 shoots at the hash marks).

Sequence 2

1. Forward 3 skates from the center circle, shoots at the hash marks, and curls left in front of the goalie.
2. Forward 4 leaves just after forward 3 and shoots quickly using forward 3 as a screen.
3. After shooting, forward 4 curls right and screens for the next shooter.

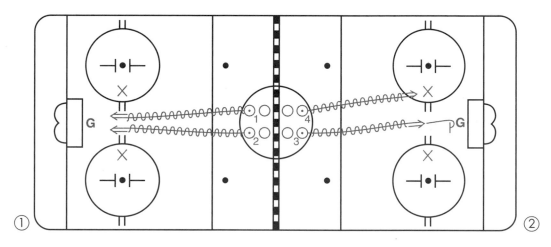

Have players perform one of the two sequences to work on goalie skills.

Sequence 1

1. Forward 1 passes to forward 2.
2. Forward 2 cuts across inside the blue line and drop passes to forward 1.
3. Forward 1 shoots quickly at the cone.
4. Forward 2 continues to skate across inside the blue line and takes a pass from the coach.
5. Forward 2 cuts around the cone and shoots.

Sequence 2

1. Forward 3 drives to the net.
2. Forward 4 passes to the net to forward 3, who deflects or redirects the puck.

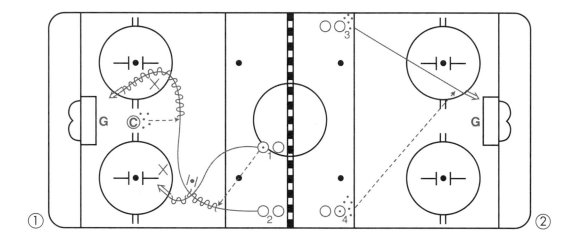

SHOOT, DEFLECT

Have players perform one of the sequences to work on specific goalie skills.

Sequence 1

1. Forward 1 passes to defenseman 1.
2. Forward 1 goes to the net.
3. Defenseman 1 shoots.
4. Forward 1 deflects or screens.

Sequence 2

1. Forward 1 passes to defenseman 1.
2. Defenseman 1 shoots.
3. Forward 1 gets a second puck, skates around the cone, and shoots or tries to deke the goalie out of position.

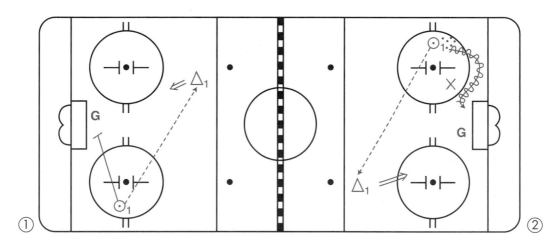

340   PASS OR SHOOT

1. Forward 1 passes cross ice to forward 2.
2. Forward 2 drives for the net.
3. Forward 2 can either shoot or pass to forward 1, who drives to the net after passing to forward 2.

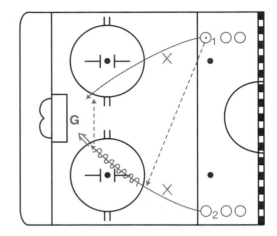

341   SHOOT, SKATE ACROSS

1. The forward shoots low at the goalie.
2. The forward then gets a second puck, goes around the cone, cuts across the ice in front of the goalie, and shoots.

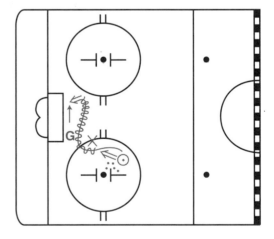

342   WRAP AROUND

1. Forward 1 skates with the puck behind the net and performs a wraparound at the far side.
2. Forward 1 then skates to the corner on the far side of the net, gets a puck, goes behind the net, stops, skates out from behind the net, and does a wraparound on the opposite side of the net.
3. Forward 2 then repeats the same sequence from the other side.

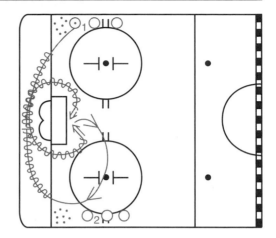

343   SIDE TO SIDE

1. The forward shoots at the goalie from one side of the near cone, then moves to the other side of the goal and shoots from the side of the opposite cone.
2. The drill continues with the player on the other side repeating the sequence and shooting two pucks.

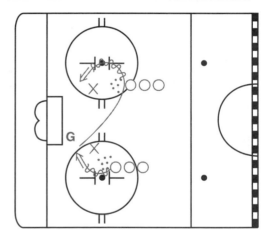

RIM OR CORNER, RETRIEVE

Have players perform either sequence to work on goalie skills.

Sequence 1

1. Forward 1 rims the puck along the boards.
2. The goalie stops the puck behind the net.
3. Forward 1 and forward 2 go to the two corners.
4. The goalie passes the puck to either player in the corner.

Sequence 2

1. Forward 1 shoots the puck to the side of the net.
2. The goalie retrieves the puck by the side of the net and passes to forward 1, who has gone to the near corner.
3. Forward 2 shoots the puck to the other side of the net. The goalie retrieves the puck and passes to forward 2 up the boards.

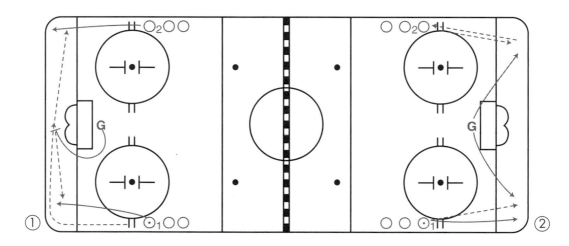

ANGLES, BOARDS

1. The forward skates around the first cone and shoots.
2. The forward then skates to the boards and gets a puck, skates around the second cone, and shoots.
3. The forward repeats the same pattern for the third and fourth cone.
4. After skating around the last cone, the forward does a wrap-around on either side of the net.

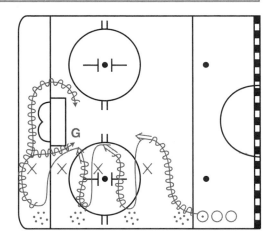

ANGLES, BLUE LINE

1. The forward starts at the blue line with a puck.
2. The forward skates around a cone and shoots.
3. The forward then skates back to the middle of the blue line, gets another puck, skates around another cone, and shoots.
4. The forward repeats this sequence, retrieving a puck and shooting around all four cones.

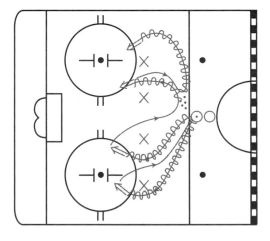

347   MULTIPLE 1V1S, SHOOT

1. Defenseman 1 passes to forward 1.
2. Forward 1 goes 1v1 against defenseman 1 and shoots using defenseman 1 as a screen.
3. Defenseman 2 then passes to forward 2, and the sequence is repeated.
4. Defenseman 3 then passes to forward 3, and the sequence is repeated.

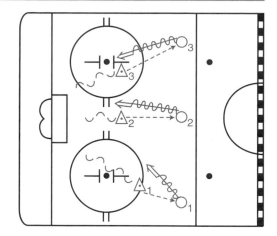

348   WRAPAROUND, POINT SHOT

1. Forward 1 skates around the cones and shoots.
2. Forward 1 stays in front of the net.
3. Defenseman 1 skates from the boards with a puck to the middle of the blue line and shoots.
4. Forward 1 screens.
5. The drill is done from both sides, with forward 2 and defenseman 2 repeating the same pattern.

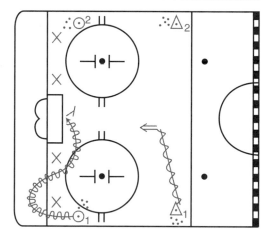

349   THREE SHOTS, ANGLES

1. Forward 1 gets a puck, skates around one of the four cones at the top of the circles, and shoots.
2. Forward 1 then goes to one corner, gets a puck, skates around a second cone at the side of the net, and shoots.
3. Forward 1 goes to the far corner, gets a puck, skates around a third cone, and shoots.

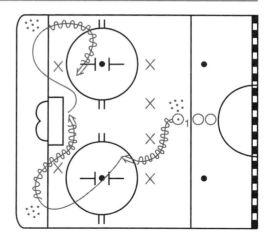

350   FIVE SHOTS

1. Forward 1 skates out from the corner and shoots.
2. Forward 2 skates out from the other corner and shoots.
3. Forward 3 shoots.
4. Forward 4 shoots.
5. Forward 5 shoots.

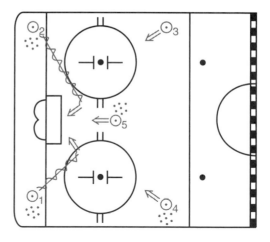

chapter 15

Power Play, Penalty-Killing, and Face-Off Drills

This chapter includes drills designed for working on power plays, penalty killing, and face-offs. They are organized within this chapter in that order. Power play drills enable players to practice breakouts, offensive zone entries, and offensive zone play. Penalty-killing drills include five-on-four, five-on-three, and four-on-three situations that involve forechecking, neutral zone play, and defensive zone play. The face-off drills are useful in developing the timing and quick reflexes needed to win face-offs in games.

Offensively, power plays should include a breakout, neutral zone and offensive zone entries, and play in the offensive zone. Breakouts may involve a number of different options that are included in specific drills. In these drills, breakouts should be executed with speed to simulate game intensity. Offensive zone entries can include crossing plays and picks at the blue line or a dump-in from a rim, chip-in or soft dump, or cross-ice dump-in. In the offensive zone, the puck should be moved quickly to create an opening for a shot. Usually, one player plays in front of the opposing team's net to screen the goalie and look for a rebound. Shooting the puck using one timers (not stopping the puck from the pass) is an essential skill for players on the power play.

For penalty killing, a team usually uses one or two forecheckers with at least one forward and two defensemen ending up across the defensive blue line. In the defensive zone, the penalty killers should stop and start quickly, using their sticks and bodies in the passing or shooting lanes to block shots. When the opponent has a five-on-three or four-on-three advantage, the team should use a regular triangle or a sliding triangle.

Running face-off drills, all forwards should practice face-offs, as the centers who usually take the face-offs in the game can be removed from taking the face-off by the referee if they do not position themselves correctly. Face-off skills such as drawing the puck using forehand, backhand, lifting the stick and drawing, holding the stick of the opponent and drawing, and shooting from the face-off should be practiced with these drills.

351   POWER PLAY, AROUND THE CIRCLE, SHOOT

1. The forward passes to the defenseman.
2. The defenseman skates across to the middle of the blue line and either shoots or passes back to the forward, who is skating around the face-off circle.
3. If the defenseman passes, the forward receives the pass and shoots. Usually, the forward is a right shot playing the left side or vice versa.

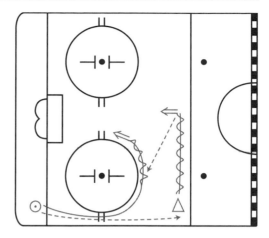

352   CROSS-ICE PASS

1. Forward 1 passes to defenseman 1 at the blue line.
2. Defenseman 1 passes across to defenseman 2 who passes back to offensive forward 1, who is skating around the face-off circle.
3. Forward 1 shoots a one-timer shot. Usually, the cross-ice shooter takes a left-handed shot on the right side or vice versa.

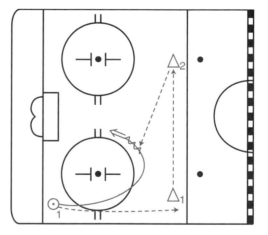

353   D TO NET, WIDE D SHOOTS

1. Forward 1 skates around the face-off circle with a puck.
2. Defenseman 1 goes to the net.
3. Forward 1 passes to defenseman 2, who shoots.

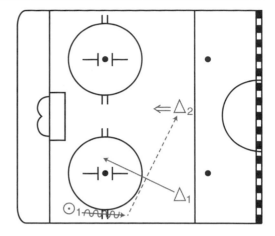

354   LOW-PLAY GIVE-AND-GO

1. Forward 1 is at the boards, and forward 2 is behind the goal line and beside the net.
2. Forward 1 passes to forward 2 and then goes to the net.
3. Forward 2 passes back to forward 1, who shoots.

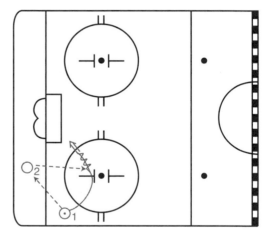

355   LOW PLAY 1

1. Forward 1 passes to forward 2.
2. Forward 1 goes to the net and screens or deflects the shot from forward 2.
3. Forward 2 skates out from behind the net and shoots.

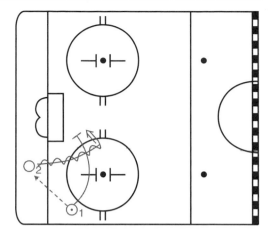

356   LOW PLAY 2

1. Forward 1 passes to forward 2.
2. Forward 2 starts to skate behind the net.
3. Forward 1 goes to the net.
4. Forward 2 passes back to forward 1, who shoots.

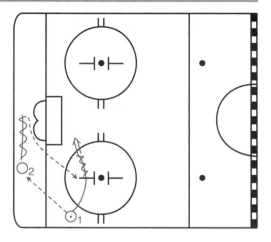

POWER PLAY, OFFENSIVE ZONE, 5V4 HIGH PLAYS, UMBRELLA POWER PLAY

Practice the following four power play options to work on offensive zone high plays.

Sequence 1

1. Forward 1 passes to defenseman 1, who skates to the middle and shoots.
2. Defenseman 2 goes to the top of the opposite face-off circle.
3. Forward 2 goes to the front of the net.

Sequence 2

1. Forward 1 passes to defenseman 1.
2. Defenseman 1 skates to the middle of the blue line and passes back to forward 1, who is skating around the face-off circle.
3. Forward 1 shoots.

Sequence 3

1. Forward 1 passes to defenseman 1.
2. Defenseman 1 skates to the middle of the blue line.
3. Forward 1 skates around the face-off circle.
4. Defenseman 1 passes back to forward 1.
5. Forward 1 passes across to forward 3, who shoots a one-timer shot. Forward 3 should be a left-handed shot on the right side or vice versa.

Sequence 4

1. Forward 1 passes to defenseman 1.
2. Defenseman 1 skates across to the middle of the blue line.
3. Defenseman 2 moves to the top of the far face-off circle.
4. Defenseman 1 passes to defenseman 2, who shoots.
5. This drill works best with the right-handed shot defensemen on the left side and the left-handed shot defensemen on the right side.

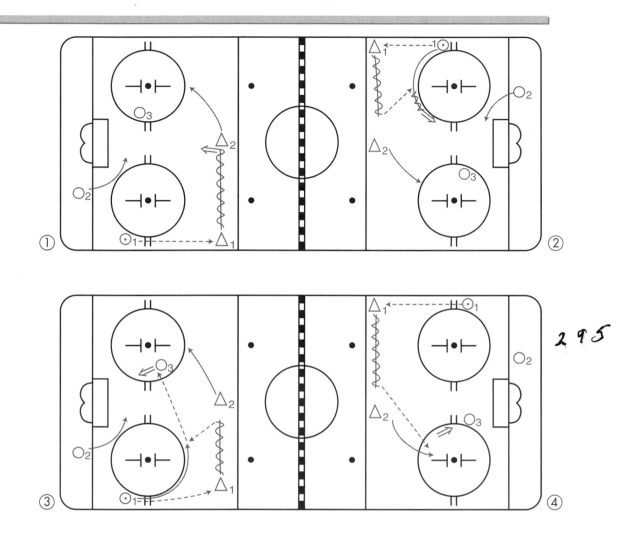

295

POWER PLAY, OFFENSIVE ZONE, LOW PLAYS 5V4 (FOUR OPTIONS)

Practice the following four power play options to work on offensive zone low plays.

Sequence 1

1. Forward 1 passes to forward 2.
2. Forward 1 goes to the net.
3. Forward 2 passes back to forward 1, who shoots.

Sequence 2

1. Forward 1 passes to forward 2 and then skates to the front of the net.
2. Forward 2 comes out from behind the goal line and passes across to forward 3. Forward 2 should be a right-hand shot for the side of the ice as shown, or a left-hand shot for the opposite side.
3. Forward 3 shoots. (Forward 2 can also shoot.)

Sequence 3

1. Forward 1 passes to forward 2.
2. Forward 1 goes to the net and forward 2 skates behind the net.
3. Forward 2 passes back to forward 1. Forward 2 should be a right-hand shot for the side of the ice as shown, or a left-hand shot for the opposite side.
4. Forward 1 either shoots or passes across to forward 3, who shoots.

Sequence 4

1. Forward 1 passes to forward 2.
2. Forward 2 skates behind the net and comes out around the far side.
3. Forward 3 goes to the front of the net.
4. Forward 2 either shoots or passes across to forward 1, who shoots.

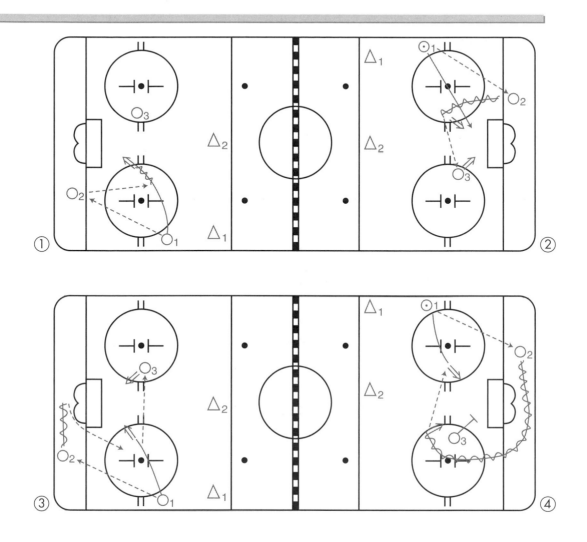

1. Defenseman 1 moves along the blue line to the middle with the puck.
2. Defenseman 2 moves to the front of the net to screen.
3. Forward 3 and forward 2 play the off side with right shot on the left side, and left shot on the right side.
4. Forward 1 plays in the corner.
5. Forward 2 and forward 3 look for cross-ice passes to one-time the puck, and defenseman 1 can pass or shoot at the blue line.
6. Forward 1 comes to the front of the net to screen with defenseman 2 when there is a shot.

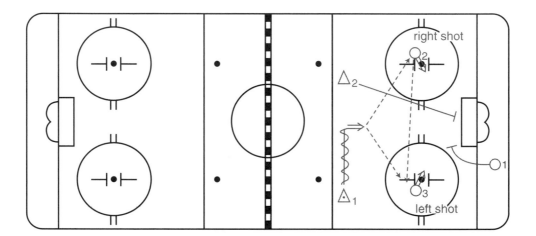

360 POWER PLAY BREAKOUTS 5V0, 5V2, 5V3, 5V4

To begin, the coach shoots the puck into the corner. The five players for the power play team are on the blue line. The five players then break out using one of the following patterns. Once they go into the offensive zone, they pass the puck to the defense, make one play, and change. The drill progresses 5v2 (two defense only), 5v3 (two defense plus one forward), 5v4 (two defense plus two forwards), with the breakout being against penalty killers.

Sequence 1: Double-Swing Breakout
1. Forward 1 and defenseman 2 swing to opposite corners.
2. Forward 2 skates across the ice at the near blue line.
3. Forward 3 skates across at the far blue line.
4. Defenseman 1 has the puck behind the net.

Sequence 2: Double Double-Swing Breakout
1. Forward 1 and defenseman 2 swing to one corner.
2. Forwards 2 and 3 swing to the other corner.
3. Defenseman 1 has the puck behind the net.

Sequence 3: Double-Swing (One Side) Breakout
1. Defenseman 2 and forward 1 swing to one corner.
2. Forward 2 skates across the ice at the near blue line.
3. Forward 3 skates across at the far blue line.
4. Defenseman 1 stops behind the net with the puck.

Sequence 4: Forwards Cross Double-Swing Breakout
1. Forwards 2 and 3 skate back from behind the center line, loop around, and cross.
2. Defenseman 2 swings to one corner.
3. Forward 1 swings to the opposite corner.
4. Defenseman 1 skates behind the net with the puck (without stopping).

Sequence 5: Double-Swing Behind-the-Net Breakout
1. Defenseman 1 stops behind the net with the puck.
2. Forward 1 swings behind the net, followed by forward 2.
3. Defenseman 2 swings to the opposite corner.
4. Forward 3 skates across the ice at the center line.

Sequence 6: Swing and Drop
1. Forward 1 skates behind the net and gets a puck from defenseman 1.
2. Forward 2 stays high and comes across the ice at the far blue line.
3. Defenseman 2 and forward 3 skate down the outside, with forward 3 cutting across at the far blue line and defenseman 2 going straight down the boards.

(continued)

4. Forward 1 drops the puck back to defenseman 1 and then skates across and down the far side of the rink.

5. Defenseman 1 passes to forward 1 to enter the offensive zone. Defenseman 1 can also pass to forward 3, forward 2, or defenseman 2 to enter the zone.

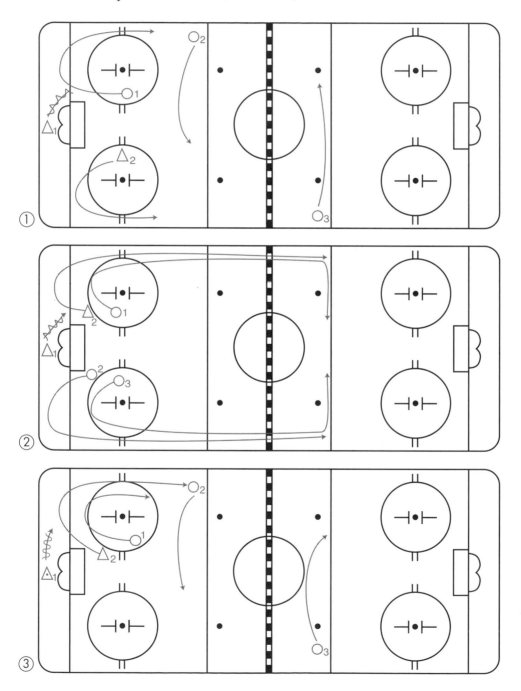

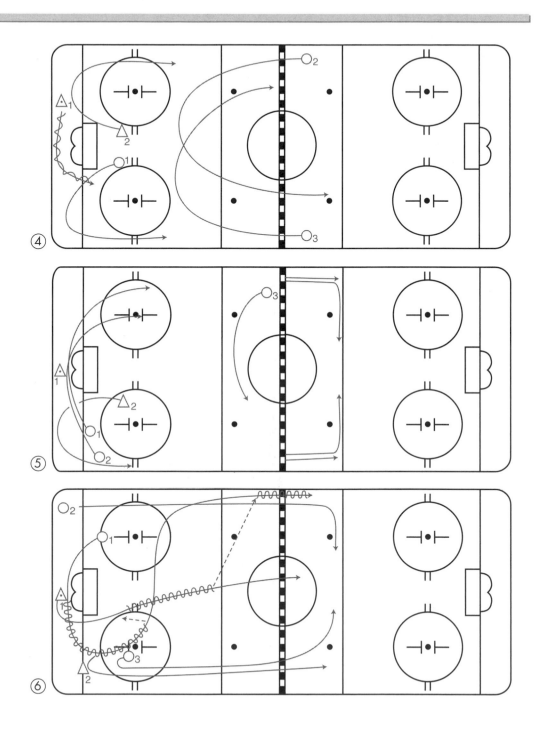

1. The five players for the power play team (forwards 1, 2, and 3 and defensemen 1 and 2) are at the blue line to start the drill (see figure 1).
2. Defensemen 1 and 2 are outside the blue line.
3. The coach shoots the puck into the corner, and the power play team breaks out against defensemen 1 and 2.
4. When the power play team enters the offensive zone over the blue line, they pass to their defensemen and set up one play with forward 1 carrying the puck to the corner (see figure 2).
5. Forward 1 then passes the puck to defenseman 1, who makes one play either passing or shooting.
6. The next five power play players repeat the drill against two new defensemen.

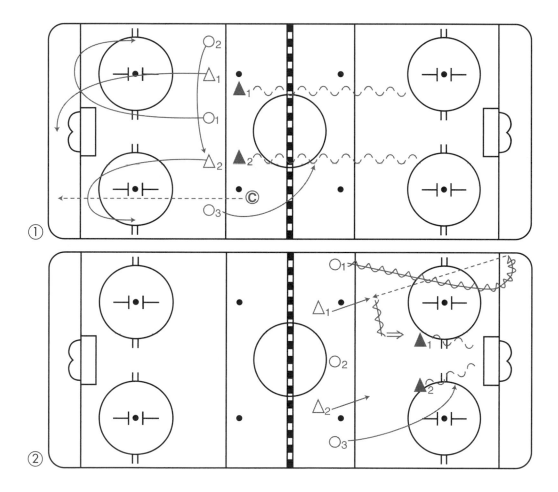

1. The five players for the power play team (forwards 1, 2, and 3 and defensemen 1 and 2) are at the blue line to start the drill.
2. The coach shoots the puck into the corner, and the power play team breaks out against defensive defensemen 1 and 2 and defensive forward 1.
3. When the power play team enters the offensive zone, they set up for one offensive play and one shot.
4. The next five power play players go against three new penalty killers in the same drill.

Variation

The drill can be done with four penalty killers, making it a 5v4.

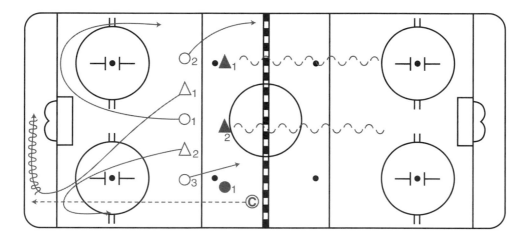

5V4, 5V3, BOTH ENDS

1. Four penalty killers (two defensive defensemen and two defensive forwards) set up in a box formation in the slot area at each end of the rink.
2. The five power play players (two offensive defensemen and three offensive forwards) set up on the outside at each end.
3. On the whistle, the players at both ends go 5v4 for 30 seconds.
4. If the puck is cleared from the zone, the coach at the blue line gives the power play players another puck.
5. Penalty-killing players switch in and out every 30 seconds.
6. The power play players and penalty killers can switch so that all players go both as penalty killers and power play players.

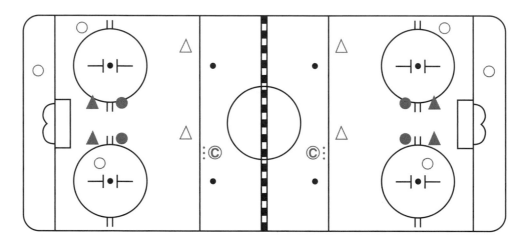

1. On the whistle, group A (offensive defensemen 1 and 2 and offensive forwards 1, 2, and 3) goes against group B (two defensive defensemen and two defensive forwards).

2. Group C (second power-play unit defensemen 1 and 2 and third-unit forwards 1, 2, and 3) waits at the blue line in the neutral zone.

3. Group D (second penalty-killing unit defensive forwards 1 and 2 and defensive defensemen 1 and 2) waits inside the far blue line in a box formation in the slot.

4. When group B (the penalty killers) gains possession of the puck and clears it out of the zone to group C, group C enters and makes two passes.

5. On the second pass, group D goes actively against group C as penalty killers.

6. Group A comes to the neutral zone at the far blue line after group C enters the offensive zone.

7. When penalty killing group D gains possession of the puck and clears the zone, group C enters the offensive zone against group B and makes two passes.

8. Group A then goes actively again against group B as penalty killers.

9. If the puck is held and not cleared, the coach gives a puck to the power play players in the neutral zone. The best entry into this drill is a rimshoot in, but other entries can be used.

10. The drill is continuous, and the power play players and the penalty killers can switch halfway through the drill.

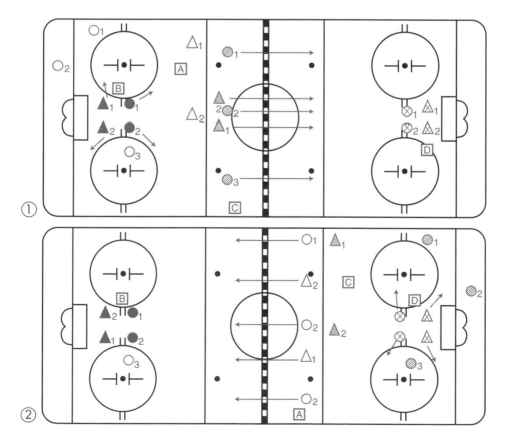

1. At the other end of the rink, five offensive players (three forwards and two defensemen) and four defensive players (two defensemen and two forwards) are set up to go 5v4 (see figure 1).
2. In the neutral zone, five offensive players are set up around the center face-off circle for one-touch passing (see figure 2).
3. At one end of the rink, five power play players are set up for a 5v0 (see figure 3).
4. In the neutral zone, five offensive players are set up around the center face-off circle for one-touch passing.
5. On the whistle, players in each zone go for 30 seconds, rest for 30 seconds, and go again for 30 seconds.
6. After the second 30 seconds, all three groups rotate to a different zone: the four penalty killers plus one player from the neutral zone go 5v4 offensively; the 5v4 power play players go to the 5v0 zone; the 5v0 players move to the neutral zone; and four of the neutral zone players go on defense for the 5v4.

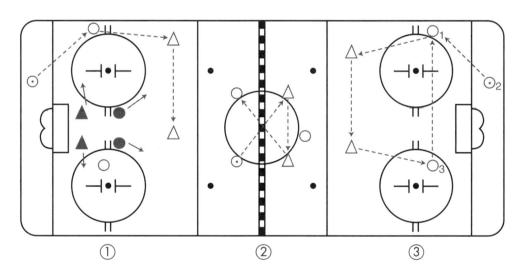

1. This drill involves two teams, a power play team and a penalty-killing team.
2. The power play team has three minutes against the penalty killers: a one-minute 5v4 scrimmage on full ice (see figure 1), starting with a breakout; a one-minute 5v4 starting from an offensive zone face-off (see figure 2); and a one-minute 5v3 full ice starting from a breakout.
3. The teams switch roles after three minutes.
4. This is a competition between the two teams, with the scoring as follows: two points for the power play team if they score a goal, one point for the penalty killers if there is no score, and three points for the penalty killers if they score.

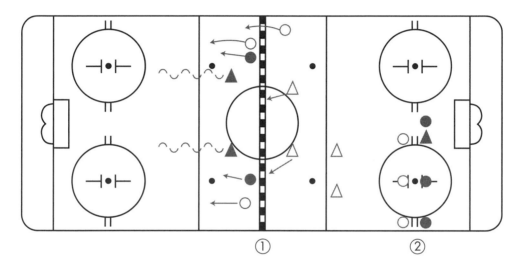

367 5V4 PENALTY KILLING, SWING AND STACK

Defensive forwards 1 and 2 loop into the offensive zone and cross. They take the outside lanes so that the defensive players are positioned four across between the center line and the defensive blue line.

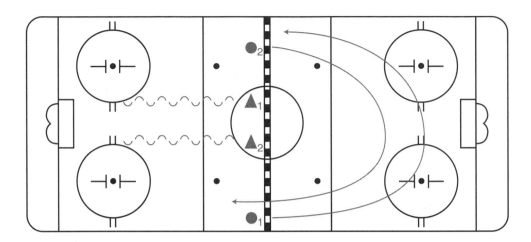

368 5V4 PENALTY KILLING, 1-3 STEER SYSTEM

Defensive forward 1 loops over the blue line and steers the puck carrier to the boards on the side of defensive forward 2.

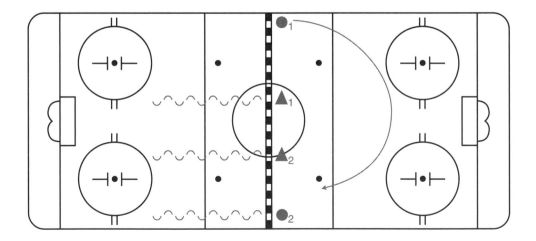

369　5V4 PENALTY KILLING, 1-3 SHOOT SYSTEM

1. Defensive forward 1 loops over the blue line and steers the power play to the side of defensive forward 2.
2. Defensive forward 2 moves forward to meet the puck carrier.

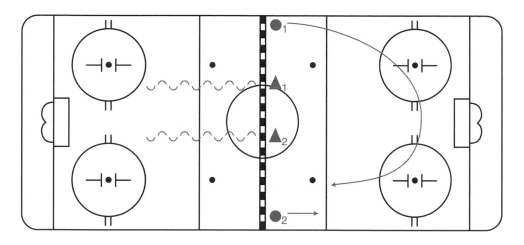

370　PENALTY KILLING, DEFENSIVE ZONE 5V4

The following are two 5v4 defensive zone penalty-killing systems.

Sequence 1

Defensive forwards 1 and 2 and defensive defensemen 1 and 2 play a box formation when offensive defensemen 1 and 2 are both at the blue line.

Sequence 2

Defensive forwards 1 and 2 and defensive defensemen 1 and 2 play a diamond formation when only one offensive defenseman is at the blue line.

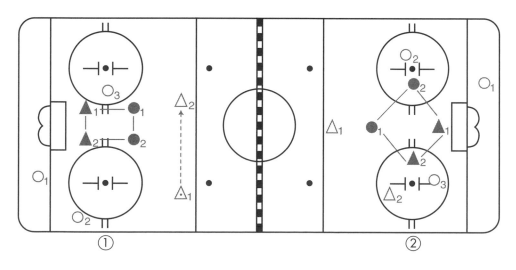

① ②

371 PENALTY KILLING, DEFENSIVE ZONE 5V3

The following are two 5v3 defensive zone penalty-killing systems.

Sequence 1: Sliding triangle

1. When offensive defensemen 1 and 2 are both at the blue line, defensive forward 1 and defensive defenseman 2 slide up and down to the top of the circles.

2. Defensive defenseman 1 stays in front of the net, staying between the goal posts. This formation is used when the power play team has two defensemen on the blue line.

Sequence 2: Triangle

When only one offensive defenseman is at the blue line, defensive forward 1 plays at the top of the triangle, and defensive defensemen 1 and 2 play at the bottom of the triangle in front of the net.

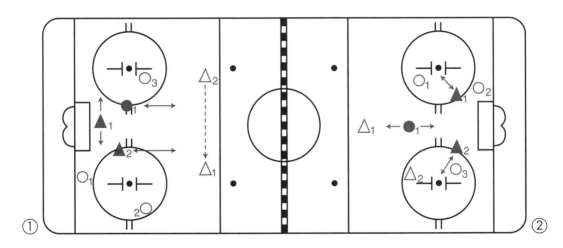

As noted at the beginning of the chapter, all forwards should practice face-offs, as the centers, who usually take the face-offs in the game, can be removed from taking the face-off by the referee if they do not face-off correctly. In the following sequences, face-off skills such as drawing the puck using forehand, backhand, lifting the stick and drawing, holding the stick of the opponent and drawing, and shooting from the face-off should be practiced.

Sequence 1

1. Forward 1 and forward 2 practice face-offs, with forward 3 dropping the puck.
2. After five face-offs, the players rotate. (The drill can also be run so that the player who loses the face-off must drop the next puck.)

Sequence 2

1. The coach drops the puck for two players practicing face-offs.
2. The players try to win two out of three face-offs, and the losing player is replaced by the next player.
3. The coach determines the winner.

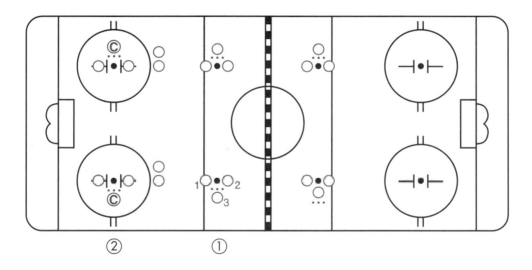

DRAW BACK, PUSH AHEAD

Use the following two options to work on drawing and pushing the puck at the face-off.

Sequence 1

1. Forward 1 draws the puck back to forward 2, who shoots.
2. Forward 3 picks or blocks.

Sequence 2

1. Forward 1 pushes the puck ahead to the corner.
2. Forward 3 goes behind the net.
3. Forward 1 passes to forward 3.
4. Forward 3 passes to forward 2.
5. Forward 2 shoots.

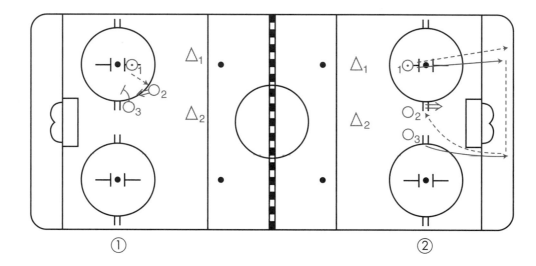

374   DRAW BACK TO DEFENSEMEN

The following two options work on drawing the puck back to the defenseman out of the face-off and what the defenseman should do once he has the puck.

Sequence 1

1. Forward 1 draws the puck back to defenseman 1.
2. Forward 2, forward 3, and defenseman 2 pick or block.
3. Defenseman 1 skates across inside the blue line and shoots.

Sequence 2

1. Forward 1 draws the puck back to defenseman 1.
2. Defenseman 1 passes to defenseman 2.
3. Forward 2 and forward 3 pick or block.
4. Defenseman 2 shoots.

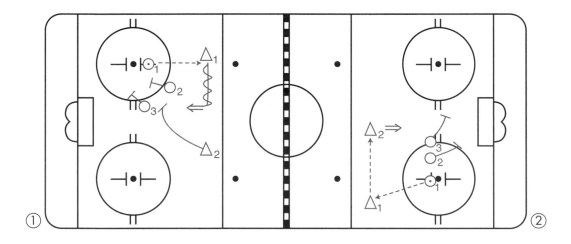

375 DEFENSE SHOOTS, FORWARDS PICK/ FORWARDS SWITCH

The following two options work on drawing the puck to different players during the face-off and provide different options for the player who gets the puck.

Sequence 1

1. Forward 1 draws the puck back to defenseman 1.
2. Forward 2, forward 3, and defenseman 2 pick.
3. Defenseman 1 skates to the middle and shoots.

Sequence 2

1. Forward 1 draws the puck back to forward 2, who is a right shot (or a left shot on the opposite side).
2. Forward 3 picks or blocks.
3. Forward 2 skates across the top of the circle and shoots.

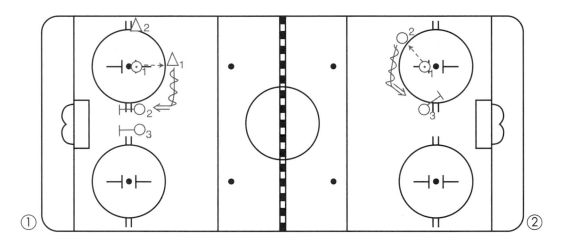

376 SIDE BOARDS

1. Forward 1 draws the puck to the side boards (the side is open with no opposing player lined up there for the face-off).
2. Forward 1 gets the puck at the side boards, skates to the corner, and passes the puck behind the net to forward 3, who has gone behind the net to the opposite corner.
3. Forward 3 passes to forward 2 in front of the net.
4. Forward 2 shoots.

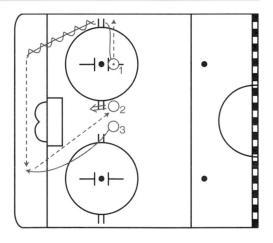

The following options incorporate more advanced face-off skills into the drills.

Sequence 1

1. Forward 1 draws the puck back to defenseman 1.
2. Forward 2 skates around the inside of the face-off circle to the high slot.
3. Defenseman 2 skates in and blocks.
4. Defenseman 1 passes to forward 2.
5. Forward 3 blocks.
6. Forward 2 shoots.

Sequence 2

1. Forward 1 draws the puck back to defenseman 1.
2. Defenseman 1 skates down the boards with the puck.
3. Forward 2 changes positions with defenseman 1 at the blue line.
4. Defenseman 1 passes back to forward 2.
5. Forward 3 blocks.
6. Forward 2 shoots.

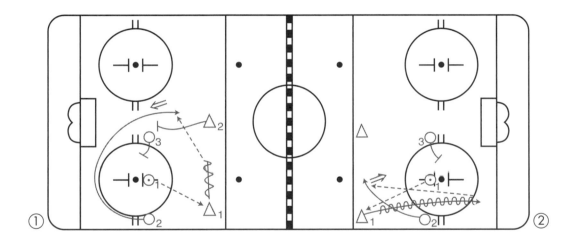

chapter 16

Competitive Fun Drills and Games

Most of the drills included in this chapter are hockey-related games that add enjoyment and competition to practices. A good idea is to include one fun drill in each practice, usually at the beginning or the end of the practice.

The drills here each contain multiple hockey-specific skills that the players can "work on" in a fun environment so, keeping that in mind, the coach should not correct incorrectly performed skills when running these drills. They are designed to be fun and competitive, providing a break from the normal work of practice. There is plenty of time during practice to make sure skills are performed with proper technique. Also, because of the competitive nature of these drills, players will likely perform them at a high intensity and, therefore, they should be incorporated into practice either after the warm-up at the beginning of practice or before the cool-down at the end of practice to prevent injury.

EUROPEAN BOGGLE

1. All the players are on the ice at one time. They are divided into two teams.
2. The red lines and blue lines are not in play, because there are no offsides or icings.
3. The game is played with two pucks.
4. The first puck scored is 1 point, and the second puck is 2 points.
5. The coach puts two more pucks into play when the second puck is scored.
6. The first team to 10 is the winner. (If the game goes on too long, play to a lower score.)

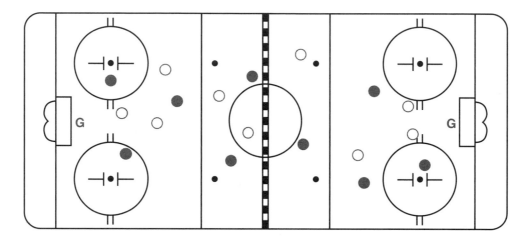

THREE-ZONE BOGGLE

1. The rink is divided into three zones. Three nets and three goalies are required for this drill.
2. Players play 3v3 in zones A, B, and C. After a team gains possession of the puck, two passes are required before shooting.
3. Teams rotate every three minutes to a different zone to play against a different goalie.
4. A record is kept of the goals scored by each team, and a winner is declared after rotation to all three zones.

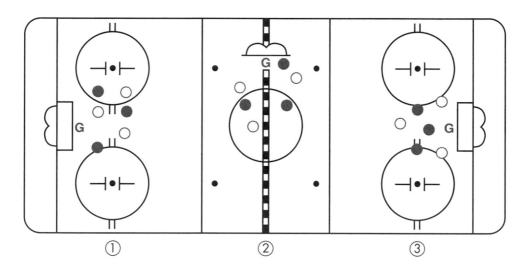

5V5 BOTH ENDS

1. Players play 5v5 at both ends of the rink, with the two teams at each end shooting at the same goalie.
2. When one team gains possession of the puck, they must pass the puck two times before shooting.
3. The coaches stand outside the blue lines and give a new puck if the puck in play goes over the blue line and out of the zone.

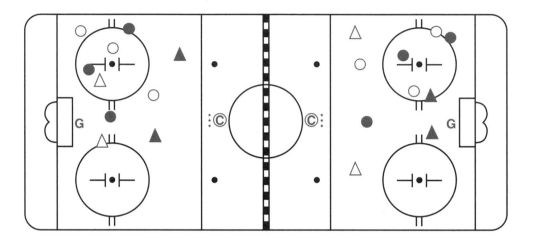

3V3 FULL ICE

1. Players play 3v3 the full length of the ice.
2. On the coach's whistle, the team with the puck passes back to their goalie, and the players change for the next 3v3.
3. The players change every 30 to 40 seconds, with the next three players on each bench entering the game.
4. Offsides are called in this drill.
5. When one team scores, they must clear out of the offensive zone, and the team scored on skates out of their own defensive zone.

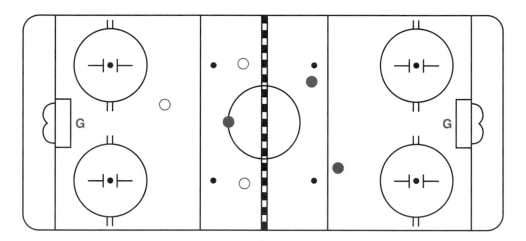

2V2, 3V3 CROSS ICE

Note: Though this drill is included in this chapter as a fun drill, it is regularly used by experienced coaches, as the confined space is excellent for developing puck-handling, passing, and shooting.

1. The nets are placed facing across the ice inside the blue line.
2. The players play 2v2 cross ice inside the blue line. The coach whistles for a change every 30 to 40 seconds.
3. If the puck goes over the blue line or a goal is scored, the coach shoots another puck in the zone.
4. The players not playing line up on the blue line and are allowed to keep the puck inside the blue line if it comes to them.
5. The game can be played 2v2 or 3v3.

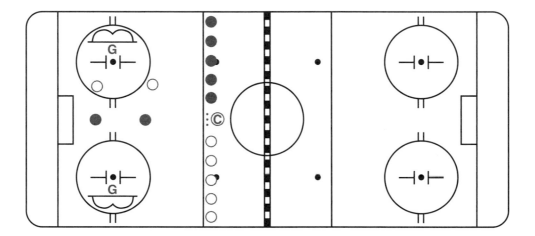

1. Players play 2v2 with two stationary players from the same team behind the net at the offensive end.
2. The two offensive players can pass to the two stationary players behind the net.
3. The stationary players must pass the puck within 3 seconds and cannot skate with the puck.
4. On the coach's whistle, the players change (every 20 to 30 seconds). The two new players take the stationary positions behind the net, and the two stationary players become offensive players.
5. If the puck goes outside the neutral zone, the coach gives a new puck.

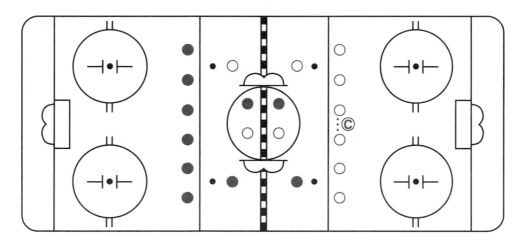

3V3 CROSS ICE, THREE ZONES

1. Players play 3v3 using cones as the goals. The cones are placed horizontal with the open ends facing inward.
2. A goal is scored by shooting the puck into the open end of the cone.
3. Goalies can play as forwards or can be warmed up separately by the coaches.

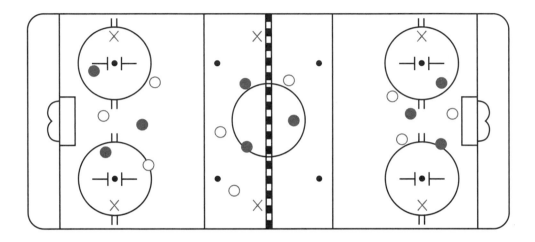

SHOOT, YES OR NO

1. Each player shoots one puck.
2. Before each player shoots, all the other players guess whether or not the player will score, and they divide into two groups (score and no score).
3. The group of players that guesses incorrectly skates one lap.

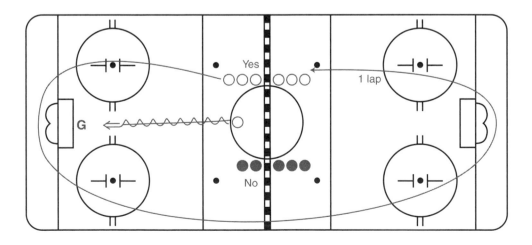

SHOOT-OUT, 10 PUCKS

1. Two teams of players are lined up along the boards on opposite sides of the center line. Each team has 10 pucks within the center circle.
2. Each player takes a puck from the center circle, skates in, and takes a shot on the goal.
3. If the player doesn't score, the puck must be brought back to the center circle before the next player goes.
4. If the player scores, he or she returns to the center circle for another puck and has another shot on goal; the player shoots until no goal is scored and the puck is returned to the center circle.
5. The first team to score all 10 pucks is the winner.

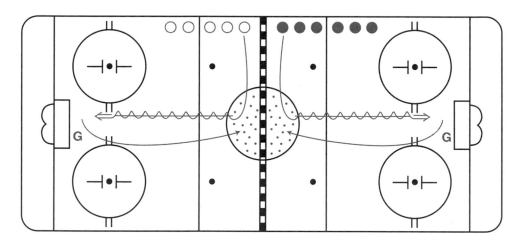

SHOOT-OUT

1. All players take turns shooting at one end on a breakaway from the center circle.
2. The goalies rotate every three shots, and the coach keeps a record of goals scored against.
3. If a player scores, he or she stays at the same end.
4. The goalie with the most goals scored against after every player has shot goes to the opposite end, along with all the players who did not score.

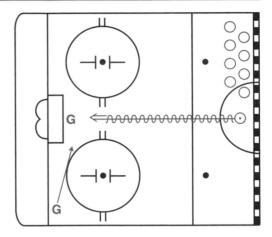

5. The players who scored go again at the same end and stay if they score until one player is left.
6. When only one player is left, that player does three breakaways from the blue line.
7. Either the goalie or the forward wins best of three.
8. The players who didn't score shoot at the other end.

388   2VO, 3VO SHOOT-OUT

1. Two or three players at a time have one minute to score as many goals as possible.
2. If a goal is scored, the players must clear the zone and retrieve another puck from the center circle.
3. The group of two or three players that score the most goals in one minute are the winners.

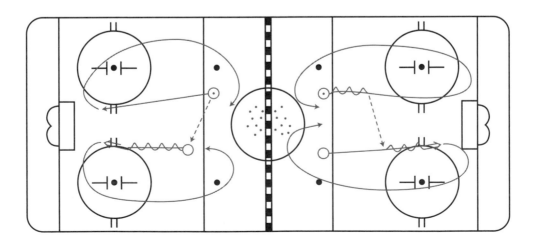

FULL-ICE SHOOT-OUT

1. Each player skates the length of the ice, takes a pass from the coach at the far blue line, and shoots.
2. The player has a designated time (usually 30 to 40 seconds) to score as many goals as possible.
3. If the player scores a goal, he or she must go outside the blue line, receive another puck from the coach, and try to score again.
4. The player who scores the most goals in the designated time is the winner.

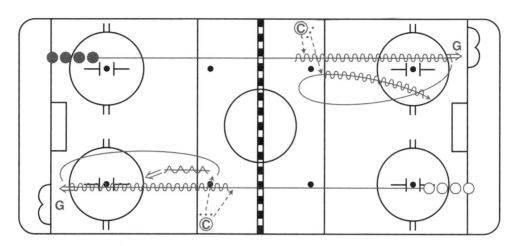

390

SHOOT-OUT, MUST SCORE

1. Players divide into teams.
2. Players get one shot, and then the next player on the team shoots.
3. Each player must shoot until he scores a goal.
4. If a player doesn't score on his shot, the next player goes, but that player must stay in rotation until he or she scores.
5. The first team to have each player score is the winner.
6. The coaches pass the pucks.

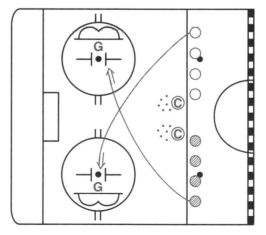

SHOOT-OUT, AROUND THE NETS

1. The nets are set up at the blue lines.
2. Players skate around the far net and try to score at the near net.
3. The game can be played to 10 goals, or a time limit can be used (with the team scoring the most goals in the specified time as the winner).
4. After shooting or scoring, the player passes to the next player in line. (If the puck is in the net, the player gets one of the extra pucks beside the net to pass to the next player.)

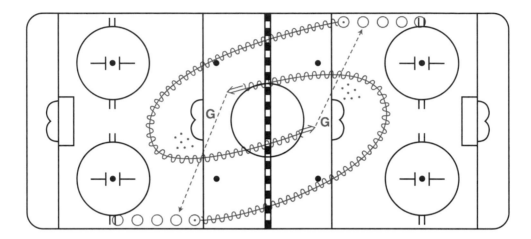

RACE FOR PUCKS

1. On the whistle, two players skate from the corners, skate around the cones, and race for the puck, which is placed on the blue line by the coach.
2. The drill is done at both ends of the rink (see figure 1).

Variation

The two players skate backward to the blue line, pivot, skate around the cones, and race for the puck (see figure 2).

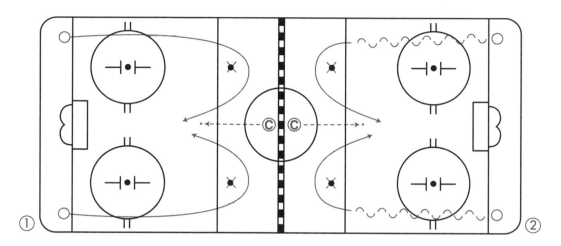

1. Two teams are in lines at opposite blue lines.
2. Two players skate around the cone at each end, passing the puck and looping back to try to score at the far end.
3. The two players must score before the next two players go.
4. The goalie cannot hold the puck.
5. If the puck goes out of play, the coach shoots another puck into the corner.
6. The first team to score a designated number of goals (usually 10) is the winner.

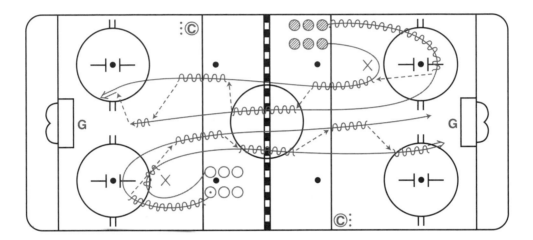

1. Two teams are lined up at the center line.
2. Each team has only one stick.
3. The first player skates completely around the line of players carrying the stick.
4. After one loop around, the player with the stick hands it to the next player in line.
5. The rest of the players repeat the same move until the last player has gone.
6. Then the first player repeats the drill going in the opposite direction.
7. The team that completes the two rounds first by passing the stick is the winner.

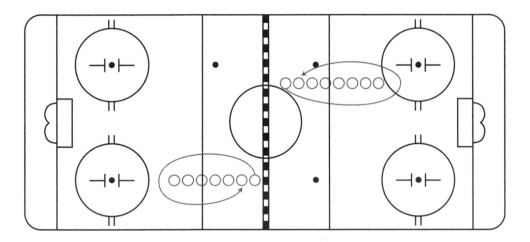

395   SKATE, STOP, SKATE, STOP, SHOOT-OUT

1. Two players start from opposite corners, skate to the center line, stop, skate to the near blue line, stop, skate around the cone, get a puck from the center circle, and go to the net for a shot.
2. Each player gets only one shot each time.
3. The next player goes after the shot on a signal from the coach.
4. The first team to score a designated number of goals (usually 10) is the winner.

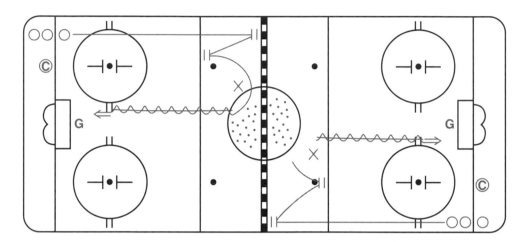

396   2V1 CROSS ICE, TWO GAMES

1. Players divide into two teams.
2. Two forwards play against one defenseman at each end.
3. The players change after each goal.
4. The first team to score 10 goals is the winner.
5. The defensemen that are at the end of the ice where the forwards lose are the winning defensemen.

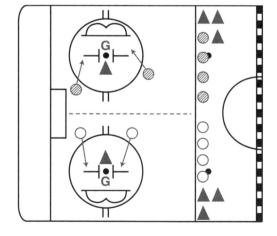

FUN, 2V0

1. The nets are moved to the blue lines.
2. On the whistle, forward 1 and forward 2 go 2v0 to the net at the far blue line. Forward 3 and forward 4 go at the same time from the opposite blue line.
3. The first two that score get 1 point.
4. Then the next players go.
5. The first team to 10 points is the winner.

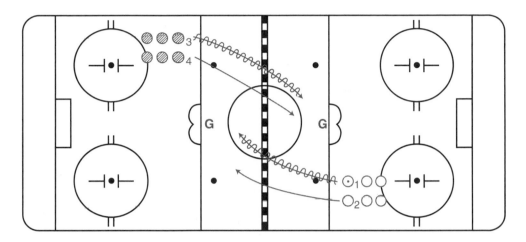

FUN, THREE-PASS SHOOT

1. The players are in two teams inside the neutral zone.
2. The coach passes to one team.
3. The first player passes to a second player on the same team.
4. The second player passes to a third player on the same team.
5. The third player skates in and shoots at one end.
6. The coach then passes to a player on the other team, who passes to a second player.
7. The second player passes to a third player, who shoots at the other end.
8. The drill ends when all players have shot.
9. The team that scores the most goals is the winner.

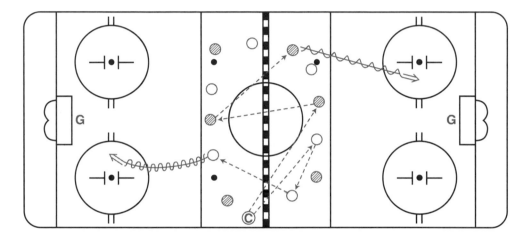

399   WRONG-HAND SCRIMMAGE

1. The players divide into two teams and play a scrimmage game.
2. The players exchange sticks so that right-handed players shoot left-handed and vice versa. Have extra right-handed sticks available, as usually more players shoot left than right.
3. All players are on the ice at once, and three pucks are used.
4. The game goes to 5 to 10 goals or a specified time limit.

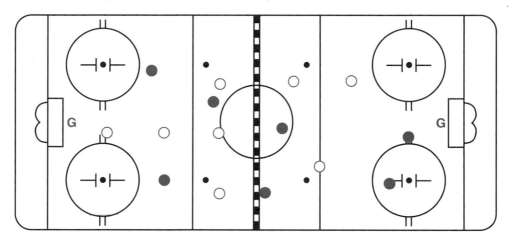

400   MULTIPLE 1V1, 2V2, 3V3, 4V4, 5V5

1. Players line up along the boards.
2. The coach places the puck anywhere on the ice.
3. Play starts 1v1, then on a signal, additional players join the game and it switches to 2v2, then 3v3, then 4v4, and finally 5v5.
4. Play continues until a goal is scored.
5. No offsides or icings are called in this drill.

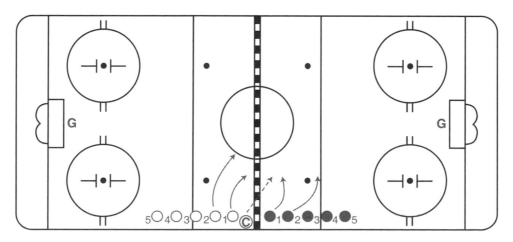

Players should form three teams for relay races up and down the ice (skating without sticks). Three different courses may be used.

Course A: Players skate around the cones.

Course B: Players skate 360-degree turns around the cones.

Course C: Players jump over the cones, which have been laid on their sides.

1. The next player cannot start until he or she is touched by the player completing the course.

2. The first team finished is the winner.

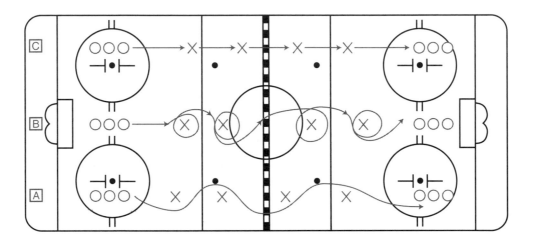

1. The forwards from the team in the corner of the rink shoot the puck anywhere on the ice.
2. The players on the other team must stop the puck and pass it three times before shooting at the net.
3. After shooting the puck down the ice, the forward from the corner must skate around the cone at the center circle and loop back to the opposite corner, trying to reach the corner before a goal is scored.
4. If the puck hits the end boards without being stopped, it is a home run; if the puck is caught by the goalie it counts as a run for the skating team.
5. If the skater gets to the opposite corner before a goal is scored, it counts as a run. If not, the player is out.
6. After three outs, the teams switch roles. (There is a maximum of four runs per inning.)

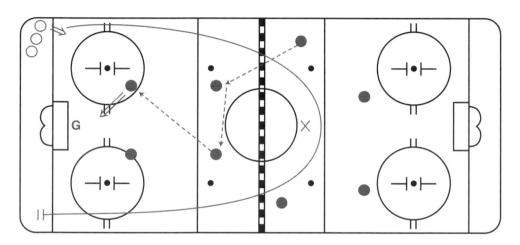

HALF-ICE BASEBALL

1. Five players are positioned inside each blue line.
2. The player in the corner passes to one of the players on the other team inside the blue line. Each player must touch the puck before the team shoots.
3. The player from the corner skates outside the blue line, around the cones, and back to the goal line in the opposite corner.
4. If the player reaches the goal line before a goal is scored, it counts as a run.
5. If a goal is scored before the player reaches the goal line, the player is out.
6. After three outs, the teams switch roles. (The maximum is five runs per inning.)

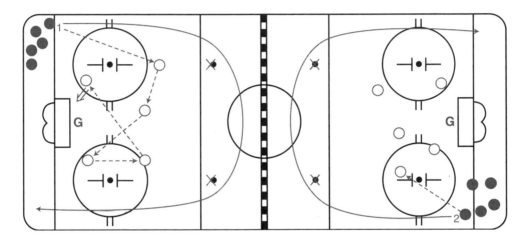

404   2V0 SHOWDOWN

1. Two players from each team go 2v0 against the goalie at the opposite end.
2. The two players must score before returning to their line.
3. The next two players cannot go until the two returning players cross the blue line where they started from.
4. The goalies cannot hold the puck.
5. The first team to score seven goals is the winner.

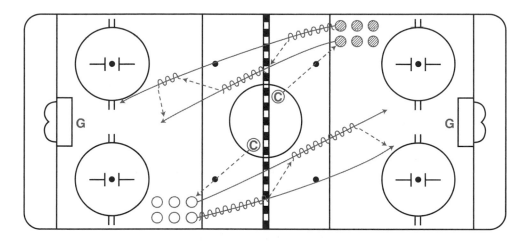

405   BRITISH BULLDOG

1. Players skate the length of the ice with no sticks.
2. One player starts in the neutral zone as the defender.
3. If a player is touched by the defender, the player becomes a defensive player in the neutral zone.
4. The last player to remain untagged is the winner.

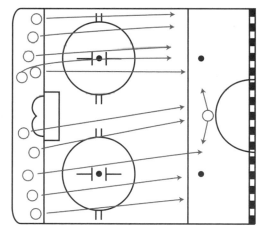

406   SOCCER (EUROPEAN FOOTBALL)

1. Players play soccer cross ice (in three zones) using a soccer ball.
2. Players do not have sticks and may only kick the ball.
3. A goal is scored by knocking over the cone.

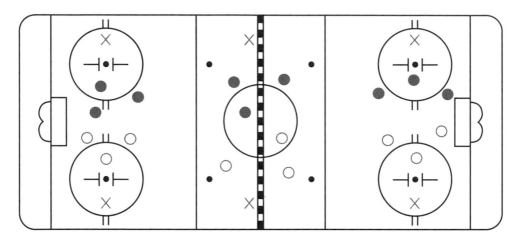

407   STICK PULL RACE

1. Two players pull a player on his or her knees using two hockey sticks.
2. They race around the cone at the far goal line and back.
3. As soon as the three players return to the hash marks at the face-off circle, the next three players go. The players can go two or three times.
4. The first team to complete the race wins.

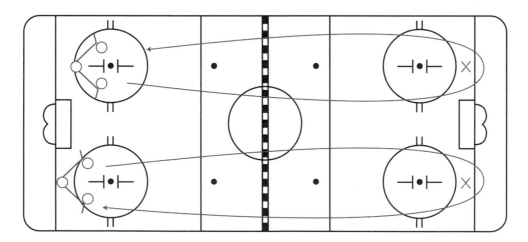

1. Four teams of five players each are in the face-off circles.
2. One player from each team tries to score at the empty net at the opposite end.
3. Each player gets only one shot.
4. If the player doesn't score, the five players in the circle skate one lap around the rink.
5. The first team to reach the number of goals predetermined by the coach at the beginning of the drill wins.

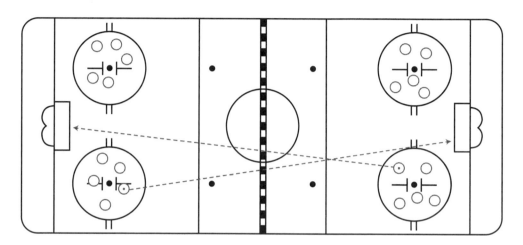

chapter 17

Evaluation Drills

This chapter includes drills that you can use to evaluate goalies, defensemen, and forwards. Evaluation drills are designed to be used when you are selecting the team, but these drills can also be used throughout the year because they are specific to the various positions in ice hockey. They can be used to find what position a player is best suited for and to help the coach determine which player belongs on which line. They can also be used to help the coach determine skills that specific players need to develop, allowing the coach to devote practice time to those skills.

Each drill contained in this chapter provides information on what skill or skills the drill is designed to evaluate. The drills allow you to evaluate skating speed, agility, and shooting and passing skills. Competitive one-on-one and two-on-two drills are included for evaluating checking skills as well as determination and motivation. Skating speed and agility, puckhandling, passing and receiving, shooting, and competitiveness in one-on-one battles are some of the qualities coaches look for in these evaluation drills.

This drill evaluates skating speed and speed endurance. Players can perform the following two sequences simultaneously to utilize the whole ice, or they can be performed individually or consecutively on only one end. To incorporate backward skating, players can alternate skating forward and backward after stopping at each line. A stop watch is used to time to 1/10 of a second.

Sequence 1

> Player 1 starts at the goal line and skates to the near blue line and stops, skates back to the goal line and stops, skates to the center line and stops, then skates back to the goal line.

Sequence 2

> Player 2 starts at the other goal line and skates to the center line and stops, skates back to the goal line and stops, skates to the far blue line and stops, then skates back to the goal line.

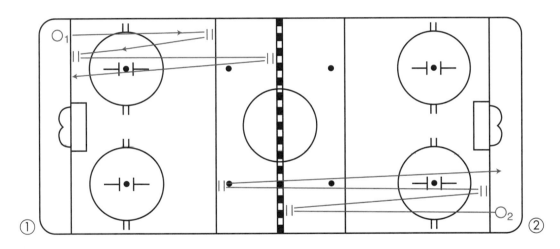

This drill is designed to evaluate the forward's speed, skating ability, shooting, and competitiveness.

1. Player 1 and player 2 are in opposite corners.
2. On the whistle, player 1 and player 2 skate around the cones at the blue line and at the top of the circles, then race for the puck placed inside the far blue line and attempt to score.
3. The drill alternates from each end, with player 3 and player 4 going next from the opposite end.

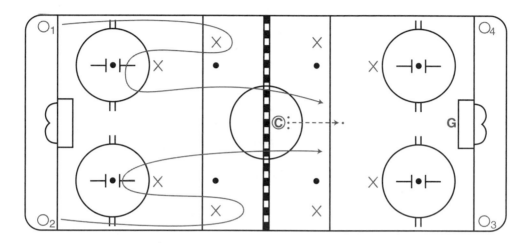

This drill evaluates skating agility, forward and backward skating, and quickness.

1. Player 1 and player 2 skate to the farthest edge of the face-off circle, skate backward clockwise around the circle until they are where they started, pivot, skate forward around the cone, and then race for the puck placed inside the blue line.

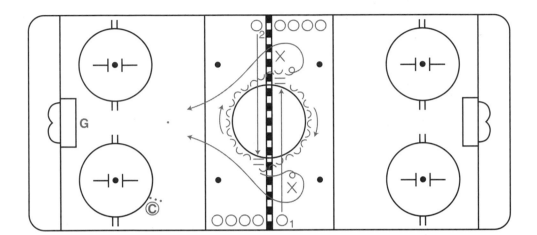

412   RACE FOR THE PUCK

This drill evaluates skating speed, agility, competitiveness, and shooting.

1. Forward 1 and forward 2 start at the center line on opposite sides at the boards.
2. On the whistle, forward 1 and forward 2 skate backward around the cone at the blue line and back to the center line, stop, skate forward, race for the puck placed inside the blue line, and attempt to score (see figure 1).

Variation

The drill is the same except that the players skate forward around the cone, stop at the center line, race for the puck placed inside the blue line, and attempt to score (see figure 2).

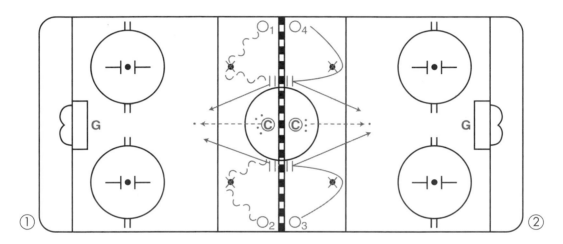

413   1V1 SMALL AREA

The drill shows players' ability to take and give a check, stickhandling in close, and shooting. It is also a good drill for evaluating goalies.

The two nets are put in the corner, and two players fight for the puck and try to score on the opposing goalie.

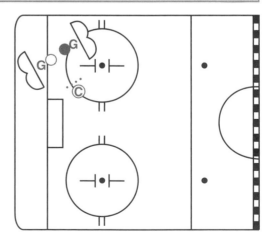

1V1 CIRCLE

This drill evaluates the players' foreword, backward, and lateral skating ability.

1. The defensive defenseman and the offensive forward skate laterally right and left to the outside of the circle, mirroring each other.
2. The offensive forward skates backward to the blue line, stops, skates forward, and receives a pass from the coach.
3. The defensive defenseman skates backward to the goal line, stops, skates forward, pivots, and skates backward.

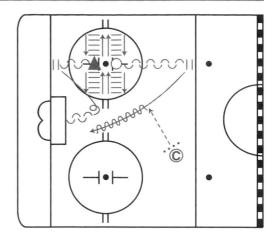

4. The offensive forward goes 1v1 against the defensive defenseman.

1V1 BATTLE IN THE CORNER

This drill evaluates puckhandling, skating ability, and competitiveness.

1. The coach shoots the puck into the corner.
2. The two players skate from the blue line for the puck, battle 1v1, and try to come to the net and score.

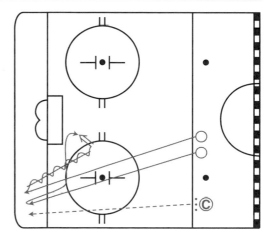

1V1 DRIVE TO THE NET

The following two sequences can be run consecutively on only one end, or to utilize the full ice, players can perform them simultaneously on both ends. They evaluate the forward's skating ability, puck control, shooting, and competitiveness, and the defenseman's defensive ability, skating agility, and competitiveness.

Sequence 1

1. Forward 1 and defenseman 1 start inside the blue line. Forward 1 has the puck.
2. On the whistle, forward 1 goes 1v1 against defenseman 1, who skates backward.

Sequence 2

1. Forward 2 is at the top of the circle with the puck.
2. Defenseman 2 is in the corner.
3. On the whistle, forward 2 goes to the net.
4. Defenseman 2 skates forward from the corner, pivots, and skates backward.
5. Forward 2 goes 1v1 against defenseman 2.

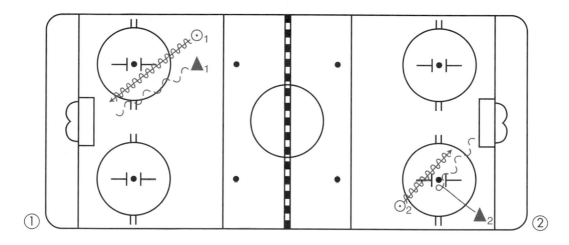

This drill evaluates skating agility, forward and backward skating, and quickness. Players can perform the following two sequences on both ends simultaneously to utilize the whole ice, or the variations can be performed consecutively by the same player on one end.

Sequence 1

1. The player starts at the face-off dot and skates backward to each quarter of the face-off circle and forward back to the dot.

Sequence 2

1. The player skates a figure eight forward then backward around the face-off circles.

2. After completing the second figure eight, the player pivots, skates around the cone, gets a pass from the coach, and shoots on the net.

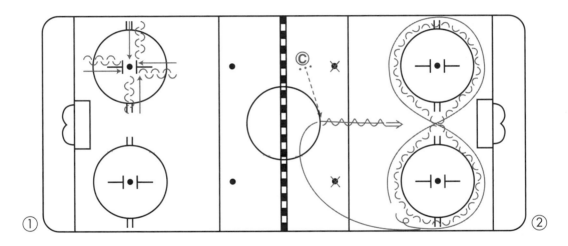

2V2, 3V3, CROSS ICE

In this drill, the players must display puckhandling, passing, shooting, and checking skills in a small area. It is also a good drill for evaluating goalies.

1. Players play 2v2 or 3v3 cross ice with the two nets moved near the boards at one end.

2. If the puck goes outside the blue line, the coach puts another puck in play.

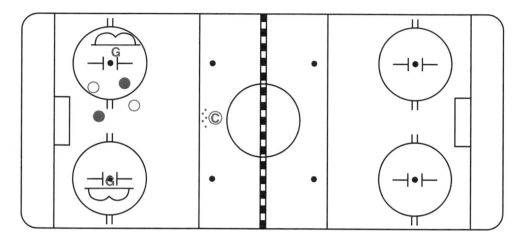

421   # GOALIE MOVEMENT DRILL

This drill evaluates the quickness and movement abilities of the goalie.

1. The pucks are placed in a semi-circle outside the goal crease.

2. The goalie skates forward and backward to each puck in succession.

Variation

The coach points to each puck randomly, and the goalie moves in and out to that puck.

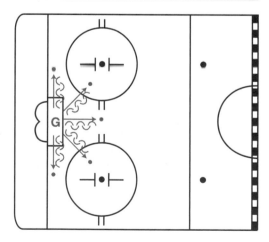

DEFENSE EVALUATION

This drill evaluates the defenseman's skating agility, puckhandling, passing, and shooting. The defenseman begins at the goal line and skates the following sequence:

1. Skates forward to the blue line, stops, and receives a pass from the coach.
2. Skates backward to the goal line, pivots, and skates forward behind the net.
3. Starts up ice, does a tight turn, and skates back behind the net.

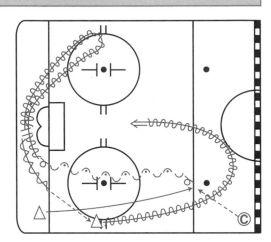

4. Stops, skates from behind the net, and passes to another defenseman at the boards near the face-off circle.
5. The defenseman on the board comes to the middle, skates the blue line, and then shoots.

GOALIE EVALUATION, SKATING

This drill evaluates the goalie's skating agility and quickness. Goalies start at the goal line and skate the following sequence:

1. Skate forward to the center line.
2. Skate backward to the blue line.
3. Skate diagonally forward to the center line.
4. Skate backward to the blue line and diagonally forward to the center line again.
5. Skate backward to the blue line.

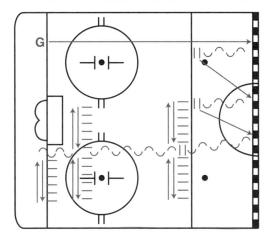

6. Perform a side shuffle right and left to each side.
7. Skate backward through the face-off circle.
8. Perform a side shuffle right and left to each side.
9. Skate backward to the goal line and repeat the side shuffle one more time.

chapter 18

On-Ice Conditioning

The on-ice conditioning drills included in this chapter are specific to the training of the three energy systems used to move the body in ice hockey: anaerobic alactic, anaerobic lactic, and aerobic. The chapter is structured with the anaerobic alactic drills at the beginning, anaerobic lactic drills coming next, and aerobic drills coming last. Also, the system each drill trains is indicated in its title. The following lists identify the characteristics of the three energy systems as well as recommendations for training each system. For best results, the drills included in this chapter should be run with these considerations in mind.

Anaerobic Alactic

- This system supplies energy for all-out efforts lasting up to 10 seconds and contributes for up to 30 seconds.
- The supply of energy provided by this system is limited.
- Training time should be 5 to 10 seconds per repetition for this energy system.
- Training intensity should be near maximal (95 percent).
- Rest time should be 30 seconds to 2 minutes between repetitions.
- Work-to-rest intervals should be 1:6 to 1:10.

Anaerobic Lactic

- This system supplies energy for efforts lasting longer than 10 seconds and contributes for up to 3 minutes.
- This is the predominant system for intense exercise of 30 to 60 seconds.
- Supplies of energy provided by this system are limited.

- This system produces lactic acid, which contributes to fatigue.
- Training intensity should be near maximal (95 percent) for this energy system.
- Recovery time should be 1.5 to 3 minutes.
- Work-to-rest intervals should be 1:3 to 1:6.

Aerobic

- This system is important for recovery in intermittent anaerobic sports such as ice hockey.
- This system can be trained using two methods: continuous long-distance or intermittent interval training.
- Long-distance work should range from 20 to 60 minutes.
- Interval exercise should range from 1 1/2 to 3 minutes.
- Work-to-rest intervals should be 1:1 to 1:2.
- Intensity should be submaximal, approximately 165 beats per minute (60 to 75 percent of maximum), as maximal heart rate is approximately 220 minus the age of the player.

All three energy systems need to be trained for ice hockey. However, during the season, the emphasis for on-ice conditioning should be on training the anaerobic alactic and lactic systems because ice hockey is a sport that requires short bursts of energy (with 5 to 40 seconds of work being the most common). Keep in mind that the aerobic system is also developed and maintained with short-interval work as well as continuous work. Therefore, an aerobic training effect will occur using anaerobic training intervals. Also note that lactic interval training drills also train the aerobic system and are more practical for on-ice conditioning as they train both systems and are more game specific.

424   ALACTIC SPRINT AND SHOOT 1

1. Players 1, 2, and 3 each have a puck.
2. The three players sprint around the cone in succession and shoot at the far end.
3. Players 4, 5, and 6 go next from the opposite side.
4. The drill is continuous with three players going each time.

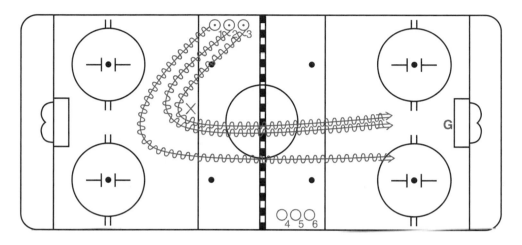

425   ALACTIC SPRINT AND SHOOT 2

1. Player 1 and player 2 each have a puck.
2. Player 1 and player 2 skate over the blue line and shoot in succession, then loop back and skate to the opposite end to take a pass from the coach.
3. Player 1 and player 2 shoot at the opposite end.
4. Players go two at a time, and when the whole team is finished, they go in the opposite direction.

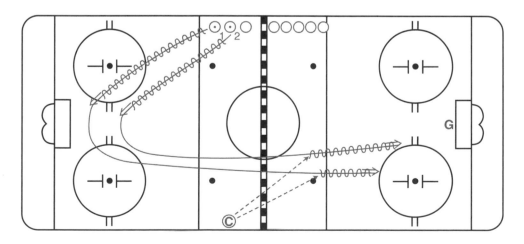

1. Player 1 skates out of the center circle, stops at the near blue line, skates to the far end, takes a pass from player 2, goes over the blue line, and shoots.
2. Player 2 goes next and takes a pass from the next player.
3. The drill goes in both directions from the center circle, with players 4 and 5 performing the same pattern in the opposite direction.

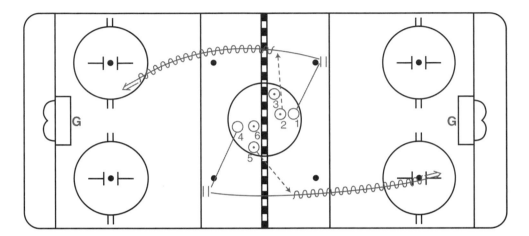

ALACTIC SHOOT WITH CHASER

1. Player 1 is just outside the center circle in the middle of the ice with a puck.
2. Player 2 is at the center line.
3. Player 3 has a puck and is in the same position as player 1 but on the opposite side of the circle.
4. Player 4 is at the center line.
5. On the whistle, player 1 skates in for a shot on the net with player 2 chasing. Player 3 skates in for a shot on the net at the opposite end with player 4 chasing.
6. All players participate, alternating between puck carrier and chaser.

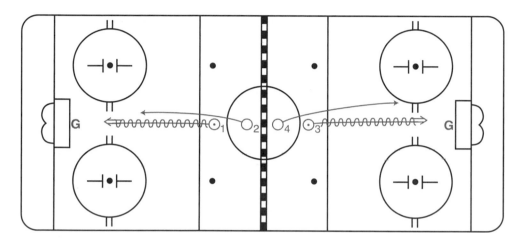

428 ALACTIC SPRINT BLUE TO RED, BLUE TO BLUE

1. Player 1 skates from the blue line to the center line, stops, and skates back to the blue line (see figure 1).
2. Each player in the line goes in succession.
3. Half the players line up on one blue line, the other half on the other blue line.
4. The players alternate from one side to the other.

Variation

The drill is the same except that the players skate from blue line to blue line, stopping at the far blue line and then skating back (see figure 2).

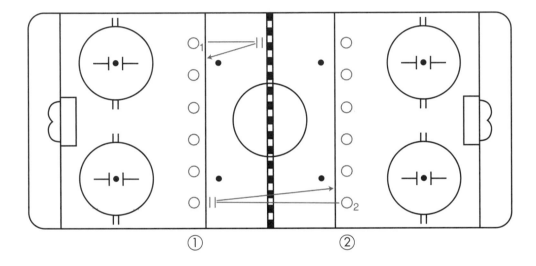

429 ALACTIC SPRINT LENGTH OF ICE, SHOOT

1. The players skate the length of the ice in succession, take a pass inside the blue line from the coach, and shoot.
2. The drill goes in both directions, with half the team going one way and the other half going the other way.

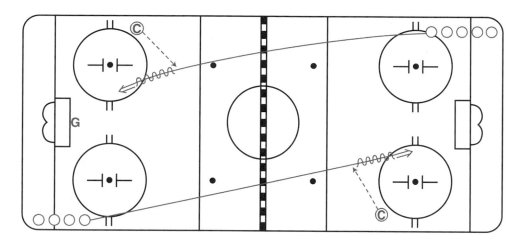

430 ALACTIC SPRINT, LOOP, AND SHOOT

1. The players skate from the blue line to the far blue line, skate around the cone, loop back in the opposite direction, receive a pass from the coach at the center circle, and skate over the blue line and shoot.
2. All the players go in one direction and then start at the other blue line and go in succession in the other direction.

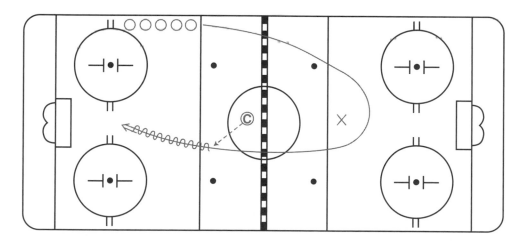

431 ALACTIC SPRINT IN FRONT AND BEHIND THE NET

1. Two players from each corner start at the same time.
2. Two players skate around the cone inside the blue line.
3. The opposite two players skate behind the net, which has been moved up to the hash marks of the two face-off circles.
4. The players skate back to the opposite corner from where they started (they will start from this opposite corner on their next turn).
5. The players from one corner always go around the cone, and the players from the other corner always go behind the net.

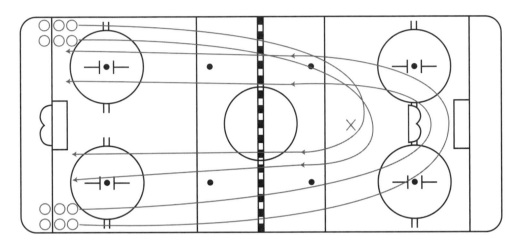

432   ALACTIC SPRINT BLUE TO RED AGILITY

1. Players are in two lines on each end of the rink.
2. The first player in each line is lying down at the blue line.
3. On the whistle, the players get up, sprint to the center line, stop, and skate back to the blue line.
4. The drill is done from both sides of the center line.

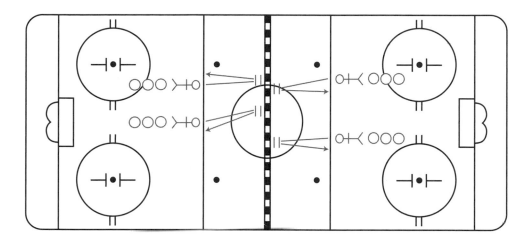

433   LACTIC DOWN AND BACK TWO TIMES

1. Players skate goal line to goal line four times, stopping at each end.
2. Divide players into four or five groups. One group skates while the others rest.

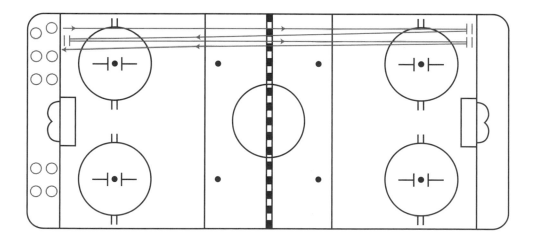

LACTIC 2.5 LAPS

1. Players are in four groups.
2. The first group skates around the rink (going behind the nets) for 2.5 laps and ends where the next group starts.
3. The other three groups rest while one group skates.
4. Group A skates 2.5 laps and ends at group B.
5. As soon as group A reaches group B, group B skates 2.5 laps and ends at group C.
6. Group C then skates 2.5 laps and ends at group D.
7. Group D skates 2.5 laps, ending at group A.
8. Each group goes two times in one direction and two times in the opposite direction for a total of four to eight times.

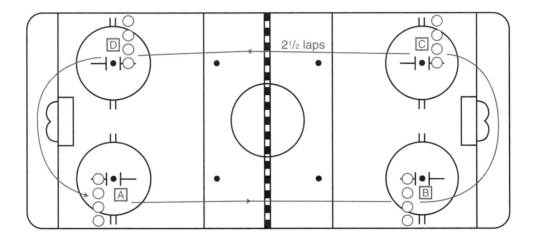

2½ laps

1. The players are in two groups in opposite corners of the same side of the rink.
2. Each time, two players from one end skate to the far blue line, loop back to the near blue line, and skate to the opposite corner at the far end to complete an S pattern.
3. As soon as the two players from one corner turn at the far blue line, the next two players go from the opposite corner.
4. The players alternate from the corners until all the players have gone and ended in the opposite corners.
5. When all the players have gone twice, the two groups switch to the opposite corners at the same end and go two more times.

Variation

The players alternate skating forward and backward between the blue lines.

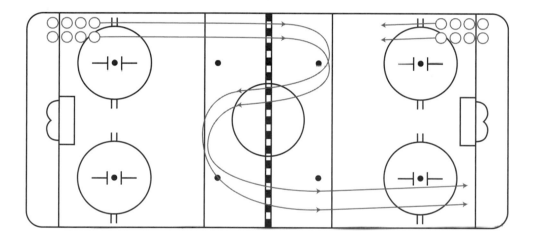

Players form four groups. The groups take turns skating the following sequence, start-ing at the goal line (one group goes while the other three groups rest):

1. Skate to the near blue line and stop.
2. Skate back to the goal line and stop.
3. Skate to the far blue line and stop.
4. Skate back to the near blue line and stop.
5. Skate again to the end of the rink and stop.
6. One group goes while the other three rest.

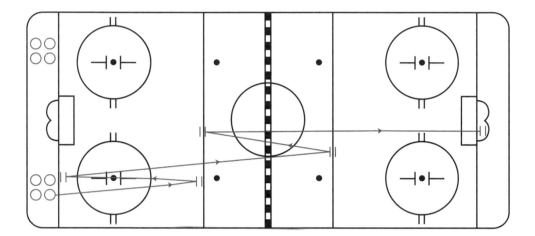

437   LACTIC FOUR FACE-OFF DOTS

1. Four cones are placed at the face-off dots in the four circles in the defensive zones.
2. Players are in four groups.
3. Each group skates around the four cones three times.
4. One group skates while the other three groups rest.
5. The direction of the skate should be changed each time a group skates.

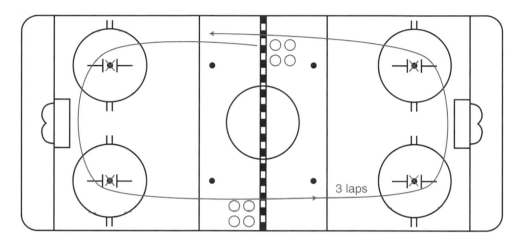

438   LACTIC ONE-AND-A-HALF PLUS ONE-AND-A-HALF

1. The players go two at a time.
2. The two players skate from the goal line, skate behind the far net to the center line, stop, skate back behind the same net, and return to the starting position at the goal line.
3. The two groups alternate from diagonally opposite corners.

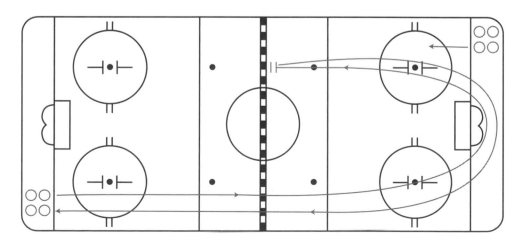

439   LACTIC RELAY

1. Players are in four or five groups, with four players in each group.
2. Players do not have sticks.
3. The first player in each line skates two laps around the rink, going behind the nets, and passes a glove to the next player between the center line and the blue line like a baton in a relay race.
4. The direction of skating should be changed for each race.

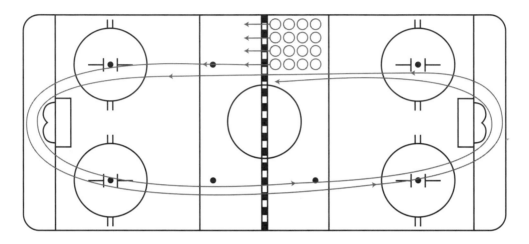

440   LACTIC STOPS AND STARTS

1. The players skate in four or five groups from the goal line.
2. The players stop and change direction on each whistle from the coach. They end at the opposite end of the rink.

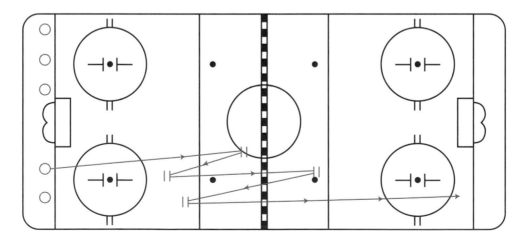

Players form four or five groups. The groups take turns skating the following sequence, starting at the goal line (one group goes while the other groups rest):

1. Skate to the center line and stop.
2. Skate to the near blue line and stop.
3. Skate to the far blue line and stop.
4. Skate to the center line and stop.
5. Skate to the opposite goal line and stop.

Variation

Players change from skating forward to skating backward at each line.

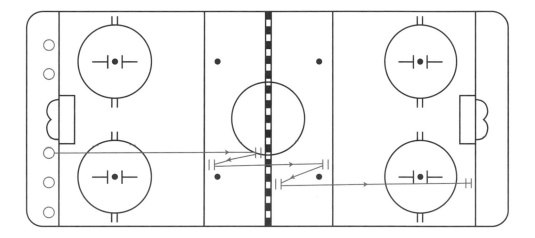

1. Players are in three groups based on positions. One group skates at a time.
2. Group A is made up of defensemen. They skate to the center line, stop, skate backward to the near blue line, pivot, skate forward to the goal line, and stop.
3. Group A repeats the sequence three times.
4. Group B is made up of forwards. They skate across the rink, side board to side board, and stop at the boards each time.
5. Group B repeats the sequence three times.
6. Group C is made up of goalies. They skate to the near blue line, stop, go down on their knees and back up two times, skate backward to the goal line, stop, and perform the double-leg-pad movement (slide quickly sideways with both legs together) to the right and left.
7. Group C repeats the sequence three times.

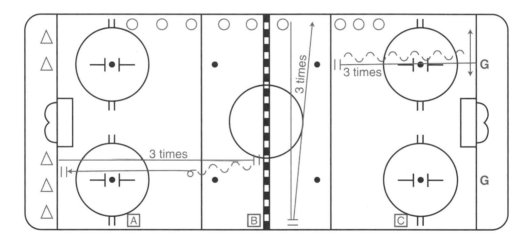

443   LACTIC TWO DEFENSE, THREE FORWARDS

1. Players are in four groups, with two defensemen and three forwards in each group.
2. The forwards skate to the far blue line, perform crossover steps right and left, and skate back to the goal line.
3. The defensemen skate to the center line, perform crossover steps right and left, skate backward to the near blue line, pivot, and skate forward to the goal line.
4. Goalies may skate with the defensemen.

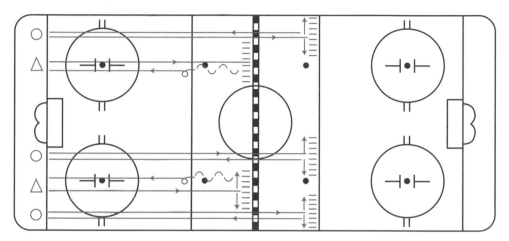

444   LACTIC DOT TO DOT

1. Player 1 skates toward player 2, stops, and skates back to the starting position.
2. The players skate from face-off dot to face-off dot and back.
3. After player 1 stops, player 2 skates toward player 3.
4. Player 1 chases player 2 back to the starting position.

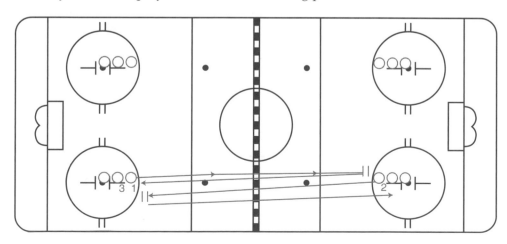

LACTIC CHASE THE RABBIT

1. One player starts ahead of the next group of players as the rabbit.
2. The group of players must all try to catch the rabbit.
3. Players skate one, two, or three laps.
4. One player of a group of five players is the rabbit, with a different player being the rabbit each time.

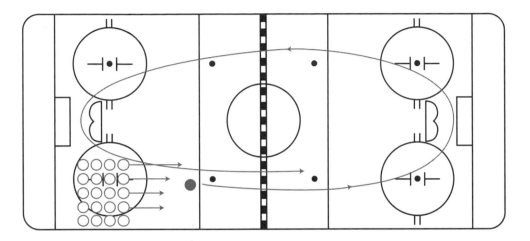

AEROBIC CONTINUOUS SKATE

1. The players skate around the nets while the coaches move the nets slowly toward the blue lines.
2. The players skate for three to five minutes, then rest.
3. Halfway through the drill, the players change direction, and the coaches slowly move the nets back to their original positions.
4. The players skate for another three to five minutes, then rest.

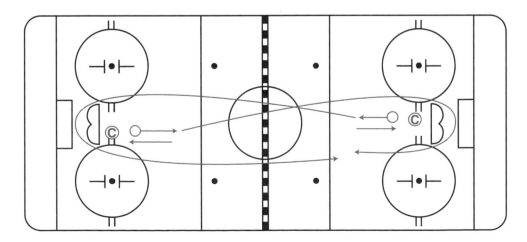

About the Author

Dave Chambers, PhD, has coached hockey for more than 30 years, from key developmental levels to the National Hockey League and international competition. His experience with all types of players and styles makes him well suited to teach the ever-evolving game that is a blend of the European and North American styles. Chambers has won two gold medals in World Championships, five university championships, and five Coach of the Year awards. He was named Master Coach by the Canadian Hockey Association and was inducted into the York University (Toronto, Canada) Sports Hall of Fame in 2005. Chambers has also written a number of books and articles on coaching ice hockey and has made numerous presentations worldwide.